BUILDING A HOME WITH MY HUSBAND

ALSO BY RACHEL SIMON

Little Nightmares, Little Dreams
The Magic Touch
The Writer's Survival Guide
Riding the Bus with My Sister: A True Life Journey

BUILDING
A HOME WITH MY
HUSBAND

A Journey Through the Renovation of Love

· RACHEL SIMON ·

DUTTON

DUTTON
Published by Penguin Group (USA) Inc.
375 Hudson Street, New York, New York 10014, U.S.A.
Penguin Group (Canada), 90 Eglinton Avenue East, Suite 700, Toronto,
Ontario M4P 2Y3, Canada (a division of Pearson Penguin Canada Inc.)
Penguin Books Ltd, 80 Strand, London WC2R 0RL, England
Penguin Ireland, 25 St Stephen's Green, Dublin 2,
Ireland (a division of Penguin Books Ltd)
Penguin Group (Australia), 250 Camberwell Road, Camberwell,
Victoria 3124, Australia (a division of Pearson Australia Group Pty Ltd)
Penguin Books India Pvt Ltd, 11 Community Centre,
Panchsheel Park, New Delhi—110 017, India
Penguin Group (NZ), 67 Apollo Drive, Rosedale,
North Shore 0632, New Zealand (a division of Pearson New Zealand Ltd)
Penguin Books (South Africa) (Pty) Ltd, 24 Sturdee Avenue,
Rosebank, Johannesburg 2196, South Africa

Penguin Books Ltd, Registered Offices
80 Strand, London WC2R 0RL, England

Published by Dutton, a member of Penguin Group (USA) Inc.

First printing, June 2009
1 3 5 7 9 10 8 6 4 2

Copyright © 2009 by Rachel Simon
All rights reserved

 · REGISTERED TRADEMARK—MARCA REGISTRADA

LIBRARY OF CONGRESS CATALOGING-IN-PUBLICATION DATA
Simon, Rachel.
Building a home with my husband: a journey through the
renovation of love / by Rachel Simon.
p. cm.
Includes bibliographical references and index.
ISBN 978-0-525-95120-9 (hardcover: alk. paper) 1. Marriage. 2. Dwellings—Repair and
reconstruction. I. Title.
HQ519.S56 2008
306.81—dc22   2008044555

Printed in the United States of America
Set in Requiem with Mrs Eaves Display   ·   Designed by Elke Sigal

For Hal—

Husband, Architect, Court Jester

CONTENTS

BUILDING A HOME WITH MY HUSBAND

PRECONSTRUCTION

House

Finally, we get married. After nineteen years of one of the most ridiculous courtships in the history of love, I move back in with Hal, and five days later, on a sunny May afternoon, I put on my wedding gown, he dons a suit, and we walk hand-in-hand through the city streets until we reach the justice of the peace. Hal is forty-nine, I am forty-one. Having survived every phase of dating, cohabiting, breaking up, and renewing, we are more in love when we say "I do" than I've ever believed possible. For the next three years we savor laughter and relief, conversation and contentment. This is it, I think, I finally understand love, and I want this to last forever.

But then one January afternoon, the next phase of our journey suddenly begins.

I do not know this when I step onto the front porch of our row house that day and pull the wooden door shut behind me. The sun is bright as it reflects off the snowdrifts on either side of our quiet, tree-lined street, so I keep my gaze down as I cross the single lane to my car, my thoughts on the flight I'm about to catch. This is why I will never know if I am alone on the block that afternoon, or if, as I unlock my car, I am being watched.

But when I look back on this moment, I realize that eyes must have been hiding in the shadows of one of the slender alleys on our street, listening to the *beep beep beep* of our house's security system, following my actions as I lower my suitcases into my trunk. Maybe they even scoped out my routine over the last many months, so they're aware that I'm a writer about to fly across the country for a speaking engagement. Of course, it's possible they've only canvassed our street since this morning but still saw Hal leave for work, blueprints in his bag. However long they've spied, *some* premeditation must have been necessary. After all, ours isn't just a neighborhood of nine-to-fivers, but also in-the-home artists, blue collars sleeping off the night shift, and retirees watching TV. And although I find our house unbearably snug, its two-and-a-half stories, with basement, bath, and seven tiny rooms have lodged large families over its hundred-year life. There's no way of assuming that once we've departed, the house will be empty.

Yet my spy remains a puzzle. Hal and I live on a lightly traveled block of row houses in the small city of Wilmington, Delaware. Pedestrians and vehicles pass only occasionally, except for rush hour, when the thirteen households come and go, and the banking and credit card professionals who work in the nearby skyscrapers deposit or retrieve their cars at the unmetered curb. But there is a delay of an hour after I drive off. Is the wait because the little boy across the street is making a snowman on the sidewalk? Are the many neighborhood dog walkers enjoying impromptu chats at the corner? Or does the course of our lives get rerouted not by design, but whim?

All we know is that at two thirty, while my bags are being screened by airport security, he—and I will take the liberty of assigning a gender and a solitary status—leaps out of his life and lands on our sidewalk. Immediately he rejects a hustle up our seven steps to the wooden front door with its beveled glass window, sure it'll be deadbolted. He dismisses a dash down the alley along the western side of the house, rightly knowing the rickety back door is locked, too.

Why bother, when there's a ragged basement door in the front?

He darts down the three steps from the sidewalk. The door is splintered, peeling, wiggly in its frame. He gives a hard shove. The rotted casing gives way, and he's in.

Beep beep beep. The security system starts counting: forty-five seconds until the alarm.

He tears past basement storage and a dank laundry room, up steep angled steps, into the kitchen. He takes in the decrepit stove, caramel-sticky cabinets, floor the color of tooth decay.

He scrambles through a doorway into the dining room. Nothing but a table piled with newspapers, walls lined with Ikea cabinets, the kind of organ found in old chapels.

He scurries ahead to the living room. A motley assemblage of used furniture, bricked-up fireplace, massive collection of CDs, library of books, *a sitar, a turntable, a bulky TV*. Models of buses on the mantel. Figurines from *The Wizard of Oz*. Would this junk even sell on eBay?

Up the stairs he flies. To the left is a pitiful-looking bathroom tiled in hazard-sign black and yellow. He barrels through the hall, throwing open a door halfway down. The room's crammed with more books, records—*records!*—exercise machines, laundry. What a mess. The door for the back bedroom opens to an unmade bed, two cats quivering beneath. Hand-me-down cabinets. No jewelry box, no fur, no designer labels, no flashy knickknacks. Of all the houses he could've hit, why'd he pick this loser? One more possibility on this floor. Feet sprinting over the crappy green carpet back down the hall, he throws himself into the front bedroom. Only—it's a home office. Jammed to the ceiling with shelves, file cabinets, storage units, desks, copier—and a laptop!

Bbbbrrrraaaannnnnkkkkkkk.

The sound comes up: ear-splitting, heart-wrenching, security-company alerting. Out, get out. No: take a peek at the third floor. He whips around the corner, up the stairs. It's one room, bright with windows, crammed with electric guitars, bass guitars, weirdo guitarlike instruments, computers, amplifiers, homemade electric drum set, microphones. Way too much to unplug.

Laptop in hand, he tears down two flights of stairs, hurls through the living room, dining room, kitchen, dives into the basement, laughs with victory as he reaches the open door—

And sees a workshop. Table saw, power drill, plywood. Lookie here: a new router.

Router in one hand, laptop in the other, he rockets outside. Down the alley, into the backyard, over the fence, onto the street. The alarm shrieking in vain behind him.

. . .

I'm not thinking of alarms as I race toward my connecting flight. I'm only congratulating myself on how much lighter my carry-on is than usual. For the past year, I've lugged my laptop on my trips, only to find that it grew heavier with each airport. This time I finally left it home.

Even so, I'm sweating when I take my seat. My layover required a breathless dash across Phoenix Sky Harbor Airport, and now, overhead bins slamming shut above me, I have only a few minutes to check my voice mail. There's one message. Expecting nothing important, I shuck off my coat while I press the code to listen. "It's me," Hal says, his voice serious. He never sounds like this, and I freeze as he continues: "Call me as soon as you get this." The message ends so quickly, it barely seems to exist.

I dial him with shaking hands. It's already nighttime back in Delaware—anything could have happened. Has someone I love been in a car accident? Had a heart attack? Please, not my sister Beth. Not my father. Friends. Even my mother. Please, please, please—it can't be Hal.

Immediately upon answering, Hal says, "Did you take your laptop to San Diego?"

My confusion at his question overwhelms my relief that he's alive. "What?"

"Your laptop. Where is it?"

"In my study at home."

"No it's not." He sighs, and explains what happened. "I'm sorry, Baboo," he says.

I try to speak, but the shake that was in my hands is radiating through my body. Though hardly as catastrophic as a flatlining monitor in an intensive care unit, losing a laptop means losing everything I've done for months. I do have copies of my recent writing, but when I backed up last week, I once again neglected my address book. I add names so often that I keep postponing this chore.

My hand reflexively covers my mouth. How could I have been so reckless? I, of all people, who measure my wealth by those I care about and those who care about me? Who, having endured a supernova of a childhood, grieves every loss, and has pursued the most impossible revivals? Yet my procrastination has lost me enough people to fill ten airplanes, and unlike Hal, and Beth, and my mother—each gone from my life for many years, then returned—I'll never get those lost friends back.

"Rae?" Hal says.

"What did the police say?" I croak.

"They didn't get any fingerprints."

"So that's it?"

"They said they'd investigate. But I think we can kiss that laptop good-bye."

Now we both sigh, and, again, I can't find words. But this time it's for a reason other than shock, and Hal knows exactly what it is. No two people can live entwined for years and not come to read whole Rosetta stones in the silences, glances, and head tilts that outsiders wouldn't even register. Hal and I generally delight in this phenomenon, and have even jokingly given it names—Friendship Wi-Fi, The Collective Consciousness of Kin, Marriage Mind Meld. But neither of us is amused now. Our relationship clairvoyance has moved on from the burglary to our one huge problem. A seventeen hundred square foot problem that isn't going away.

Finally Hal says, "I'm going out tonight to get a replacement for the basement door. It'll be secure by the time you get home."

"Thanks. But—" Don't say it, I tell myself, as the flight attendants check that the passengers' seat belts are buckled. Hold your tongue. But the shake in my body is now coursing so mightily in the opposite direction that my mouth just won't stop. "I mean, there are so many other things I haven't liked," I say. "Now I won't even feel safe in that house."

Then I lock my lips, and without a word we go through it all over again. The house. The one quarrel we've had since he carried me over its threshold. It's ironic, because the house—or, really, any house—is such an unlikely dispute for us. When we met, I was twenty-three, he thirty, and neither of us thought about owning a house. An aspiring writer with low-paying jobs that meant little to me, I was content scribbling stories in libraries. Hal, in the apprenticeship of his archi-tectural career, and at his own low-paying jobs, spent his off-hours at home practicing guitar. Home ownership was as absurd as time travel—and not only because of our callings or income.

The truth was that I couldn't commit to him. I loved him, he loved me, we were utterly compatible, but something I had yet to understand kept me from saying that he was The One. Nonetheless, we so enjoyed being together that after a year of spending every night in his or my dumpy Philadelphia apartment, we moved into our own dumpy Philadelphia apartment together. Five years later, after savoring everything from our vegetarianism to our fondness for offbeat films and modern art, we rented a modest house in the suburbs. But I felt no closer to what I wanted to feel. I groped toward advice, but each friend contradicted the last, and therapists mostly said, "Tell me more about your family." Hal grew aloof, sometimes patronizing; I burrowed into writing and friends. Eventually the highlight of our time together was zoning out before the TV, numbing ourselves with pizza. When I was alone, thoughts assaulted me: *I have to leave! But he's so funny and caring and smart. I have to find The One! But how can I hurt him?* My head felt caught between two crashing cymbals. I developed rashes. I ground my teeth in my sleep. And finally, after thirteen years—I know, *thirteen years*—we called it quits. For the next six years, I lived in rented rooms, over garages, in basements. I dated a little, but mostly I was alone. Hal was so convinced he'd failed at love that he didn't even try to date. He took up Buddhism and environmental sustainability and eventually became a first-time homeowner—of the very house we're not talking about now.

He says, "We'll deal with the house when you get back."

"Right," I say, as my brain sends him an instant message: *This is the final strike.*

"We'll work it out."

"I know." *The time to move has come.*

"Turn off all electronic devices," I hear overhead.

I don't want to end our call like this: stunned about the burglary, agitated about the loss, angry about the house, longing to comfort each other. In the moment we have left, Hal and I hold each other's gaze through the phone. "Love you," he whispers. "Me, too," I say. And, remembering how much easier it is for him to say those words—and how accepting he is of why I find love so hard to express—I feel tears come. That's when we hang up.

Then the plane is accelerating down the runway, and I suddenly realize that this moment has launched me into a new leg of my life's journey. I don't want it to. I don't want to have anything to do with whatever awaits: expenditures of time and money to replace the laptop, the return of our debate about moving, and, heaven help us, if we decide to stay and finally renovate, possibly even our hard-won solidarity going up in smoke. I cannot guess that in the end all this will indeed happen, and some of it will be a great trial, though not in any of the ways that I fear, and not only with him. In fact, it will blow open the tight seal around everything I think I know about myself, about family, about the misunderstandings and resilience of love; and all my memories and aspirations and regrets and joys will come bursting out, some old beliefs disintegrating, others surviving transformed. But it's only a house, people will tell me, and, with Hal demystifying for me how construction proceeds, step by step, I will not refute that it is. Yet the lessons I get in the physical world of building will, at the same time, deliver so much more: locked rooms leading to the depths of myself, forgotten closets brimming with wrinkled relationships, falling walls exposing conflicts of the past, sudden calamities enlightening my spirit, newborn windows opening their eyes and looking out into the future.

But of course I do not know any of this as the plane tilts up into the sky. I simply feel stiff with anxiety, and envision quarrels stirring beyond the horizon. How different I might feel if I could see past the dust, and glimpse the gems that this journey will reveal.

Two days later, I drive home from the airport, determined to press my case to move.

It's not that I don't appreciate Hal's affection for the house. That's been clear to me since we reconnected after the breakup. I think about that time now, as I grip the steering wheel, dreading the dispute that awaits. Soon after Hal bought the house, we reestablished a friendship, one that neither of us thought would blossom into a romance. For a while after that we visited through casual phone calls and the

occasional meal out, and that's where I expected things to stay. But
then Hal began waging a gentle campaign to win me over.

First he invited me to the wedding of a friend, where I was reminded of traits I'd forgotten, such as Hal's sense of humor and easy
affection toward his friends. Then our calls began growing longer and
more frequent, often occurring while we lay in our separate beds in
our separate homes, late into a weekend morning. Our dinners out
became more relaxed, too, and went from monthly to weekly to twice
a week. Slowly I saw that I was no longer focusing on all that he was
not, but was letting myself see what he actually was: a man with a rare
combination of dependability and playfulness, likeability and intelli-
gence, humility and confidence, vulnerability and strength. Still, I
didn't think that anything more would happen until he invited me
along on a business trip and suggested we share a room—"as friends,"
he clarified when I asked. Yet it was there, in a nondescript hotel along
a highway in Pennsylvania, that our friendship turned into romance,
and by the time the weekend was over, I realized that he was a man
cuter than I'd ever acknowledged, with angular cheekbones and hazel-
green eyes and hair so fine that the gray he'd acquired now simply
shimmered in the blond. Such a contrast to me, with my dark curls
and brown eyes. Yet we were both slim and short-statured, and we
both smiled easily, he playing the court jester, me laughing merrily at
his silliness. We do fit, I thought, numb with amazement. After nineteen years, we actually fit.

A few days after our transformation in the hotel, he invited me to
dinner at his house. I'd been there a few times before, but this time, I
realized, I'd be seeing it with different eyes, just as I was now seeing
him.

On the appointed day I drove from my apartment in Pennsylvania to Wilmington, Delaware. There, after turning off the main road
into a grid of one-way streets, I made my way down a slope of hundred-
year-old row houses, which were sandwiched between the downtown
office towers at the hill's peak and a genteel park at the hill's bottom.
Although the neighborhood bumped up against a major hospital and
was close to an interstate, when I parked I enjoyed an uncommon
quiet, one I hadn't noticed before.

Hal ran down the street from his house and hugged me hello. Then we proceeded to walk down his block, a tucked-away haven one lane wide and one block long. I was struck, as I'd previously been, by the majestic sycamores, then by the surreal way that several of the trees displayed the remnants of NO PARKING ANYTIME signs—rectangles of metal that had been affixed to the trunks so long ago, the bark had grown over all four edges, swallowing most of the words, leaving nothing but TIME on one sign, the biblical fragment ARK on another. I laughed at how appropriately symbolic the signs were for us, and Hal said they were one of several things he loved about living here. There was also the sociable atmosphere in the neighborhood, which I witnessed moments later, when he exchanged warm words with a little boy and his mother who were sitting on a porch across the street from Hal's house. Hal reminded me also that the block was informally known as Teacher's Lane, because once upon a time it lodged several prominent educators, one of whom, Eldridge Waters, had sold Hal his house. Then Hal and I turned toward his house. He ushered me up the steps, we crossed the terra-cotta porch, he opened the heavy oak door, and we were in.

Instantly, the pleasure he took in the hardwood floors, deep baseboards, plaster walls, and operating transoms—and the promise he saw in the rundown kitchen and bathroom, the cramped bedrooms, the paucity of closets, even the miniscule backyard—endeared him to me even more. I already knew what everything looked like, yet now every detail seemed important and interesting. I felt different, too: as we emerged from the stairs into his third-floor music studio, where sycamore leaves were draping one set of windows and sunlight was streaming through the other, and he tentatively reached out to hold my hand, it seemed as if we were in a glass ship sailing down a river of row houses and trees, embarking on a voyage that transcended our failed past. As we stood with the sun pouring in from the south, it occurred to me that if this man could see so much that was worthy in such an unexceptional dwelling—and make me see it, too—then his heart was more generous than I'd realized. If, with all of its imperfections, he could say, "I love this and want to stay forever," he could say the same to me. A few months later, he did.

But soon after we walked home from the justice of the peace, I learned that the third floor was also bone-chilling in winter and suffocating in summer. It lacked insulation, as did the entire house, which also sported no central air. The kitchen cabinets were laminated with a sticky veneer that no amount of scrubbing would clean. The kitchen window looked out to a decrepit aluminum porch. The bathroom was tiled in bumblebee black and yellow, its pipes clogging so frequently we had them replaced, leaving a gaping hole in the ceiling below. Without funds to repair the hole, we then had a porthole between the bathroom and the dining room. It leaked, too: when we showered, water dripped onto the first floor. Electrical outlets were meager in number, and the wiring was knob and tube. The furnace was old, the stove ancient, the windows with aged, wavy panes failed to stop drafts. Transom glass was missing. Hardwood floors bore the blemishes of decades of rotting carpets. The banister was an ugly metal railing. In heavy rain, puddles speckled the basement.

I tactfully admitted to Hal that I lacked his enthusiasm for the house. But I hardly commanded the resources to move to a place more to my liking, like a sunny, ample-sized, detached house, preferably in a suburb with generous yards and garages. You mean, Hal would respond, a place with the kind of muscular mortgage that would kick sand in the face of our scrawny payments? He'd go on. Small, attached houses are more energy-efficient, we can walk to do most errands, and we enjoy long strolls along the Brandywine Creek in the park. I still protested. "Okay, then," he'd say, "where and what would your dream house be?"

Up until now, this was where my thoughts—and our quarrels—stopped. I'd lived in all kinds of places as a kid: apartments and houses, cities, rural areas, and suburbs. But perhaps because I was more concerned with the crumbling foundation of my parents' marriage, and then, after my father left, with my mother's ability to function, and *then*, after she went off the deep end and disappeared from the face of the earth, with the resumption of my life with my father as well as living at a boarding school, I came to feel no attachment to any kind of housing. I like historic homes for their curbside appeal and idiosyncratic crannies, but I like youthful town houses for their brawny plumbing and vigorous heating and windows distinguishable from rice paper. I like the urban ease of being able to walk to the dry cleaner, but I like the elbow room of the suburbs. I like the way a small footprint permits me to blast through whatever housework I care to do, but I like spacious rooms and multiple baths and broad views. It seemed that I was just as commitment-phobic about my housing preferences as I'd been about marriage.

It became even more difficult to focus on the house after a book I wrote, about my sister Beth, came out a year after we married. Beth has developmental disabilities, and it turned out that my account of our lives together struck a chord among many people who had family members with disabilities. She also has an unusual passion—she rides city buses all day, every day. I joined her in this lifestyle for a year—and my chronicle of that experience caught the eye of celebrities, who started talking about making a movie. By the time I celebrated my second anniversary with Hal (known in that book as Sam), I was being deluged by calls from all over the country, as people in the disability field and public transit industry invited me to give talks at conferences, fund-raising dinners, award ceremonies. I found it exhilarating to advocate for the rights of people with disabilities and their families, so I seldom declined. But my trips had become so ceaseless, it was all I could do to keep up with my marriage and a part-time job teaching writing. I had no spare moments in which to make up my mind about where to move, much less convince Hal.

Now, as I park before our house for the first time since a burglar brought matters to a head, Hal runs out to greet me, and our hug is far longer and closer than any I thought possible during the six years apart. Then he kisses me, and his body makes abundantly clear what his voice has yet to speak: yes, we can at last leave this woeful house behind, without any more argument from him. "Well, that was easy," I say, giggling inside our kiss. "Marriage Mind Meld's awfully efficient," he says.

"Okay," I say the next night, as we sit in front of my new laptop. "Let's see what houses are selling for around here."

We click on some sites. Recent sales are in the ballpark of

$175,000, which would give us a huge profit on the $95,000 that Hal paid. "That's terrific," he says.

Then we remind ourselves that we can't approach a real estate agent without remodeling the kitchen and bathroom, which would reduce our profit to—

"What do you think those projects would cost?" I ask.

"Some architects have a better handle on costs. I'm among those who don't."

"So how can we figure out what we'd have left over for another house?"

"We just have to estimate."

"But certainty would be much more to my liking."

"One order of certainty, hold the mayo," he says in the phony voice of a short-order cook. "Aw, you're outta luck, lady. Certainty ain't on the menu."

"Fine. Let's just look at what houses are going for." We tool around online, checking out towns between the college where Hal manages construction projects and the college where I teach. Then we plug in three bedrooms and one bath. I want to add proximity to the airport, plus an accessible entrance, since I'm friends with many wheelchair users. Aside from being green, Hal *must* have a design that's not so gauche that it would call into question his architectural creds. But the search lacks these parameters. So we click on "No maximum price."

Sixty-three options appear, but only on the final screen do we find affordable possibilities—and every one is hideous, ramshackle, adjacent to sewage treatment plants, on four-lane commercial strips, in areas oft-cited in the police reports, or too snug for our sofa.

Hal lifts a bottle of water off my desk and holds it to his mouth like a microphone. "Yes, ladies and gentlemen, it's true," he intones in a radio announcer's stentorian voice. "There is no hope for our two heroes."

"Other people find ways to move," I say, slumping in my chair. "We could, too, if only we'd started saving in our twenties, instead of being artists."

"For our two pauper heroes," he amends. "For them, there is only doom."

January eases into February. We debate our house all the time. I'm adamant about moving and Hal's completely cooperative, but real estate prices remain uncooperative. We do get an unexpected shot of hope when we learn that my book is going to be adapted for a television movie, but then realize that the funds won't be nearly enough to rescue us from the final screen on the real estate sites. To make matters worse, at one of our many neighborhood parties, when I'm sounding off about our burglary, a former resident who's back to see old friends says, "I moved away because I wanted to be in the suburbs. The day after we moved, we were robbed. Everyone in our neighborhood has been robbed. It can happen anywhere."

"Yes," say other people at the party. "My pocket was picked in Princeton." "Our car was broken into in Cherry Hill."

"Nowhere is safe," I say to Hal as we walk home from the party.

"We could stay," he suggests.

We reach the house. The local planning office says it's "of a vernacular Second Empire style." I prefer to think of it as Forgettable Flawed.

"We could," he repeats.

"You hate mansard roofs. This has a mansard roof."

"A Victorian one, so that makes it more bearable."

"And the downspout doesn't work," I say.

Spring advances. Buds dot the sycamores outside our windows, then open like the relaxing of fists. Neighbors sweep winter off their steps, let their children ride tricycles without coats, hang Japanese lanterns on porches. The park fills with daffodils and ducklings.

So it is that on a glorious April day, we're out for a stroll in the park. We've just cracked jokes with a dog walker we know from neighborhood parties, and as we resume our loop around the Brandywine Creek, I mention how much I like the friends we've made in our neighborhood.

"You know, we like a lot of people here," Hal says. He directs my gaze. Nearby is a picnic table where a red-haired mother draws pictures with her red-haired daughter. He gestures toward a man collecting seed pods along the cobblestone road, Monkey Hill, that slopes up from the park zoo. He nods toward a couple jogging past the fountain with classical statues. We know all their names. We have spoken with them in shorts and bad hair, in down coats and good spirits, with groceries in our hands and worries on their minds, in front of the mural a resident artist painted on his wall and beside the toy truck the little boy plays with across the street. Newcomers or old-timers, black or white, gay or straight, corporate or Bohemian, they are talkative and open. "We live in a great place," Hal adds.

As we cross the nineteenth-century stucco bridge over the Brandywine, then continue beside the river until the small dam at the bottom of the steep street that leads to our neighborhood, I think, for the first time, about how our house, boring and decayed though it is, is right in the middle of the very characteristic that everyone seeks but that's never a parameter on real estate Web sites: an actual community. I've never even thought about community when I've conjured up my fantasy smorgasbord of housing possibilities, but I sure am glad we have it.

Is it possible that I'm beginning to see less of what isn't and more of what is?

We turn toward the river. There, in the shallow water beneath the dam, stands a great blue heron, the same one we saw last summer and the summer before. We've even named him. "Look," Hal says. "It's Edward, back for the season."

"Hi, Edward," we call out, as we always do.

Hal turns to me. "Please. Let's fix it up and stay."

"No, no, no, no. It'll be hugely expensive."

"We can get a home equity loan, add in the money from the movie, and make up the difference with our savings."

"But you're fifty-three! Our savings are already nowhere near what we'll need if you're ever going to retire!"

"So we'll just use *some* savings, and if we need to, refinance the house when we're done."

"But it'll be so much work!"

"This is what I do for a living."

"What if things go wrong? I hear all the time about the terrible things that can happen. What if they happen to us?"

He shrugs. "They just did."

I laugh. "I guess so."

"And we lived to tell the tale."

"We did."

"So?"

I can resist. I can spend the next year hoping to stumble upon a just-listed suburban charmer that miraculously pleases us both. But frankly, I don't want to take the time—and the petals are opening, and Edward is here again, and Hal is looking at me with his big green eyes.

"I ask you, Professor Simon," he says. "Aren't we already on Teacher's Lane?"

Yes, somehow, by a twisting route that took me from love to doubt to anguish to loneliness to regret to searching to reconnection to standing here with my husband as he waits for my answer by this river, I am a teacher, and I have come to live on Teacher's Lane. And somehow, like the parking signs and their trees—and like Hal and me—I have come to be part of this neighborhood, and it a part of me. Maybe our destinies are already growing together.

"All . . . right," I say.

"Ow-wow-wow-owf!" Hal calls out, and he lifts me up and twirls me around. Then he takes my hand, we wave at Edward, and head up the hill toward home.

D·E·S·I·G·N   P·H·A·S·E

Love

Hal wants to start off small. The smallest room in the house, actually. "It'll ease us into the process," he says, as he parks before the bath and kitchen store. "Get you acquainted with renovation before we start the bigger changes." That sounds like a wise plan, though when we walk inside and come face-to-face with the maze of tubs, sinks, toilets, and cabinetry zigzagging on into infinity, I suspect that the only thing his plan will end up doing is acquainting the client with her accommodating architect, and the architect with his clueless client.

We venture into angled aisles. "Tell me what you like," he says, clipboard in hand.

"I have no idea."

"Look. Look around you. Look at these displays. The cabinets are all different. The fixtures. What appeals to you?"

"They're all fine."

"*Fine?*"

"They're all nice. Nice store displays. But I can't see myself living in a store display."

"What can you see yourself living in?"

"Beats me."

He looks over the top of his glasses with amused annoyance.

I smile weakly at him. "Sorry," I say, "but it's true."

He can hardly be surprised. I told him on one of our first dates that I've always been ill at ease with the third dimension. Because Hal thinks in terms of things you can see or hear, he was sure I was exaggerating, despite the fact that my conversation seldom strayed from emotions and memory and relationships and the meaning of life. He even teased me about the frequency with which I had epiphanies, playing off the bossa nova song "The Girl from Ipanema" by calling me "the Girl from Epiphanema." Still, for a long time, Hal remained unconvinced about my 3-D ineptitude. But after two decades of my balking at such inscrutable feats as lacing my shoes, giving up on fax machines and CD players, discerning no distinctions between models of cars, likening televised sports to moving wallpaper, and delaying driving until my thirties—all while he glided through the triple rings of height-length-and-depth with the grace of a bareback rider—he's had to concede that I was right.

Now he says, "It's that darned third dimension again."

I nod, adding a pout to induce extra sympathy.

"Then we'll just deal with it, okay?" he says, his annoyance softening to alliance.

"I'll do my part," I say, as he takes my hand. "Whatever the heck that is."

Our familiar imbalance now out in the open, we walk into the labyrinth, winding past bathrooms so well-appointed they look like Disney World sets, so unsullied they look like alternate realities. I want to make a joke, but this is serious business.

Finally he stops between two displays. "Okay," he says. "Let's compare these sinks."

"One's white, one's gray."

"Right. But look. That one's freestanding. The other's set into a cabinet. That one has shiny fixtures, those fixtures are burnished. There's tile, there's marble. What do you like?"

I look forlornly at the displays. There are too many details for me to assess, and anyway, they look like the sort of places *other* people live in—people like my older sister Laura, who's decorated her Arizona house with kitschy collectibles from yard sales. Or my brother, Max, whose New Jersey house is done in stately Americana. Or the millions who watch renovation TV. I admire the knowledge those people possess, any one of whom would make a more suitable match for this thoughtful architect than I. Instead, he got a client and wife who's never cared about owning things, and has felt at home among only two decorating styles: Whatever's Already in Place When I Move In, and Eclectic Mementos with Good Stories Behind Them.

"Well," I finally offer, "I like the shiny faucets."

He frowns. "You do?"

"You don't?"

"I like the burnished kind better."

Now it's my turn to give a withering look. "Are you the architect, or the husband?"

He grins. "I'm the husbitect."

"What does that mean?"

"The architect will do the work. But the husband's not a tyrant. This is about *us*."

Relieved to hear this, I turn back to the faucets. Okay, I'm more drawn to shiny faucets, but enough to make a case out of this? It's not like when I was looking for the love of my life and had a clear image of what I wanted down to every detail. I've never even thought about faucets, and it's not as if I couldn't live with Hal's preference. I suppose I *could* take a stand just to assert myself. But that's one of the earliest lessons I learned about love, back before kindergarten, when I was playing dress-up with Laura and she always had to be the princess, I the queen: choose your battles. And this is one of the lessons I learned about love during the years away from Hal: it's awfully easy to invent battles when none actually exist.

"Well, husbitect," I say, "just tell me what you like. If I feel strongly against it, I'll say so. But since it doesn't matter much to me, I probably won't."

He squeezes my hand. "Think of all the lawsuits that could be avoided," he says, "if every client in the world was like you." He makes some notes on his clipboard.

A week later, Hal announces that he's ready to move ahead. He'll buy a new sink, toilet, and tub, hire an installer, and pry off the bathroom wall tile himself. Although this plan has the virtue of economy, it makes me think about all the mug handles that have been waiting a decade for glue. I ask, "Uh, honey, how much would it cost to pay someone to do the whole bathroom?" He tries to reach some contractors to get estimates. Phone tag ensues for a few weeks, then slacks off into silence.

This is when I reveal just how unideal I am as a client. "Maybe this is a sign," I say one morning as he's paging through issues of *Architectural Record*. He looks up. "A sign of what?" "A sign that we should, well, just postpone this renovation. You know, like indefinitely." And this is where Hal reveals just how husbandly he is as an architect. "Yeah, right," he responds, reaching for his clipboard, where he begins writing notes under columns he's already labeled: "First Floor," "Second Floor," "Third."

I stare at him for a moment, but we both know that I'm not going to press my case. For one thing, I have too much respect for his expertise. But for another, I have recently become preoccupied with something far beyond the scale of the renovation—something I told him about last night, when we were getting into bed, and I casually mentioned that I was embarking on "my search for my life purpose." Hal, having endured my existential crises in the past, laughed and said, "Again?" And when I got offended, he suggested that there was a more accurate way to put it: "The Search for Your Life Purpose 2.0."

He was right. My initial round of searching, which happened in my younger years, basically consisted of me pulling the lever over and over on the slot machine of my life, hoping for just one solid win in work, home, or love, but having all the reels keep spinning to blanks. Now, for the first time, I'm post-jackpot, and my pockets are jingling with happy stability, so I'm finally free to consider loftier goals. Not that I wish to give up writing, teaching, or speaking, nor could we survive financially if I did. But there are extraordinary second-act successes in this world, people who, after a stellar career in one field, take on noble causes—think Jimmy Carter, Bono, Bill Gates. Or lesser-known Samaritans I've met in my travels who, after midlife milestones like remarriage or sobriety, started making documentaries, directing early-intervention schools, running rural transit systems. I want to do something like that. Something that would be transformative for others and a fresh challenge for me—without jostling the very agreeable life I now have. Something that would, dare I say it, change the world. If only I could figure out what it is.

"You know," Hal says now, eyes turned to the clipboard, "your Search for Life Purpose 2.0 is well-timed." "How's that?" I ask. "Because I know that even though you might be anxious and tentative, you have something more important on your mind, so I'll be able to think freely about this."

He makes a wry smile at me, and I do the same to him.

And just like that, our start-small project becomes the complete renovation of our house.

"Here's what I've been thinking," Hal says when we're at a café a few nights later, getting him a soy mocha latte. He presses his hand to his shirt pocket, making the architect's pledge of allegiance to find his ever-present mechanical pencil, then brings the lead to the back of a receipt.

I observe from my usual upside-down position. "Since we want to catch the light from the south," he says, "we need to take down the wall between the dining room and the kitchen."

He draws, and I do my best to make sense of his developing sketch, though, as always, his first many marks seem incoherent to me. This is probably true of everyone who lacks the ability to visualize space, though maybe it's an even more formidable exercise for me. But over the years I've learned to be patient when he draws. Because look: within moments, he adds the stroke that gives me the perspective I've needed, and his lines cohere into meaning.

He spins the receipt around. I follow him completely as he walks me through what I now understand to be a floor plan. "Here's the western wall, the back porch along the southern wall, the three windows along the eastern alley. This jutting intrusion is the stairwell to the basement. And you know the pantry wall that separates the kitchen and dining room?"

"There's no pantry wall on this sketch."

"Right. If we take it down, the light from the south can penetrate deep into the house."

"It'll be a nice big room."

"So you like it?"

"From what I can tell, yes. But how can I be sure?"

"But you think you do. That's a start."

"Where are the stove and the sink?"

"I haven't worked that out. I want to reconfigure the whole kitchen."

"What about the disgusting cabinets and floor?"

"There's an order to all this, and getting the overall design comes way before appliances and flooring. But eventually I'll probably design new cabinets and research new floors. I'm getting ideas for a new study for you, too."

"You are? A whole new study?"

He flips the receipt over. "It's a cool idea," he says as he draws.

I resume my gaze, waiting again as the differences between our minds become apparent, then, with a single jot of his pencil, disappear.

"Wow," I say.

"You like it?"

I look at the paper again, marveling at how it takes only one small notation to create a whole shift in perspective. "Are you kidding?" I say. "It's beautiful." I look up at him and he's beaming.

Around this time I begin to experience something I never imagined might happen.

I grasp this at about two a.m. one night, when Hal rustles in bed beside me and then gets up to go to his music studio to put his latest ideas on paper. He's been doing this for weeks now, so, as usual, I mumble, "Come back soon," and try to go back to sleep.

But by the time his feet mount the stairs to the third floor, I know that once again I, too, will remain awake, and I realize that every night, as Hal's thoughts have unfolded from room to room in the house that is and reshaped themselves into the house that has yet to be, my thoughts have rolled backward in time, leaving the life I now live to visit the times I left behind. I don't know why this is happening, just that the first few nights my thoughts were about the journey of reconnection I began when I was riding buses with Beth, and then, the next several nights, about the journey of forgiveness I began after my mother's disappearance. Lately, though, my thoughts have flowed toward the errors I made in those first years with Hal—and I finally see what's been linking all these nights together. It is love I've been thinking about, in all its messy permutations, and my long struggle, one person after another, to understand what love is.

How hard I once focused, I now let myself recall, on the ways that Hal and I differed. He spoke *slowly*. My words came out like a ticker-tape machine. He had a handful of friends who he saw less and less over time, I had a cast of thousands who multiplied by the day. On the rare occasions when he exercised, he did yoga. I worked out every day—power-walking, aerobics, weight-training—anything but yoga. He stayed up late and slept late; I went to bed early and rose at dawn. He drank coffee; I, tea. He liked summer; I, winter.

None of these differences truly irked me, but that could not be said of the effort he put into composing music on his guitar. This would seem to be less a difference than similarity, since I devoted so much energy to writing. But Hal's compositions were influenced by such nonmainstream performers as Captain Beefheart, Ornette Coleman, Gong, and obscure psychedelic bands, and my listening preferences were the Beatles, National Public Radio, and silence. Also, he drifted from one half-finished piece to the next. I'd sit at my desk, losing my concentration as his snippets drifted into my study—and I'd steam. Why create atonal music when he was equally fond of melody? How could this man live with himself if he didn't finish things? And, the big one: if we have such fundamental disparities, how could this be true love?

True love—*that* was the crux of the matter. The couples at college who were so in sync, they'd dance for hours at parties with their eyes closed. John and Yoko, who shared dreams of peace and iconoclasm. Hepburn and Tracy, Bogart and Bacall—celluloid lovers with witty repartee. As for *my* true love? I knew just who he was. An unwritten but very exacting list.

It was a list of my own tastes and traits (well, the good ones), as well as specific physical attributes, and early in my love life, one boyfriend had even satisfied most of it, assuming I overlooked his determination to never love me. Yet I believed, as did friends still prospecting for their own soul mates, that a perfect fit merely awaited discovery. In fact, large swaths of my conversations with friends were given over to analyzing why we'd failed thus far. So even though I met Hal under circumstances that were so against-all-odds, so miraculous, that in a movie he'd *have* to be my true love, even though his looks were strikingly aligned with my fantasy, even though all my friends thought him a man of fine character, and even though he made me feel cherished, inspired my imagination, and accepted my weaknesses, a few checks were missing on my list. Therefore, how could he possibly be The One?

Only during the six years of our breakup did I start wondering if my idea of love was just a teensy bit askew. Actually, as I lay on the air mattress in the attic where I lived our first year apart, I came to feel horrified with myself. Look, I started saying to myself, even more insistently than Hal had in the bath and kitchen store. Look at what's right in front of you. Suddenly my mind defogged. The couples I'd known in college had all gone down in flames. Yoko threw John out of the house for years. Movie couples often resulted from matches made in adultery. As for friends who'd championed soul mates, only those who'd chucked their own lists had become well-partnered—either to the steady spouse they'd finally come to hold dear, or to even-tempered true-blues they'd have never noticed in the past.

I hadn't wanted a man. I'd wanted a mirage.

Ashamed at having duped myself for my entire life, terrified that I was already thirty-six, and feeling too guilty and played-out to ask Hal to resume, I decided that if I was ever going to have a relationship again, I had to approach love as an apprentice. Only this time, rather than rely on Romeos and Juliets I saw purely from afar, I'd look at happy couples I knew firsthand.

Initially, I looked to my parents, seeking enlightenment from the original source. Although they'd failed to achieve a lasting *pas de deux* with each other, they'd created rewarding marriages with other partners. But how? I rarely saw my mother, who lived in Florida with her third husband, Gordon, and I was feeling too foolish to ask them about love over the phone. Though I adored visiting my father and his second wife, Theresa, who lived a few hours from me, I felt even more tentative querying them. So at first my apprenticeship yielded no insights.

Over the next few years, though, seeing that I had friends in satisfying partnerships, I grew bolder. When one told me that his wife was less talkative than he, I asked how he could stand it. "When she doesn't feel like talking," he said, "I just enjoy my own thoughts." Another mentioned that her long-term girlfriend lacked the charisma of previous partners. I asked if this was hard. She sighed. "I'm so done with drama." A third friend, married to a woman raised in Central America, learned Spanish and bought a vacation home in her country. "If you embrace another person," he told me, "your life doubles."

But the big breakthrough happened on a simple phone call. I was speaking with a friend, Harriet, who was still devoted to her husband, Vic, of forty years, as was he to her. In the background I heard piano music. I knew Vic owned many recordings of jazz greats, so I asked Harriet, "Who's Vic playing?" She said, "That *is* Vic. He's taken piano lessons for years." I'd never known this, and I asked, "Do you like what he plays?" She laughed. "I like jazz okay, but he's terrible." I gasped. Then I asked, "Doesn't that bother you?" "Why should it?" she said. "It makes him happy. That's what matters to me."

Her words provided the missing line in the sketch. Of course. My chatterbox mother didn't garden all day like quiet Gordon, nor did he read mysteries at night like she did, but they gave each other the regard to indulge in their pursuits—and personalities. Unlike my brilliant father, the equally brainy Theresa didn't spend her days reading the *New York Times,* preferring literary novels. But they encouraged each other's differences while relishing their similarities. I brought this up one day when I was on the buses with Beth. Her long-term boyfriend, Jesse, was as passionate about riding his bicycle as she was about riding buses, leading me to ask, "You don't mind that he does something you don't do?" She looked at me like I was out of my mind. "Why should I *care*?" she said. "Thiz way I see him enough—and not *too* much."

So when Hal reached for my hand on the third floor of his house and I fully embraced the second incarnation of our relationship, I decided to adopt Harriet's perspective. The effect was instant. No longer did I judge Hal's enthusiasms by whether I shared them or had them on my list, but by whether, in *his* opinion, they made his life more worth living. How quickly my life doubled then. How easily we got along. All I had to do was open myself to asymmetry.

If I could walk the path of my thoughts tonight and enter my old study and see my younger self sitting in judgment of her boyfriend's music, I would pull up a chair. Trust me, I'd tell her, the certainties that you hold about another person, and yourself, can change. One day years from now, Hal won't talk as slowly anymore and you won't talk as fast. You'll like summer, he, power-walking. Though you're now the metaphysical one, guess who'll become Buddhist? Why make such a big deal over differences? What do you think love really is?

Now, lying in bed without him as I did for those six long years, but feeling able to give and receive the love I'd craved all those years before, I understand why Hal's architectural ideas are unleashing ideas inside me. Architecture is a blend—of form and function, solids and voids, scale and proportion, weight and mass—and love is a blend, too. Of two people's pasts and presents, similarities and differences, flaws and strengths, respect and forgiveness. It, too, is a design, ever-evolving. Especially if you can admit you could be wrong.

It takes the whole summer, but finally Hal finishes the plans—and what a marvel they are. The grandest feature is my new study, a heavenly third-floor addition reached by a spiral staircase up from the back bedroom. Southern light will pour through its large windows, illuminating the high-ceilinged room all day long. I won't need to leave all day, either—a private powder room and kitchenette will cover all my needs, and when weather permits, I can even meet Hal on a new roof deck that will lie between my new study and his studio.

He has left no floor untouched. Walls will go down between the two smaller bedrooms, as well as the kitchen and dining room. The back porch will vanish, the first floor will lengthen by five feet, the bathroom and kitchen will completely transform. A powder room will replace the ratty toilet and sink in the basement, which itself will be refloored, re-walled, and made dry with French drains. New wiring, pipes, and ducts will go up throughout the house.

He's also included many eco-friendly features. Solar panels. A high level of insulation. Kitchen cabinets made of wheat board with formaldehyde-free adhesives. Paint with no volatile organic compounds. Environmentally friendly linoleum for the kitchen and bathroom floors. Maybe even a geothermal heating and cooling system.

I ask if we can put a wheelchair lift on the front or a ramp in the back. He says there isn't enough space if we want to do it safely. I'm disappointed, but hope that he'll figure something out, because, aside from this, the house might as well be a cathedral.

In early September, Hal takes an afternoon off from work so he can take the plans to the city building department for permit approval. Before he leaves, I ask to see the whole package. His face glows as he opens the envelope and sets the plans in my hands.

They're magnificent, intricate—and forty-three pages. "Geez. It's as thick as a book."

"I guess so," he says, smiling. "Now, let's see if they approve it."

I watch him walk down the street toward the municipal offices, a spring in his step. I feel that way, too, whenever I walk to the post office with a finished manuscript.

Thirteen years wasted over differences. Rome was probably built more quickly.

"I thought so," Hal says when he gets a call a week later. "We need a zoning variance."

The building code, he explains, requires that new construction be set back at least five feet from the side property line, and my new study will not. In October, Hal begins the first step for getting a variance: sending certified letters of our intent to every household whose property abuts ours. This is not as easy as it sounds because some neighbors are renters and don't respond to requests for their landlords' addresses. Other neighbors never bother to reply. A friendly guy across the street expresses surprise when we mention the proposed addition while we're all out shoveling snow one day. "We sent you a letter about it," we say. "You did?" He barks out a laugh. "I probably thought it was junk mail and threw it away."

By New Year's Eve—almost a year since the break-in—I'm pretty disgusted. After Hal labored nonstop for months on his design, we've been spending months just sitting around. I admit that I'm feeling less generous than usual. I've been traveling relentlessly for speaking engagements, then coming home to teach, then heading out the next day, and I need a break. I already notified the college where I teach that I'll be taking the fall semester off. But can I also cut back on my talks? We can't possibly make that decision before we find out about the variance.

As midnight nears, and we settle down on the third-floor staircase beside the window, Hal with hot chocolate, me with hot tea, I'm in a surly mood. It doesn't matter that in a few minutes we'll be able to see the New Year's fireworks going off over the city's center. All I can think about are the neighbors at our property line. These aren't the ones who come to neighborhood parties. I don't even know who they are. "Bums," I say, looking out the window. "You're all bums."

"Man, you're a ball of cheer."

"Doesn't this get your goat?"

"No."

"How could it not?"

"Why should it?"

"Because you're a human being."

He laughs. "You know, it might have gotten to me more before I started studying Buddhism."

"How did that help?"

He sips from his mug, and as we wait for midnight, he tells me about Buddhism. Apparently, there are four noble truths, with the first two saying that suffering exists, and is caused by attachment and aversion. We crave possessions, people, and pleasant experiences, and we push away the unpleasant. "Attachment and aversion," he says, "are both based on the idea that you can somehow freeze or control reality. But since everything changes, we create problems for ourselves by being fixated on the notion that we must have this thing or experience exactly when and how we want it."

The third noble truth, he goes on, says that you can end your suffering, and the fourth says that there is a path to ending it. "They say the way to end suffering is right thoughts, right words, right actions.

You can study that for a lifetime, but what I mostly think about is not being attached to results. If you keep thinking you'll be happy if things go just as you want, then you'll suffer. But if you let go—if you stop being attached to results—you can free yourself from your self-imposed bondage. Then you can have compassion, generosity, loving-kindness, and suffering can cease."

"Have you done that?"

He laughs again. "Yeah, right. I am nowhere near it. But I'm trying."

"Do you think you'll get there?"

"Buddhist teachers say, 'Everything changes.' People's bodies show that the organic world changes. Our relationship has shown us that the inner self changes. The deterioration of buildings shows that the material world changes. If you just accept change, you know that attachment is problematic. But you also realize that you yourself will change. I just believe that I'll get better at being unattached to results, because I believe that I can change."

A light catches our eyes outside the window, and we turn. Framed by the office towers behind our house, a streak of white races up the sky and then bursts open like a nebula.

We watch the fireworks begin, and I think, I *want* to feel attached. Yes, it's brought me suffering. But think of all the attachments I've had—my father and Theresa, my mother and Gordon, Beth and Laura and Max, rafts of friends, years of students. Maybe suffering is sometimes worth it. It brought me back to Hal, and so many others. Suffering, in a way, has been teaching me what love is.

But—and I imagine my younger self castigating me to remember what I just told her—only because I let myself change.

"To the new year," Hal says, clinking our mugs together.

I want to say, "To change," but the truth is, I don't want change. Not anymore I don't. I just look to the fireworks and put my arm around him, and quietly I clink my mug back.

"Dan Bachtle's here for the walk-through," Hal yells up the stairs.

I yell down from my study, "Who?"

"The contractor a lot of the neighbors use. The guy who runs Edge Construction."

"I thought you already talked with him."

"I talked with Artie, who did the houses down the street. And George, who someone at work recommended."

"How many more are there?"

"I've got calls out. We'll see."

It is April, two months after we got the variance, one year after we decided to renovate, and I listen from the top of the stairs as Hal answers the door. I should be down there with him. But since Hal will be managing the project and knows how to spot a scam artist in this field, I've let him run these auditions.

It might seem that I am making no contributions to this project. But in fact over the last few weeks I took charge of one of the few in-the-world realms in which Hal has no aptitude and I feel knowledgeable, and researched home equity loans. I found a good rate, and a week ago we signed the papers for an $88,000 loan, less than we'd hoped for, but as much as the appraisal of our house would allow. Added to the funds from the movie, we have a $130,000 budget.

"What if it's not enough?" I'd said to Hal. "What if there are"— and I plucked out of the air a term I know from living with an architect—"change orders?"

"Then we'll deal with it."

"How?"

"By not being attached to the results."

I laughed, thinking he was joking. He laughed back, but he was not.

Now I come downstairs and shake Dan's hand. Tall, clean-shaven, and soft-spoken, with brown hair and preppy clothes, Dan does not inspire thoughts of incompetence or treachery. Still, the contractor stories I've heard have left a comet trail of wariness. I tell myself to trust that Hal will keep this job from catastrophe, yet what I feel is close to foreboding.

I watch Hal lead Dan into the dining room for their walk-through. I'm attached to our savings and low mortgage. Completely attached. No noble truth will ease that kind of suffering.

Eventually, contractors Artie and Dan say they'll bid on the job. Hal sets a date. The night before, Dan asks for a week's extension. Hal gives it, then calls Artie to let him know there's more time. When Artie answers the phone, he tells Hal, "I can't do your job at all."

"That's obnoxious," I say to Hal. "Putting you through all that."

"Oh, well."

"Doesn't it make you upset? George jumped ship after five calls, now Artie says no."

"I'm not happy. But they have a lot of work. They can afford to blow people off."

"So it's down to one guy?"

"That's right."

"What if he's no good?"

"Dan's reputation is excellent. He's done several houses we like. And I liked him."

"So you're not going to worry?"

"What good will worrying do?"

"You are way too relaxed for this. It's a lot of money and time and our lives will be completely at this person's mercy."

"Why get upset?"

"I'm not upset. I'm envious. I don't grasp how you could be so la-di-dah about this."

"This is my prayer wheel," he said in a guru voice, picking up a lint brush. "I have removed the lint of my attachment."

"Please stop it. I am not in the mood for comedy."

"Okay." He sets down the brush. "The problems that happen in the construction world are not the machinations of evil people who wish others ill. They're about the circumstances of each project and the particular stresses of our times. Anyway, what's the worst that could happen? We don't do the renovation and instead we stay in a house that would be a palace for ninety-nine percent of the world? Besides, why get upset *now*? There's so much more to go through."

"That's what I'm worried about."

"Getting worked up never solves problems. Whatever happens, we'll deal with it."

"You know all your books on Buddhism?" I point to a shelf behind him and, with a straight face and joking tone, I say, "I'm going to dynamite them right now. And that stupid lint brush, too."

Dan calls the night before his extension. He'll drop the bid in our front door by noon.

Hal hangs up the phone with a smile. "He's very professional, too," he says.

"He's also a *fortune*," I say the next afternoon, envelope in one hand, phone in the other.

"What's the bid?" Hal asks from his office at work.

Laughing, I reply, "$320,000."

Hal groans.

"What do we do now?" I ask. "Do we bail out?"

"Are you kidding?"

"But that's more than every penny we have! Even if we sell all our belongings!"

"We negotiate."

This is news to me, but it's all news to me. Not that I'm in a position to pay much attention—I'm running around, dealing with the media that's crashing down on me because of the movie, which is airing in a week. I am so overwhelmed that I am not much good for anything, so Hal fills me in on how he and Dan work it out. He tells Dan, "We can't even come close to that. I'll redo the drawings." Out goes my new study—the year-long zoning wait was for naught. Out go the roof deck, finished basement, solar panels, geothermal system. We'll still have sustainable features, but far fewer. Getting a wheelchair inside just isn't going to happen.

"We're eliminating so much!" I yell.

"I know," Hal says calmly.

"Aren't you bummed about everything we're cutting out?"

"No. I let go of the results."

"Well, at least you could shout a little!"

"I don't need to," he says, smiling. "I've outsourced the yelling to you."

He sends the revised documents to Dan. The figure comes way down, but not enough. So Hal eliminates awnings he designed for the southern windows. He calls for white paint except for one "accent" wall in each room. He keeps one major feature: a full-height wall of windows on the back of the kitchen. But he scales down other goals. When I get agitated, he just says, "My job is problem-solving, and that's what this is. That's *all* this is."

In this way, the price drops to $171,000—way more than we'd hoped to pay for far less than we'd wanted. But we will get what Hal has come to feel, and I actually do agree, is essential: the demolition of several interior walls to create bigger, sunnier rooms on the first and second floors, the demolition of the rear kitchen wall, the extension of the kitchen by five feet (eliminating the back porch and requiring a hand-dug foundation), remodeled bathroom, remodeled kitchen, new wiring, new plumbing, new ductwork, new insulation, new windows, central air, new appliances, new cabinetry, new finishes, brick cleaning outside, brick painting.

Relieved, I ask whether we'll be signing a contract. "The architect-contractor relationship—and the client-contractor relationship—is set up to be adversarial," he tells me. It's a good idea to do whatever you can do to mitigate that. People who are less familiar with the industry than I am should almost certainly negotiate a more formal contract, but I feel comfortable with a letter agreement from Dan." The letter, which Hal adds is legally binding, has a payment schedule, a list of items to be purchased by us, and a statement that Dan carries all insurance—something that, though we can't possibly know it now, will become radiantly important later.

"Are you okay with this?" Hal asks, his pen poised above the letter.

My face feels tight. Such a huge bill won't mean debt, but it will mean digging deep into our savings, as well as my filling the next years with talks instead of cutting back. But Hal is confident that everything will work out. "Yeah," I say, hiding my wince.

That night, although I go to bed early, I lie awake. This renovation journey has already dragged on way too long and we haven't even started. Of course, we also haven't suffered—yet. But even if we escape suffering all the way to the end, the experience will not culminate in the house of our dreams. So far it is, in fact, like so much of life: the incandescent promise that you'll receive every glory that you want, followed by the hard shock of regular old reality.

I get out of bed. At the top of the stairway to the third floor I see Hal, not in front of the drafting table, but with a guitar in his hands, for probably the first time in months.

"Can't sleep?" he says.

"It's just so expensive," I say, "and so far away from the fantasy. And I'm afraid."

"I'm nervous, too."

I know he is, yet his eyes have a serenity that I do not feel.

"Come on, Baboo," he says. He sets down the guitar, stands up, and takes me in his arms. "Few things in life are gained without risk. It's time to do this."

His skin is comforting. But even as we are standing in this embrace, and I know we are going to be on this journey together, I now grasp that we will be traveling separately. He will be more involved. I will, if I choose, be free of whatever crises arise—and be the one who agonizes. I feel lucky that the client has a husbitect. Yet I also feel oddly alone.

We hold each other for a long time, our bodies moving with our breathing, our thoughts synchronized one moment, far apart the next. It is, I realize, our own awkward dance. And I suddenly understand a new lesson about love: that when your life doubles because you accept another, and you're happy because he's happy and he's sad because you're sad, and you enter the biggest decision that the two of you have ever made, this unbalanced dance might be the dance you'll do most often. I wonder if it is even what love is.

MOBILIZATION

P·A·C·K·I·N·G

Friends

"You're joking," I say to Hal.

"Would I joke about this?"

"Move out of the house? Like *completely*?"

"When they demo these plaster walls, dust will go everywhere."

"We can wear masks."

"Every day they'll start bright and early at seven in the morning."

"I'll get up at six."

"What about the power tools? They're loud and they'll be going all the time."

"I'm still traveling a lot—and I'll just spend my writing days at the library."

He sighs, then perks back up. "Okay, contestants. It is now time for Final Jeopardy."

I turn to the cats. "See what I have to put up with?"

He continues in his best Alex Trebek voice. "Excessive exposure to take-out meals, Porta Potties, and thermal underwear." Then he hums the Jeopardy jingle: "Do do do do, do do do."

"I have no idea what you're getting at."

"*Ehnnk.*" He makes the sound of the cut-off buzzer. "The question is, What happens when Dan's guys gut the bathroom and kitchen and shut off the heat?"

"All of that's going to happen?"

He raises a brow and nods.

"At the same time?"

"Well, we *could* pay them for an extra year of work."

I remember something a friend told me when I visited during her renovation and watched her husband and son almost come to blows. "I once saw a cartoon," she said as her son slammed into his room. "The devil is standing before two doors. One door leads to hell with all the flames. The other one is living in your house while it's being renovated."

"Okay," I say to Hal. "We'll move."

The night we make this decision, I walk into my study—and almost collapse in despair. Like probably ninety percent of the world, I dread packing. This is not, though, because I get overwhelmed by the prospect of organizing. The problem is far more seismic than that. Actually, the problem is many layers of problems, with each one going deeper than the last until you hit the molten core at the center of them all.

The most obvious layer—the one that stops me right off the bat—is the sheer volume of my belongings, most of which are crammed into this room. I've moved over twenty times in my life, the last when we married, at which point I felt buoyed by the certainty that I'd reached my final destination. Then I learned that the house, with its four closets and miserly square footage, was unfit for forty years of possessions. Within a week of our honeymoon, my belongings were straining every drawer, shelf, and cabinet. We added storage units in the only available room, my study, going right up to the nine-foot ceiling. But after three more years, the dam burst, overflowing even the chairs, windowsills, and rug.

Aside from not being able to walk into my study without wading through recent flotsam—souvenirs from my travels, paperwork from my classes, correspondence from friends (I'm a devotee of handwritten letters), newly laundered clothes, books, mugs—there's the peril of the enormous amount of furniture wedged in here, some of it jutting way out into the room. A seven-and-a-half-foot IKEA wardrobe. A dresser we rescued from an abandoned house twenty years ago. A chest of drawers I shared with Laura in elementary school. A quirky end table from my grandmother. Wooden crates that were Hal's first design-build project.

Now we're approaching the real issue. I'm still not all the way there, but just knowing I'm getting warmer makes my knees weak. Because the next layer to the problem is that every item in here has a story behind it. Some, like Hal's wooden crates, tell vignettes, whereas others that are strewn around the room add up to novels. But regardless of how extensive the narrative, each item captures a particular story with a particular person. Some of these relationships are ongoing. Some survived interruptions. And some were with individuals I will never see again.

The end table from my grandmother, for instance. She's been gone for twenty years. The finger cymbals from the year I studied belly dancing, where I met Amina, a beautician with a strong shimmy who shaped my unruly mop into a flattering cut, then passed out of my life following our final performance. The Tupperware container I once borrowed from Frankie, the hot dog–eating bookkeeper at my food cooperative. When he began dying from AIDS, I visited him every week at home, relieving his partner from duty, and as Frankie and I grew closer the container grew more important until I couldn't bear the thought of returning it.

Those stories all ended without regret or ill will. But I have keepsakes from more complicated pairings. The Monty Python album I listened to with my teenage boyfriend before he ended our romance and I cried for months. The crystal night light I kept on during calls with my friend Ethan, whose despair over having married a woman who was not his soul mate ended when he left her, and, to my shock and sorrow, stopped calling me. The scarves I wore as a college student to visit my friend Marie in her dorm room, where she would strum her guitar while we sang Beatles songs—a habit we indulged in, on and off, until our thirties, when one day on a phone call, she insisted that I had to have children right now, as she had, even though Hal and I had just broken up and I was too depressed to think straight; in mere seconds, my affection for her drained away. The single earrings from pairs I shared with Sandy, my best friend from fifth grade, who went through many inner trials, which we discussed in letters for decades.

Usually I forget that I'm surrounded by relics—after all, I rarely use most of them. Then a pen rolls under my grandmother's table, or I'll open a drawer and find a box of old letters, and that's all it will take to put me in a memento trance. I'll recall how, after I first learned Monty Python routines with that boyfriend, we went outside to a wintry golf course and kissed in the moonlight. A Chinese silk jacket will return me to dancing with Marie at a friend's wedding reception. The stained glass I bought because it reminded me of Sandy's love of the shore will take me back to a summer day on a boardwalk when I realized that drugs were ruling her life.

So I stand here, knowing that as soon as I start to pack, I'll be at my mementos' mercy. Every story I've ever lived through—some essential to the person I am now—will return to me, possibly leaving residues of remorse about compassion that arrived too late, resentment about apologies never offered, or wistfulness about vanished affinities. Yet I must pack, and since our four closets will drop to two after the renovation, I *have* to exile some of these belongings. But how can I leave the many persons I once was, and the many people who once loved me, for good? And how can I face the innermost problem with packing, the one even deeper than these?

I shut the door and walk away.

Dan sets a starting date of August 8. The first order of business isn't packing, but finding a temporary home. I expect this task to prove daunting, but I've always been someone who makes friends wherever I've lived, worked, visited, shopped, exercised, even dined. In fact, one of my goals in life has been to meet everyone in the world, and it so happens that in June, Natalie, a gracious Delawarean and new friend who once hosted me at her book group, moves her mother out of a twin fifteen minutes from our house. With the market so robust that she's in no rush to sell, she offers to rent it to Hal and me. We drive over, find it acceptable, and say yes.

Thus able to set a moving date of August 1, I finally return to my study. It's already late June, but I feel emboldened. Not only has an unexpected generosity saved the day, but the stress surrounding the film made from my book is over, Hal's negotiations with Dan are behind us, and ahead lies only the future. This isn't to say that I've come to any conclusions about that future. In fact, with more time to mull over my Search for Life Purpose 2.0, the quandary has worsened. I can't pursue a cure for cancer or a career as a psychotherapist, as I have no aptitude for science, and our compromised savings prohibit a return to school. Nor, since I want to keep waking up with Hal and am not especially adventurous, will I be joining the Peace Corps. Founding a beneficent nonprofit briefly enticed me, but then I acknowledged that I had no single-minded vision, zero funding, and just enough wherewithal to know how little I know. The truth is that every idea that's come to mind is so impractical or at odds with my personality that I'm as aimless as I was months ago.

So packing feels like a superlative diversion, and I'm able to commence with vigor.

In the first few days, I energetically thumb through all my clothes, decide which ones are inconsistent with my current tastes or have never complemented my physique, bag them up, and toss them into bins at Goodwill. Equally brisk is the weeding out of books that I will never reread. Thousands of dollars at cash registers disappear into donations at the library.

But come July, I pry open cabinets and wardrobes—and there they are, my mementos, each item a page in my book of life. Immediately my momentum comes to a complete halt, and all moments rush inside this one. I pick up the Tupperware container. Behind it, I'm surprised to find, I stored my old bottle of sandlewood cologne. I dab a dot of fragrance behind each ear, and then Frankie is resurrected before my eyes. He's in his bed, singing along with a video of Bette Midler on his big screen TV, and I am entering his room for a visit. Even though I don't make a sound, and he recently became blind, he turns toward me. "Umm," he says, "I love your perfume," and I go toward him, both of us laughing again. I push the Tupperware to the side. There is the Maxfield Parrish address book I bought a few years ago because it reminded me of Marie's classic beauty. Inside, I secured pages of song lyrics, each in her writing, and as I flip through, I am again sitting with Marie's family on a steamy July Fourth, and she and her brother are trying to one-up each other on their guitars, and we are all singing these songs to the high heavens. In the next drawer is the crystal night light. I plug it in, and hear Ethan again, over the phone, reading me the bedtime story that he wrote for his little daughter, and that inspired me to buy a pop-up *Alice in Wonderland* book. Oh, and on this shelf is the green dress I wore to Sandy's wedding, and I am again at the reception with Hal, watching Sandy dance with her groom. "Maybe she'll be okay," I'd whispered to Hal, and we'd exchanged looks of guarded hope.

Then it is all at once: the phone call where Frankie's partner tells me that Frankie died moments ago, my stagger away from my office desk after Marie tells me how to live my life, the long hug with Sandy at her father's funeral, where she is hiding the depths of her addiction from me, as well as her then ex-husband.

Knowing I'll never finish packing at this rate, I force myself to move to another cabinet. But when I open that door, I discover photo albums, as well as one unfinished task. Having been advised by a lab tech years ago that photos deteriorate when improperly stored, I've long wanted to remove my pictures from the sticky-back Woolworth albums where they've lived for decades. Look: on a shelf beneath the albums are archival boxes, waiting for this very opportunity.

It'll go quickly, I tell myself, and I might as well get it done. But as soon as I open the first album, I see friends and family marching me through time. It's as if the novels strewn about the room had been collected into these albums. I must pack! No, I must read. I lower myself to the floor and set the first album in my lap and become even more ensnared in timelessness.

So many people long gone, some to a less earthly existence like my grandmother, others, like, for a while, my mother, to paths beyond our personal intersections. I cared for them all, even those whose words caused me to back away, or who, due to my own lapses in judgment, would never receive me with open arms again. And looking at Sandy laughing in the schoolyard in fifth grade, I remember the great revelation of my adolescence: family is different from friends. I'd certainly been told when I was a child that you can choose your friends but not your family, but when I was a teenager I discovered another distinction. Family was the very house in which my thoughts had come into being, and they remained around and inside me all the time. Plus, family was a *they*—all I had to do was start talking with Beth about our mother, Laura about our grandmother, and the conversation would ignite everyone's presence all around us. But friends? In the house of me, my friends were the rooms themselves, each a private haven where I could be a different version of myself, as could they, each decorated by our unique camaraderie. That, I remember thinking when I was a teenager, was what friends were—two people who so delight in each other's company, they make their own sanctuary from everyone else, including (maybe especially including) family. What a sanctuary it was, too: a place of songs only you sing together, of earrings only the two of you share. This is why, when the teenage me had a falling out with a friend, it was never I who encouraged the termination. I couldn't imagine ending a friendship. Each of those private rooms was far too precious to me.

I reach for the next album. My twenties. Here is my mother the night I saw her again, at age twenty-two. Here I am with Hal, who entered my life a month later. Here are so many others, some still traveling through time with me, others so long past that I wonder if they remember my name. Here, for instance, is Marie, smiling in my college room, and as I once again feel that gut-punch from knowing that our friendship was over, I remember a new understanding that I learned in that decade of life: friendship requires more than delight in the friend's company. It also requires trust, depth, and the ability to contend with history, and if it lacks those, it might not be in my best interest. That moment with Marie, for instance, slammed me into a mistrust that I knew I'd never shake. Belly-dancing Amina and I lacked the depth for continued effort. And when I looked up my teenage boyfriend when I was thirty-one and we met for dinner, I thought that if we were meeting now, we'd be friends—but I also knew that our history made any friendship impossible.

The photo albums move into my thirties. Author readings for my first books. The breakup with Hal. Running events in a bookstore. Starting to teach. Riding the bus with Beth. There is Ethan, right before he left his wife. Although I remain baffled and saddened by being left behind, I feel the aperture of my heart open when I see this picture—and I remember that in my thirties, I came to yet another conclusion about friends. Though I might have no understanding of why someone moved out of a friendship, or find the stated reasons cowardly or frivolous, I need to grant them the same right to act in their own best interest that I grant myself. Besides, I still think of my former friends with a full heart. Maybe they do the same with me.

Now, my forties. Look at Hal, back in my life after long loss. Look at Beth and my mother and recently even Laura, with whom the same is true. Oh, and look at Sandy: sober at last, living in a house at the shore. Taking in all these faces—moments in stories still being written—I know something new. That only by going the long haul with these people, forgiving them their errors as they forgave mine, did I learn that each individual is so much more than a single foolish action or ill-considered word or self-centered time in life. Believing I can fix someone conclusively, as in these photos, as in each object, strains rationality. I can no more pin a person down than I can pin sand to the wall. This is why my friends are still with me, even if our friendships have ended. This is why my resentment of a rejection is accompanied by affection. And this is the core of why packing can be so daunting. It is a reliving of how all that once was slowly became all that is now. It is a lamenting of all that is no more—and gratitude for all that's survived. It is, I'm stunned to admit, grieving.

In the kitchen, Hal, unplagued by even the slightest trace of grief, is whistling a made-up tune as he rolls up our glasses in newspaper. I reach for a glass, thinking I'll distract myself by being useful. But something about me—the swirl of memories on my face, the scent of sandalwood behind my ear—awakens his Marriage Mind Meld. "What's up, Simon?" he asks.

"Nothing," I say in a telltale lying falsetto.

"It's so nothing you look like you're about to fall over. Have it out."

I slump in a chair and tell him what I've been doing. Or haven't been doing.

He says, "Lots of people can't get rid of things, probably for these same reasons. Maybe that's part of why the square footage of new houses keeps growing, and the self-storage industry's booming. But we can't put in more closets and we're not renting extra space."

"I thought you architects were space magicians."

"Ah, foolish lass, now you see the folly of your thinking."

"So what can I do?"

He thinks a minute. "When a building loses its original purpose, like a factory goes out of business or a church closes, Americans tend to take one of two approaches: they neglect the building for years, then tear it down and build something new, or they regard it as a precious gem that has to be kept precisely as it is. But in recent years we've been finding ways to do what's called adaptive reuse, which is more like what the Europeans have been doing for a long time—turning the factory into a school, the church an office. It's funny. We have a tendency to see only two options—throw it away or preserve it with awe. They allow for a middle ground."

Pyrex bowl in his hands—a gift from Beth—I say, "But how do you adaptively reuse objects that mean so much to you?"

"Beats me," he says. "Maybe an epiphany will strike in your sleep. Aren't you the Girl from Epiphanema?" Then, grinning, he sings lyrics he's made up to go with the tune: "Short and cute and smart and lovely, the Girl from Epiphanema goes asking, and then she's musing, it's quite amusing, then—Pow!"

I make a small smile. "Nice try. Except I don't feel any Pow."

"I know you," he says. "You will."

And he's right—by the next morning, I know what to do. But it didn't come to me in my sleep, and it didn't hit with a *pow*. It came while I was talking with Hal in our bed, late into the night. There, our conversation lit by the turtle lamp I bought when we were apart, listening to a CD of Portuguese guitar music he found at the same time, thinking beyond the most obvious options, we came to the solution with ease.

Now I return to my study, dig out the Maxfield Parrish address book, and set it aside to give to the amiable receptionist at my chiropractor's office. I reach for a box, insert the crystal night light, and label it for my sister Laura. I run through my date book for the last few years, looking for new friends. Marni, the jewelry maker I met in

Boulder, will love the single earrings. Bonnie, the author who answers my e-mail when I'm on the road, will love the pop-up Alice. When I am outside later in the day, I wave to my neighbor Susan as she walks down the street. An education director at a church, she's a new friend I already feel will continue through my life with me, so I immediately tell her the story about Sandy, and that I have a stained glass panel that I love but that holds a memory I need not keep. Does she want it? She almost weeps as she says yes. In the next days, as I send out packages to one friend after another, I start to think of myself as a story giver: here is how this Chinese jacket, Tupperware container, pair of belly-dancing cymbals, came to me. Now I am giving them to you.

I am not regifting, but spreading memories. Nor am I demolishing my past. I am adapting it for the future.

Finally, the night before the movers arrive, my closets are empty. My steps unburdened, my spirits revived, I walk through the house, ready for tomorrow. But now I am also ready in another way. I am at last realizing a truth I have suspected but resisted all along: that although nothing in this life is fixed—not friendships, not houses, not kisses, not perfumes, not whirling belly dances, not even a fifth grader's laughter—we can still, every day, make some mark on another person's page. We can sing a song together. We can share a wave on the street. We can give each other a story.

Family

This is how our moving day begins:

"I should tell you something," Hal says as we stir awake. "Your huge IKEA wardrobe?"

I rub my eyes. "What about it?"

"I, uh, I broke one of the mirrored doors."

"But I saw the doors last night. They're leaning against a wall downstairs."

"No, you saw a healthy door. I turned the broken one so the glass faces the wall."

"You *hid* it?"

"Not exactly. I just sort of . . . delayed its discovery."

"You're telling me *now*? On *moving day*?"

He hurries through the details. Four nights ago, hoping to shave a few minutes off the movers' bill, Hal began hauling everything he could carry down to the first floor. But as he was maneuvering the towering mirrored door down the stairs, he slipped. The mirror canted out of his grasp, skied down the stairs, and slammed into a wall.

"Why didn't you tell me when this happened?"

"You were at that talk in Orlando."

"And when I got home the demands of packing conveniently postponed this confession?"

"You could say that."

I turn toward the ceiling with a loud sigh and feel him bracing for my reaction. There are so many possibilities. An exasperated *What in heaven's name were you thinking?* A guilt-inducing *Moving day disaster always finds me. Me!* An icy *I'm getting dressed now.* But I discard all these options, because only one response truly encapsulates what I feel.

"Well," I say, turning back, "stuff happens."

He smiles. "Exactly."

"Maybe the broken door will get us off the hook. Maybe this'll be a good move."

"Whatever that is."

"Hey, you can't be the pessimist today. That's my job. You need to be the optimist."

"On moving day, anything can happen."

Knowing just how true those words can be, we laugh, memories brimming in our eyes.

"So no truck accidents?" I say.

"This time," he replies in a Beatle accent, "we'll pass the audition."

He looks at me with hope, I respond with trepidation. And so our moving day begins.

Stuff Happens. Almost anyone who's U-Hauled, Mayflowered, or just lugged their worldly goods from one home to another is acquainted with this unwritten law of moving. The language is sometimes coarser when first imparted by a wizened sage, typically outside a dorm while a thunderstorm is pounding sage, siblings, and overpacked boxes into misery. Sometimes, too, it's dismissed as cynicism, especially by those fortunate enough to have emerged sound of body and mind from a move. But for veteran movers like me, for whom Stuff sure did Happen on moving days past, all we can think when we wake up on moving day morning is: Please, God, spare me anything unexpected. Let no Stuff Happen again.

Stripping the bed as Hal jumps in the shower, I think about my first exposure to this harsh wisdom. I was a month shy of the end of second grade, and although my family had relocated from a city apartment to a suburban house when I was a year old, this was essentially my first move. Indeed, until that day, enjoying what I now regard as the most carefree period in my childhood, I'd had little experience with change. Every day bloomed into a cheerful routine: a welcoming school, a neighborhood teeming with kids, a generous heap of freedom. Plus, I felt much like everyone else in our New Jersey town: Jewish, with a working father, stay-at-home mother, and kids close in age (Laura, the oldest, was nine, Max, the youngest, four, Beth and I in between). It never occurred to me that moving would bring the curtain down on this all.

Perhaps if I hadn't been seven, I might have acknowledged that in the bedroom across the hall from mine there was evidence that the unexpected does occur. But as a sibling, I didn't view Beth's disability as bringing anything unexpected to my family. Sure, I knew the story: right after my first birthday, when Beth was five weeks old, my mother noticed that my sister was not responding to anything, from other people's smiles to her own hunger. Only after months of rising dread did my parents learn the diagnosis of mental retardation (or what would now be called an intellectual disability). Where had it come from? They didn't know. What should we do? Consider an institution. But my father, who'd grown up in an orphanage, knew firsthand about the despair of institutional life, so my parents kept Beth at home. By seven, I'd certainly noticed that the families in schoolbooks and on TV and along our street included no children with disabilities, but since Beth was completely stitched into our everyday life, I didn't find this omission notable, nor think about the unanticipated issues that disability brought into a family. I knew Beth *had* a disability—she was slow to speak, sit on her own, and move on from diapers. But she laughed boisterously, was sneaky and willful, and was fun to play with. My parents made clear that all of us were to protect her from the world's cruelties, though this also seemed unremarkable. Families stand up for each other, I believed. That's simply what families *do*.

But Beth's disability was not the only evidence of the unexpected that I might have seen in my family. Laura, with her fourth-grade eyes, was beginning to observe something else, which she would whisper about in our bedroom at night. Our mother was smiling less, struggling to keep up with the four of us, Beth's extra needs, housework, and classes for a master's degree. Some days she just started crying.

Our father—the only father on our block who worked four jobs—seemed more delighted by us kids than his wife. But our parents never fought in front of us, so it was easy for me to refute what was already vivid to Laura. Easy to refute, but not ignore; one night I had a dream in which my father was stoking the fire in our fireplace when the flames leapt out and encircled him. As they rose higher I screamed at him to jump to safety, but he calmly replied, "I can't, Rachie. I'm stuck."

Then my father got a job in Pennsylvania, four hours away. I was distantly aware that through the winter and spring, our house was being sold, a new house was being bought, movers were being hired, boxes were being packed. But I kept playing with my siblings and neighbors, especially my best friend, Naomi, a sweet blond girl who lived next door. I knew moving day was approaching, but with all the contentments of dandelions and bicycles and Naomi's mother's tuna fish and watching *Let's Make a Deal*, moving felt as otherworldly as college.

Then moving day arrived. A truck longer than our school hallway pulled up in front of the house. Naomi and I kept going from her lawn to ours, watching. Laura did the same with her best friend, Lucy, who lived across the street. A crowd of neighborhood playmates gathered as movers carted each room, piece by piece, into the truck. Then our parents called Laura, Beth, Max, and me inside to "say good-bye to the house," and things started to get strange. Walking through the rooms was like seeing someone naked for the first time. The house was too large and inhospitable to be the house we knew. It even talked back, echoing our voices. A feeling of unease began engraving itself on our faces.

My parents said it was time to go. Max and Beth sat in the middle of the station wagon while Laura and I settled in the rear, taking the seat that faced backward. All of our friends—most prominently Naomi and Lucy—planted themselves at the fender of our car. "Bye," they said in a civilized way. "Write to us." We giggled at how serious we were being. Then my father swung the door closed, and our loyal companions burst into tears. The car pulled away and Laura and I bawled our eyes out as the wailing group ran after us, reaching out their arms.

We drove crying toward the rural Pennsylvania area where my father was helping start a community college, and that night we stayed in a hotel. Hotels had always been a delicious treat, but I couldn't even doze off. Is this what moving was? Something that yanks you out of your place in the world? That carves moods no one understands and thoughts no one wants onto your brother's and sisters' faces—and deep inside of you? The next day, the movers carried our furniture into the new house. We stood taking in the neighborhood, a desolate subdivision of muddy lots, backhoes, and just-built split levels, and when no kids materialized, we knew that here we'd just have each other. The movers drove off, and when we went inside we noticed that our glass coffee table was missing. "Where is it?" I asked. "The movers dropped it," my mother said, and my father added, "It broke." "But we love that table!" Laura said, and Beth and Max and I agreed. "Stuff happens." My father shrugged. "You have to expect that when you move."

With our first round of chores out of the way and half an hour until the movers arrive, Hal and I now have to deal with our pets.

"Okay," Hal says. "You hold Zeebee upstairs while I cage up Peach."

I herd the younger of our two cats into the room with the exercise machines, now unscrewed down to their skeletons. Black-and-white Zeebee, who has not been through a move, has been bounding around the cardboard playground springing up in the house. But orange-and-white Peach, a seasoned mover, has been hiding under the bed. This is why we're separating them now, lest Peach's distress at the sight of the carrier lead Zeebee to catch on and panic.

I sit on the floor and stroke Zeebee, but I can see by the worried confusion in her eyes that our strategy is foundering. I wish I could reassure her that her imminent captivity is only for a trip to the vet's so she won't be underfoot during the move, and that when we pick her up tomorrow, she'll have a new home with sunny windows that she'll grow fond of. But I'm no pet communicator. Even if I were, how do you reassure anyone when you yourself are on edge?

Of course, I remind myself, not all pets suffer at moves. Dogs in particular can be comforting or even adventurous, especially if they sense that their owners are eager to fold their cards on one round of their lives and try their hand at the next. Or so I learned on the second move of my life, which happened precipitously after the first.

Laura and my dream had been right. Three months after my family moved to that friendless subdivision in Pennsylvania, my mother got a job as a librarian in the community college where my father was working. But it failed to usher in whatever spark she was lacking in her spirit, and his new job failed to extinguish his discontent with her. Two months later, he packed a suitcase, called Laura and me into their bedroom, and told us, as my mother sobbed on the bed, that he was moving out. We would still see him, but he needed to go. Would we be strong for Beth and Max? We promised. Then we walked him downstairs as our mother stayed in their room, hugged him with stunned desperation, and watched his car leave.

But even as melancholy came down on each of us, snow on the frost that had never melted from the move, all was not grim. Laura was turning ten, and for her birthday, my mother said she could get a dog. So a month after my father moved out, my mother picked herself off the bed and drove us to a house where our new puppy lived with his dog family. We brought him home, and soon we became his family and he ours. A small black dog with tan paws, he was named Ringo, for the Beatle who wore rings. What uncompromising happiness he brought us. We ran around with him in the houses under construction. We slept with him in our beds. And when our mother decided she needed to lean on her own mother, we spent our first, and only, winter in that house driving back and forth the four hours to New Jersey, my mother seeking a respite from her pain, the four of us playing word games, Ringo entertaining us all.

When we moved back to New Jersey at the end of that summer, we embraced the change. I'd made friends only at school, and wasn't as close to them as to the few kids from our old house who wrote me letters, which, sadly, did not include my blond friend Naomi. A new home might mean new friends, and also that our mother might stop crying. Plus, my father, in a new job, was already living near the apartment we'd be renting. Maybe he'd even come back. We could be a family again. We cuddled Ringo, following the moving van, singing to the radio.

Now Hal says, "I'm ready." I open the door, we wrestle Zeebee into the carrier, and while Hal waits for the movers, I secure the cats at the vet.

"They were due ten minutes ago," Hal snaps, unearthing his inner pessimist.

The dormant optimist in me replies, "I'm sure they'll be here soon."

In the already sweltering heat, we stand on the front porch, waiting.

"Well, if they're not here at nine o'clock," Hal says, "I'm calling the main office."

"A lot of our neighbors like them," I say. "Don't worry. It'll be fine."

Were any neighbors outside—and there are not, because the rates for Dinkins & Sons are lowest on weekdays, so we picked a Monday for this move—Hal and I would appear to have swapped our roles. I suppose we have, but as he well knows, I'm saying these words as much to crank up my hope as to reassure him. Late movers were the next Stuff that Happened in my growing up, and optimism, however misplaced, was all I had left to cling to.

The day we moved on from the apartment in New Jersey the movers came egregiously late—just as I was hoping they would. I was eleven by then, and for two years I'd hungered for my father's return. At the same time, I knew that moving brought so much newness into a life that it almost seemed to sow new selves inside the original self. In the past two years, the four of us had acquired a darker humor and a mistrust of our own lovability, and my mother had begun wearing a hangdog face. So what if we were moving to a house on a pretty lake in another part of New Jersey? All I could think as we waited for the truck to show up that morning, then afternoon, then evening, was that if it never arrived, history would have only one move to reverse. Then there'd still be a chance to restore the personalities—and family—we'd been.

Finally, after dinner, the movers showed. "How could you do this?"

my mother wailed. We hit the road at ten, reached the new house at eleven, and at two a.m., the movers finished. My mother's expression grew even more powerless. My hope was unmasked as naïveté.

"You're right," I say to Hal on the porch. "We should call the home office now."

"Let's not worry just yet. It's only quarter to nine."

Cicadas thrum in the humidity. Our roles have switched again. We wait.

"I'm Albert," says the lead mover. "This is Jimmy and Melvin."

Tall and muscular, they have two moving trucks, which they parked in the center of the street, right beneath the leafy sycamores. I am glad that they'll be shaded as they work.

Albert, a Montel Williams look-alike, has a no-nonsense persistence that the ninety-three degrees and ninety-eight percent humidity do not shake. Trim, gangly Jimmy seems cut from the same cloth: efficient and serious. Melvin smiles—and jokes, and goofs off, and carries the lightest pieces of furniture, one per trip. Melvin's clothes are the most colorful, and his eyes are lit with a sense of play. Under other circumstances, like an office cubicle we shared, I'd adore the jovial atmosphere in our foxhole. But now, when he's manipulating the giant wooden desktop out of my study and saying, "Sure is a big desk," I simply say, "Yeah," suspecting that Hal would be irked if he knew I were chatting with someone on the clock.

Of course, Melvin, who hasn't the faintest idea about our history, can't possibly know that Hal often found my inclination to talk with strangers disruptive in our first relationship, as brief exchanges with waiters, postal workers, even telemarketers turned into animated social affairs, and he waited beside me, steaming. By the time we split up, I knew that when I was around him, judiciousness was called for. Even now, if Hal and I are out for a walk, I'll try to assess his tolerance level before a nod to a stranger watering her lawn becomes an hour-long garden party. And today is undoubtedly not a tolerant day.

"There's always one who doesn't keep up with the others," Hal says, coming up to me when I'm standing in my study, watching the movers from the window.

"Yeah, but Melvin lends comic relief."

"I'm not paying for them to take time doing their job."

I guess it's wise that I'm keeping my mouth shut—this sure won't be a good move if we start fighting. Though I wish Hal would be more zen about this, more like the Master Thich Nhat Hanh I have just become. He's probably wishing I would be more vigilant, more the eagle-eyed worrier he has just become. It seems we have reversed ourselves yet again.

Too bad we can't trade our memories, too, I think, as Hal heads downstairs to keep an eye on the movers and I stay at the window. Until adulthood, he was a charter member of that elite group of people whose moves were harmless. He was familiar with the logistics; along with his parents and little sister, he moved three times around the suburbs of Washington, D.C. But each transition was unexceptional, and his family was stable, so he remembers nothing of those moves. The ones he does recall were on an ocean liner, at the start and finish of two years in London, where his father had gotten a job. On the way, fourteen-year-old Hal was repeatedly chided for unbecoming behavior at state dinners, but on the way back, at sixteen, he had a grand time running around the twisting passageways with his sister, infiltrating the first-class decks.

That's the kind of moving day memory I'd like—frolicsome, picturesque. But in fact, the move I made at sixteen, which happened to be my next move, is the very one I would not wish on anybody. Not only is it a moment in my family's history that is so extreme that it hardly seems real, but whenever I unscrew the lid on my remembering to tell the story, the old ice storm comes alive so ferociously in my chest that I get the telling over with as fast as I can.

So: I am sixteen, and it is a sleeting February afternoon, and Max and I are in our mother's driveway, shoving our things into our father's car. In the five years since we moved to this house—the house on the lake—my mother's insecurities and loneliness have led her through a succession of testy boyfriends, each more kid-allergic than the last. As she drifted more fully into their arms, we four kids spun our aches into sarcasm, our longings into contentiousness. My father moved back to Pennsylvania, where he'd begun living with Theresa, though the animosity between him and our mother became so severe that we saw him only every few months. Even today, as we are leaving her house, he will not step inside.

Four weeks ago, my mother met an ex-con in a roadside bar. A drinker and smoker of Dionysian proportions, as flinty-eyed as Rasputin, he sweet-talked her into believing that he was a secret agent leading a life of excitement, and that, if she ditched her children, he'd give her the adventure of a lifetime. Astoundingly, my mother, a nondrinking, nonsmoking librarian, bought into this. Two weeks later, he moved into our house. Two weeks after that, on this very morning, Laura, Max, and I were told to leave. Beth can stay—my mother still feels affection for her. Laura quickly departed for a rented room, though she will soon resettle at our father's, which is where Max is going tonight and where Ringo will end up, too. I'm being placed in a boarding school—right now. Yesterday, we were just an excessively messed-up family. Now, as Max and I get in the car and look through the cascading sleet to the front door and see Beth holding Ringo and waving good-bye, we are a family in ruins. Whatever family means.

The next morning, I sit down in a phone booth at the boarding school and call my mother collect. I want to tell her I'm all right, but she refuses the charges. I go cold with disbelief, which only gets worse when, two weeks later, my mother marries the ex-con, takes Beth on her honeymoon, and disappears. Our grandmother sells the house, as well as whatever belongings hadn't made it into my father's car. My insides are a blizzard. For the first time I taste hatred.

Even when Beth is returned to us four months later, my hatred remains. Because then we find out that my mother has been living a life on the run, and that her new husband, who's violent, paranoid, and heedless of social conventions, had them living in hotels, riding buses across the Southwest, squandering my mother's savings, running from skipped bills. The whole last night before my mother put Beth on a plane to my father, Rasputin held a gun on my sister.

Drunk on my hatred, I tell friends that I don't care about my mother, I don't believe in maternal instinct, I loathe every schoolbook and TV show and charming suburb that perpetuates the propaganda we call family. What in the blazes is family? A bunch of fractured selves yoked together by blood. I'm not going to think about family again. Each person, sure, I'll think about Laura and Beth and Max and my father and Theresa, but only one at a time, as I try my best to get along with each. But don't you dare call them my family. In the deep freeze that has become my soul, family is the most piercing word there is.

Could I have imagined myself now, thirty years later? Calmly driving through a city in Delaware on a moving day? Being so ordinary that I'm about to start a home renovation? Savoring marriage to a man who can easily say "I love you"—yet who understands why, even when I'm feeling a rush of romance so great it alchemizes distress into merriment, I cannot?

This is what happened a few minutes ago, when Hal came upstairs and found me at the window, watching the movers. Seeing no value in my standing there, beset, as he knew, by memories, he suggested that I go on to the new house, have lunch, and wait for him and the movers to show up. Then, with the trucks blocking our street, and my never having mastered driving in reverse, he backed my car out to the adjacent block. "I love you," he said, kissing me when he rose out of the driver's seat, then ran back to the house before my usual awkward reply.

So, cruising down the road toward this next lock in our moving day canal, I accelerate through the memories, taking them up to just before we met.

After that fate-bending February day when I was sixteen, there followed many moves, from boarding school to my father's during the summers, from my father's to college, from college into a house in Philadelphia with two friends. On the rare occasions when my mother came up in conversation, I would cut it off by saying that she'd disappeared, which, for all intents and purposes, she had. But in fact I *had* learned where she was. One day, my father happened to see her name in the local newspaper among the public notices of bankruptcies. It couldn't possibly be her—she'd never been to that part of Pennsylvania. But when Laura and Beth drove to the address, there was our mother, living only half an hour away. It was a short, tense visit. She told them where she worked, and that she was no longer with the ex-con, but expressed no interest in us. Furious and confused, they left, and we heard nothing for years.

Of course, once hatred has coursed down your throat and entered your veins and soaked your bones, it seduces you. It has so much to recommend it—its flair for absolutism simplifies decisions, its fervor incites self-importance, its potency generates arrogance. Besotted with hatred, I felt new selves deploying inside me: incisive, disdainful, battle-ready.

Except that they failed to crush my now prodigious self-doubt. Otherwise, why would I have selected college boyfriends who were hostile to relationships? Why would I have felt breathless with envy when friends talked lightheartedly about their families? Why, when a therapist dared suggest that someday I should track my mother down, did I not slam out of his office? Apparently hatred, for all its bluster and might, hadn't utterly overpowered me.

Perhaps that's why, the spring before I graduated, I did look up the number of the library where my mother had said she worked. Not that I was going to call, as the therapist had urged. I was just going to . . . carry her number around. I did this for a year until, at a particularly de-spairing moment during my first job after college, I pulled it out and my fingers dialed the number and I kept the phone to my mouth and asked for her department. It was six years after I'd left the house on the lake—the same amount of time I would later be apart from Hal. My mother picked up. I said who I was. Instantly, she started crying, thank-ing me for calling, gushing her desire to see me. I was speechless. Why, in all this time, hadn't she called *us*? Wasn't *she* the parent?

I didn't get my answer until I saw her face-to-face soon after, when we arranged to meet for dinner. Hatred roared inside me as we sat down and ordered our meal, yet I kept it to myself, surprised to see that she carried herself with the same old meekness and lack of self-regard. And when I contained myself enough to ask why she hadn't called, I was just as surprised at her answer: "Because I thought you'd reject me." Wait, I wanted to say, you've got the whole thing wrong! Instead, I was so taken aback that I went to collect myself in the ladies' room.

I stood in front of the restroom mirror, and let the hatred surge through me. Leave right now, it demanded. Dump her. But when I stepped back into the restaurant and looked at her from afar, I saw a little, forlorn, gray-haired woman who was so unable to see how family was supposed to work that she thought her children had authority over *her*. Why she was this way—what storms she'd weathered in her own childhood—I had yet to discover, and I didn't ask myself that now. Rather, standing in the restaurant watching her, I felt something unfamiliar rise inside me. I had heard the word for it before— "forgiveness"—but having viewed it as the realm of the gullible and small-minded, I'd never considered it pertaining to me. But there it was, and it said to me, You have a choice. You can keep on hating her, or you can decide to forgive her, and as accustomed as you are to the lures of hatred, it has not done well by you.

I walked back to the table, sat back down, and, without saying a word about what had just happened, committed myself to forgiveness. It was not easy then or for a long time, and it never intoxicated me like hatred. But it stilled the storm. Over the next three years, I helped Laura, then Max, then Beth come back to my mother, and as I did I said to myself that maybe family isn't propaganda any more than forgiveness is. Maybe I just have to recognize that, behind the storybooks and TV shows and every door in every house is indeed a bunch of fractured selves. Just like me. Taken over by hatred, too, or hatred's cronies: rage, sanctimoniousness, judgmentalism, self-loathing. But I knew now how awful all of that felt. I knew, too, as I came to understand my mother's story, that she had acted not out of malice, but weakness. That she had not schemed to make me feel shattered by her actions, but had just felt so compelled by her own misery that she couldn't help herself. This, I now knew, was what most of us do all our lives. Or until we find ourselves standing in the back of a restaurant, making a choice we'd never known was there to make.

Leaving behind hatred and my narrow view of family, I never sought out either again.

Look at how ahead of schedule we already are! We thought the movers would get to the rented house at one, but it's only noon. Might we

escape unscathed? Don't hope too hard, I think, as they take the opportunity of the halfway mark to break for lunch, and Hal goes into
the kitchen to nibble on leftover pizza. But I try to influence fate. I
plug in fans to cool the house down. I find the checkbook. Then I run
out of things to do, and perch on a box and fidget.

It's just not like me to sit around. It's sure not like me to keep to
myself. So, despite the risk of annoying Hal, I find a jug of water, go
out to the boiling driveway, walk up to the movers standing in their
truck, and ask, "You guys want something to drink?"

"That's all right," Jimmy says, wiping his brow with the back of his
hand.

"We picked up Gatorade when we dropped the second truck off
on our way here," Melvin adds. He lifts a bottle to show me.

"This whole thing must be brutal," I say. "Just keeping going. The
heat."

Jimmy says, "Yeah, it's rough."

I could just walk off and find some shade, and if Hal were out
here, perhaps I would. But as I learned whenever I moved, every single person is so filled with stories that all I have to do is strike up a
conversation with genuine curiosity and a patient ear. Then the
weightiest of concerns will make way for new fascinations, and soon
my discomfort will lift. Or, as I've always seen it, moving, more than
anything else, is how I learned to speak to strangers.

I dive in. How did they come to work for Dinkins & Sons? Jimmy,
an electrician, has had trouble finding work in his field. Melvin, a me-
chanic, is earning money to open a garage. Albert, the only one who
sees himself as a moving professional, is studying for a degree in business before his body gives out. Each story, brief though it is, moves me,
as Jimmy and Albert become more expressive, and Melvin's liveliness
is further fueled by his ambition.

What *is* a good move? I ask myself as I listen. I've always thought
it meant that nothing gets broken. But might it also be a move where
something unexpected is gained?

The move into the house begins. While Albert and Jimmy hoist the
sofa and Melvin tackles the IKEA panels, I linger on the front yard,

examining this building that I will soon call my home. A two-story brick twin, it resembles the house that Hal and I rented after our first five years of living together. We remarked on this to each other when we came here to decide if we wanted to rent, but we didn't talk about it at length. Although we have fond memories of that other twin, we associate it with the two lowest times of our previous relationship, which were, predictably enough in this chronicle of ill-fated moves, the day we moved in and the day we moved out. I rarely mention these occasions to friends, since anyone who already knows about my family would think, Surely the girl's hit her Stuff Happens quota by now. But if life had any regard for quotas, then when two people leave their families of birth and enter their family of maturity, they'd arrive with the most resplendent of personal traits rather than such a huge sack of ragged old junk that they don't even know what they're carrying.

Our move into that other twin took place on a steamy August day just like this one. I was twenty-nine, Hal thirty-six, but unlike today, we'd enlisted friends rather than movers. That morning, while Hal went to U-Haul to get the truck, I stood in front of our Philadelphia apartment, waiting for our friends. I was concerned about parking— the street was almost as narrow as Teacher's Lane—but after all our friends arrived, there was still a vacant space right across from the house. Then Hal returned, steering the enormous U-Haul up the street. He pulled the truck up to the space and threw it into reverse, and, as I stood watching with our friends from the front stoop, Hal misjudged the angle and demolished a neighbor's parked car.

I wish I could say the crash was the worst of it. But then Hal lowered his head to the steering wheel. "Are you okay?" I asked, running over. Our neighbor emerged from his house, more shocked than angry. "My new car," he kept saying, dazed. "Are you okay?" I repeated to Hal. He raised his head and stared straight ahead. I asked again. He opened the driver's door. I stepped out of the way and, without meeting my eyes, he crossed the street and said to our gaping friends, "Let's get going." "Wait," I said. But he had become mechanical. He took no breaks, spoke to and looked at no one. He's become another person, I thought, and as our friends pretended nothing was amiss, I worked beside him as he appeared to prefer: a pair of hands no more intimate than a stranger's. Finally I cornered him in a room where, too hurt and selfish to offer solace, I let other considerations take over my mouth. "The insurance will cover it, right?" I said. Eyes on a chest of drawers, he said, "I didn't buy insurance at the U-Haul." I gasped. "How much would it have cost?" "Fourteen dollars," he said. We didn't speak for the next ten hours, then ended the day not at the thank-you dinner we bought everyone at a Chinese restaurant, but on the curb while they ate inside, screaming at each other like banshees.

Hal and I eventually resumed conversation after our old neighbor presented us with an eight-thousand-dollar bill. But that moving day, with its eruption of selves we'd never seen in each other, crowded our table and bed, convincing me even more that we were destined to part. When we moved again seven years later, we moved separately, I leaving first. That move, which he and I packed on one end, friends and I emptied on the other, was oddly, for two people breaking up, as tender and cooperative as the other was not. After we wedged everything in place, we kissed good-bye. Then I drove off, and in seconds it was just as bad as Naomi, and Beth. I pulled off the road and Hal buckled against our door, and we each crumbled, alone, in tears.

With the truck almost empty, I peek into the smallest bedroom—now my study—and the medium-sized bedroom, aka Hal's studio. Everything's in place. I'm not ready to say that this was a good move—bad luck could still lie in wait. But I can almost let myself think it.

I poke my head into the master bedroom, assuming I'll see Albert and Jimmy shifting furniture. But they are kneeling on the floor, the bed frame a square around them.

"What are you doing?"

"Making the bed," Albert says, screwing the metal pieces together.

"You're kidding me. I've never seen movers make the bed."

"It's part of the job," Jimmy says.

"It's the last thing we do," Albert says.

Melvin, coming out of my study, adds, "The last thing we do here, that is."

"What do you mean?" I ask—at the very moment as I hear Hal ask the same.

I turn as he comes upstairs, and our gazes meet. I expect him to be irritated for my chatting up the movers, but his eyes are filled with respect. It's a look I did not see much during the years in the other brick twin, nor did he see it much on me. I guess that, when we first met, we saw only the traits that most appealed and either did not know about or looked past all the rest. But over the years, inevitably, stuff happens. And even though I emerged from my family with a few priceless nuggets of awareness, when it came to adulthood—to making a new family with another fragmented self—there was an enormous amount to learn.

Such as what I see right now, as Hal turns to Melvin and says, "You mean it's not the last thing you do because you do something else after you leave here?"

"Yeah," Melvin says. He gestures toward Hal's studio. "I play music, like you."

"What instrument?" Hal asks.

"Accordion," Melvin says. When we express happy surprise, he adds, "A lot of people think it's weird."

"The accordion can be very cool," Hal says.

"You really think so?"

Hal says, "Sure. Do you know about Guy Klucevsek?"

They start talking about avant-garde accordion music, and I shake my head. Some people cannot drive in reverse. No one, no matter how desirous of a lost time, can reverse history. But successful reverses abound, if you know where to look. A pessimist can become an optimist, a hater can become a forgiver, a man who once shushed his girlfriend can become as outgoing as his now-wife. Yes, we all cart our fractured selves along as we move through our lives. But we can choose whether we keep plodding along the same rutted road, or take a turn we'd never thought was ours to take.

Hal keeps talking, but we're smiling at each other. This is, I now know, a good move.

There was another good move.

After our last kiss at the other twin, we went into separate lives. The disaster of that August move seven years before remained in our memories, yet as time passed we came to realize that we could not forget the many selves that were strewn about inside each other, most of them praiseworthy, a few flawed, an uncountable number still undiscovered. And because of Hal's Buddhist teacher and my bus rides with Beth, we spent those years trying to learn how to embrace the mysterious sum of other people, including the selves we might have found fault with or misunderstood. Traveling similar paths separately, we worked hard to see the whole of another person, and to hold it, shortcomings and all, in esteem. Finally I moved one more time, into Hal's house to marry him.

Now as I tear the check off the pad and we shake hands with the movers, a light is on in all their eyes. We know them at this point, though not as intimately as friends—I do not know about the misery in their families or the crashes in their romances. They do not know that this past spring, Naomi saw an ad for the movie of my book and knew it was me and tracked me down on the Internet and we wept at being together again. But Hal and I know our movers about as well as they, having carried our desks and treadmill and bed, know us. And as they walk out the front door, I answer my question. A good move is not a move where nothing you own gets broken, but a break where you own up to who you've been, and move a little closer to good.

"Why don't you call the vet?" Hal asks. I can barely hear him, with the movers backing the truck down the driveway. Speaking louder, he says, "We can get the cats tonight."

"Great idea," I say. I find the phone, raise it to my face—and the dial tone cuts off dead.

I no longer hear the truck.

We open the front door. The movers have stopped the truck. Apparently they drove into a low-hanging wire on the way to the curb and severed the phone line for our house.

They emerge, effusive with apologies. Dinkins & Sons, they say, will make good on any costs to fix the line, but it's our first day in our new house and now we won't have phone service and they feel terrible. They seem as shaken as I was my first night in boarding school, and as Hal was when he smashed the neighbor's car. This time, though, a calm Hal goes inside to call the phone company on his cell phone, and an angerless me walks up to the movers and says, "We're not upset, guys. Stuff happens. It's okay." And as I now know, it is. The hot day will cool down tonight. The box-filled house will get unpacked. The snapped wire will get fixed.

In the silky pink light at the end of moving day, we flop on our bed. It faces a view into our new backyard, and a sky that is melting into dusk. Zeebee and Peach, freshly sprung a night ahead of time, poke inquisitively around the house. I take in the bedroom, and although I see this moment right now, this final lock in the moving day canal, I also see another dusk, one that fell right at the end of my six years away from Hal, when we sat on this very bed, talking about whether we should marry. I was worried at all that could go wrong—because, once before, it *had* gone wrong. "But we don't have to live that relationship," Hal had said. "Now we're in this one." "I know," I said, "but what if stuff happens?" "Stuff will always happen," Hal said, putting into words what I was finally understanding about every kind of love, "but that doesn't mean that the universe is against us or that we'll never get over it or that we've received some sign that we're doomed." "Then what does it mean?" I asked. "Not a darn thing," he'd said, and I'd laughed. Now, night takes over the sky, and as Hal's sleep starts becoming mine, the less celebrated law of moving day makes itself clear to me at last: repair can happen, too.

Self

"**B**ut have you been trying the doorknob?" Hal calls into the hall from his shower.

"I *am* trying!" I shout back from outside the bedroom door, twisting for all I'm worth.

"We haven't had any trouble with these doors since we moved in. Did you lock it?"

"There *aren't* locks on these doors!"

"Then it should open."

"I *know!*" I stick my head into the steamy bathroom. "But the knob's not turning at *all!*"

"That's impossible," he says from behind the shower curtain.

"It sure is. But—" I jump back into the hallway and seize the bedroom knob with both hands, "this stupid thing isn't rotating an inch!"

"Ah, Simon, once again it's that darned third dimen—"

"It *better* be. Because if the problem's not me—if the problem's the *door* itself—then I'm in big trouble."

"Don't panic."

"Who's panicking! I'm not someone who panics! I just need to get into this room!"

"Well, hang on," he says. "I'll be out in a minute."

I scowl at the bathroom, leave him to the blather of *Morning Edition* on the sink radio, and keep trying to prove to the Lord of All Matter that I'm capable of opening a *door.*

How swiftly I went from zero to spin-out. At sunrise on this, our second morning in the rented house, I got up with my customary cheerful grogginess. In the fifteen minutes since, while Hal went into his studio to select his clothes for the day and headed into the bathroom, I threw on the outfit I'd tossed on the bedroom floor last night (green shorts, aqua tank top, sneakers), stumbled out of the bedroom, *closed the door behind me to keep out the cats,* downed a quick breakfast, hauled myself back upstairs—and discovered that the knob was stuck.

No, not today. Hal went back to work yesterday, but my out-of-the-house responsibilities don't resume until eleven this morning, when I'm giving the keynote speech for an incoming class of two hundred medical students. That's four hours from now. And it's in Philadelphia—an hour away. Yet here I stand on the far side of a wooden door, with my suit, pumps, stockings, make-up, wallet, driver's license, car keys, cell phone, and host's contact information sealed off like the tomb of King Tutankhamun a mere two feet from my reach.

I try to rattle the knob. I try to pull the knob toward me. I shove my shoulder against the wood. But the door's new identity is a wall.

Okay, be rational. Only overly manipulated fictions contain such critically timed impasses. This is real life, which is so insistently chaotic that it makes a mockery of well-calibrated plots. Besides, this door-and-knob did yeoman's duty for Natalie's mother for years. What could possibly have caused them to abandon their station *today?*

The radio moves on to the next news story, and I tell myself to concentrate on how this morning will be saved. It will be—it *has* to be—even if the hero isn't me, chronic stumbler through the space-time continuum that I am. I'm just fine with it being monk-mannered Hal. I even try to envision it: within moments, my husband will burst forth from the shampoo-scented bathroom transformed into the barrel-chested 3-D Man that he really is, apply his ground-penetrating radar to the innards of the latchset, hone in on the single part worn to a nub, flick his wrist with exactitude, and vanquish the knob and its accomplice.

Or if he doesn't, then at least, with his clothes in his studio, *he'll* be spared.

I sink to the floor and hug my knees, a damsel in distress.

This should not be happening. After all, I learned my lesson about first mornings when I was nine and my mother moved us to the apartment in New Jersey. It just so happened that we arrived the night before I began fourth grade. Too tired to be functional, we kids unpacked little more than our school clothes and shoes before we fell into bed. In the morning I remembered that I still needed socks. Opting not to wake Laura and Beth in our darkened bedroom by putting on the light, I felt my way through boxes until I retrieved two anklets. Then I left for my new school, and soon enough filed into my classroom, wondering if I'd still be the person my teachers had told me I was: a good student, someone who made friends easily. A half hour later, as the teacher was discussing the routines of our day, I heard snickering behind me. I turned. "Why are you wearing different colored socks?" a girl asked as her friends giggled. I looked. Sure enough, one anklet was yellow, one blue. I blushed, crossed my feet—and laughed. "I just moved." I shrugged sheepishly. I described the dark room and the box, and they smiled. By milk-and-cookies time, I felt an ease developing with my new classmates. Walking home from school, I still didn't know whether I would remain a good student or an easy friend maker. But I knew that I didn't take myself too seriously, and that was a nice surprise to me.

That incident bequeathed in me a dread of the curse of first mornings, which has led me ever since to plan in advance. It's why I write my syllabi for the fall as soon as school ends in the spring, and calculate my April 15th taxes at Christmastime. For this move, I strategized for weeks, mindful that a medical school talk would call for a well-put-together image. I even pressed the suit and stored it in the bedroom days ago, a fact I revealed with pride last night to Hal. He laughed when he saw my ensemble waiting in the closet. "That's so you," he said.

"All right," 3-D Man says, appearing beside me in his underwear. "Let's take a look."

I rise from my moping and watch. He jiggles the knob and joggles the knob. He bobbles the door and parries the door. He kicks the door. "Yup," he says. "It's stuck."

"Would a screwdriver help?"

"The spring latch inside the spindle doesn't seem to work. A screwdriver won't help."

"What will?"

"I have no idea."

"This can't happen! Natalie's mother lived here for eight years and it dies on us *today*?"

"Blame the machinations of a malevolent universe? Cosmic whim?"

"I want a superhero, not a philosopher."

He shrugs. "I guess it's a two-for-one deal."

"What about taking off the hinges?"

He points. "There aren't any hinges outside this door. They're all inside the room."

"What if we unscrew the part of the knob that's screwed to the door?"

"The spindle will still be stuck. And I have to leave for work in ten minutes."

"You can't leave now!"

"I'm sorry, but I have a big meeting this morning. I can't even be late."

"There *has* to be a way out of this."

"Call your host at the medical college and tell him what's up."

"I can't call anyone, remember? The movers severed the phone line."

"Oh, right. What about your cell phone?"

"It's in the bedroom, along with yours."

"Hmm. It's a right pickle, I'd say."

"How can you be so laid-back? What's wrong with you?"

"Just bend gently like a reed, Grasshopper."

"I won't get upset. I won't get upset. I won't, I won't, I won't—"

"There's always the train. An hour's ride right up to Philadelphia."

"The station's miles away, and you don't have time to drive me there before you leave—I haven't showered, and I can't give a talk in a tank top and shorts. Argh! What can I *do*?"

This is the point where, in a sci-fi blockbuster, Keanu Hal would take the red pill, learn the truth about the permeable quality of the door, and in the world's first noncinematic use of bullet time, foot-bang the blasted thing open. Or, in a fantasy epic, Hermione Simon would revolve her time-turning necklace back half an hour, get out of bed all over again, and leave the door ajar. But as 3-D Man stares at me with his early-morning stubble and I frown back without the hint of a plan in my head, it's blazingly apparent that we—mere ordinary folk— are powerless in the face of the fiendish plot twists of the universe.

"Wait," Hal says. "I don't think my cell phone *is* in the bedroom."

I tear downstairs—he *did* leave it in the living room. Then I have the amazing good fortune of finding a phone book. I dial a locksmith. A woman answers. I explain the riddle of the stuck door. "I'll have him call you," she says.

"Aren't *you* the locksmith?"

"This is the answering service, ma'am. Can I have your number for a call back?"

"Uh, how soon?"

"Sometime after nine."

Already knowing the futility of a call that late, I read off Hal's phone number, then notice that his battery is running on fumes.

"Where's your recharger?" I call upstairs as I hang up.

"In the bedroom," Hal says.

I've always wondered what I might do if, in my on-the-road life, a similar mishap occurs. Infrequent travelers might suspect that the worst fate is a missed plane connection, but I find doors to be far more fearsome. On every trip, I think about tales of travelers who step out-side their hotel rooms in their underthings to retrieve the complimen-tary copy of USA Today only to hear the door swing shut behind them.

Then I remember that, thanks to my paranoia about planning, when I printed out the information for my talk this morning, I set a copy in my car—and when I did, I happened to notice that my host, Dr. Charlie Pohl, doesn't live in Philadelphia, but *right here in Delaware*.

"Hal," I call upstairs, "maybe Dr. Pohl can drive me in! Where are your car keys?"

As usual, even though we've just moved, his keys are in the wicker duck in the dining room, and they include the extra key for my car. If only my driver's license weren't locked in the bedroom, or I were reckless enough to drive without a license. But still, progress might be at hand. I run outside. Yes! There are the numbers. I run back in and dial.

"Everything's fine," I lie when Dr. Pohl picks up, "but," and I explain.

He listens with the sensitive bedside manner befitting of a physician. "Unfortunately," he says, "I'm already halfway to Philadelphia. But maybe my wife, Janice, can bring you to the train station. She has a meeting this morning, but I can see if she can work this in."

"Well, I do have the slight problem of getting more appropriate clothes."

"I'm sure someone in my office has something you can wear."

I ask him if anyone there is five feet tall. He pauses. "I don't know about that . . ."

I hang up, and collapse to the sofa—or I would, if it weren't sagging beneath boxes.

Get a ladder from the other house. There's no time. *Call a neighbor for help.* I don't know anyone around here. *Call Natalie.* She's on her morning walk, and I need a solution *now.*

I hear the wire hangers in Hal's closet upstairs chime against each other as he finishes getting dressed for work, and the tide of self-pity starts to rush in. This is it, I think. It's all over.

But then I turn myself toward a different thought, or perhaps it manages to turn toward me. It is a memory of one of those serendipitous conversations I favor, this time at a disability conference in Denver. Dan Wilkins, an activist who became a quadriplegic after a car accident, told me, over a table of his thought-provoking T-shirts, something he'd learned after becoming disabled. "It isn't life on autopilot anymore. If you want to figure out how to do something, you give it a shot, and if Plan A doesn't work, you go to Plan B, and then Plan C, and then Plan D. You're not locked into the whole fixedness of life. You come to understand that there's no wrong answer—except thinking that there's only *one* answer."

I can't imagine why I think of Dan Wilkins at this desperate moment. Do memories rotate back to the front of one's mind because of the divine latchset of the universe? Or do I think what I think and do what I do because of the ordinary chaos of me?

I hear Hal go into the bathroom for the final step in his routine, a quick brushing through his hair. The radio is still playing, and he shuts it off. It's all over, I think, except for Plan D, whatever that is. And then, as easily as a reader turns a page in a book, the solution is there.

At eleven o'clock, Dr. Pohl delivers my introduction. I stride to the front of the lecture hall and look up at the students. I am fresh off the train, the ticket paid by his wife, Janice. I am also freshly made-up, my cosmetics courtesy of Janice. But most important, I am dressed.

Quickly—Hal had to leave within minutes—we went into his studio where, two days before, we'd hung his clothes. Hal is seven inches taller than me, but long ago, when we were fooling around in that way that people do when they're newly in love, I'd tried on his pants and found that they sort of fit. "Try these," he said to my request this morning, and I heaved on the white jeans in his hands. Although they kept sliding down and ended way below my sneakers, they did the job. An hour later, Janice loaned me a cardigan to cover my tank top. Then Dr. Pohl's assistant Joyce gave me a scarf, which I knotted around my waist to hold up the pants.

The medical students look at me. One part Hal, one part Janice, one part Joyce, one part me, I tell these doctors-to-be about my morning. "Whatever personal struggles you're having as you move on in life," I say, citing the lesson I learned from Dan Wilkins, "there is always Plan D." We share a laugh, and I continue with my talk. But later, when I make my way back to Delaware as a patchwork self, amazed at discovering a three-dimensional facility I'd had little inkling I possessed, and then when I wait for the locksmiths, who will take two hours to break into the room, I feel much more than mirth. Yes, first mornings might be cursed. But at the same time, on first mornings, I also have the opportunity to unlock the fixedness in myself, and discover something new about me.

That night, as I step inside the newly opened room, and turn around and around, gratefully taking in everything that was waiting all day just beyond my reach, I ask myself, Who will I be by the end of this renovation, so many first mornings from now? What limitations—

or new abilities—will I find in myself? I stop turning, and as I look at the door, now gutted of its entire knob assembly, a small historical anecdote awakens inside me. It is not a first morning from my own history, but from the archeologist who'd spent years and years seeking King Tutankhamun's tomb. The story goes that when he finally discovered what he believed to be the site, he found himself facing a sealed door. With shaking hands, he drilled a peephole into the door, and as hot ancient air from inside the tomb sighed out, stirring the Egyptian sands in the chamber, the archeologist leaned close to the hole with a candle to take the first look. Behind him his benefactor asked, "Can you see anything?" The archeologist strained to see within, the candle flickering as golden treasures emerged from the mist. His expedition in suspense, his life about to change in ways he could not possibly predict, it was all he could do to find the words. "Yes," he replied at last. "Wonderful things."

THE JOB STARTS

D·E·M·O·L·I·T·I·O·N

Children

"They've started the demo," Hal says as he unlocks the door to our house. "Be careful. You never know what might come loose—you could easily step on a nail."

A week after we left, we walk through the vestibule into the living room, and I take in the very first phase of the job. The wooden floor stretches before me, revealing that the golden brown hue I'd never noticed is graffitied with stains and rug shadows. The mantle mirror is playing truant. The refrigerator, draped in protective plastic like a ghostly trick-or-treater, is hanging out by the fireplace. Catcher's mitts of dust wait open-palmed in the corners.

I wasn't expecting that the job would start with such small but noticeable changes. Nor was I expecting that it would feel vaguely unreal, as if we'd passed through a portal into a counterclock land, where the time is running backward and only a single survivor remains. I want to tell Hal how strange this feels. But when I glance at him, he seems to be carrying himself differently, as if he's gone through a portal, too, transforming from the-husband-who's-an-architect to the-architect-who's-a-husband. I just ask, "What's been happening?"

"They've started by removing the doors and trim." He gestures toward the hobbit-sized closet under the stairs, now doorless and trim-free. "Soon all the kitchen appliances will come out, then the dining room pantry will go, then the interior walls will get erased, and finally they'll take down the exterior kitchen wall."

"So basically a lot of the house is going to disappear."

"That's demolition."

"How long will it all take?"

"It'd be really fast if we didn't care about preserving the floors or the plaster walls. But we do, so they're being careful, which means it'll move forward steadily but not swiftly."

"How much do you think will change during my visit to my father and Theresa?"

He looks at me, knowing that in the past few days, my father's been calling a lot about a possible medical crisis that Theresa's facing. I've been shaken, but now I try to act calm. "Since that's a few days off," he says, pretending not to worry along with me, "and you'll be gone only a day, just a little. But believe me, before you know it, the place'll look really different."

"Well," I say, "it's funny timing. Having so much coming down in the house when—"

"Rae, you don't know that the worst is going to happen."

"Theresa did have cancer before."

"We won't even know if she'll need a biopsy until she sees the oncologist next week."

"But my father's scared, and . . . and . . . I just think about what could happen . . ."

"I'm concerned, too. But all we can do is wait." He gives me a hug, and I feel his love wrap around me. "Let's look at the rest of the house."

We walk forward. The graceless stair railing has vanished, rooms have shed doors, and in my former study, the only second-floor room that will keep its walls, the mantel mirror sits in the closet. All that Dan plans to reuse—doors, moulding, trim—is piled up like kindling.

I look at Hal, and he's beaming.

"Nice moment for the architect, huh?" I say.

"The ship has set sail!" he replies.

"Yeah," I say. "Too bad we might run into sea monsters."

"Ah, not to worry, matey," he says in pirate-speak. "I have a cutlass!" I smile, not reassured, but amused. "I might end up with a patch on my eye and going *Arrr, Arrr* at Dan and we might limp into port— just like so many ships I've steered. But by golly, I'll get us there!"

We walk back into the hallway, and Hal, now openly excited, begins to elaborate on the imminent removal of the corridor and bedroom walls. The air is memory-scented, as if the taking apart of the house has uncorked the past, and as he speaks, I imagine I see into last week, as he's bouncing a cat toy down this hall for leaping feline Zeebee and I'm cheering them on. Then I see into four years ago, as I emerge from my study in my wedding gown, and Hal bursts into tears at the sight. Still in the reverse flow of years, I envision Eldridge Waters and his wife saying good night to their children in this hall, and before them, stretching back to 1905, babies crawling to mothers in this doorway, children dressing in these rooms for school, widows entering the bathroom to weep. I haven't thought of these people before, and now I almost wish I knew something about them, even their names. Because they've probably all died, and very soon the house as they knew it—the last physical witness to their memory—will be no more, too.

And as I'm thinking this and listening to Hal and wondering how my father and Theresa are holding up, the oddest phase that's happened so far in my renovation journey—the one I'll find most embarrassing to admit, the one that will revive an inner duel I thought I'd settled in a draw—begins: I realize that since we walked in the front door, I've been experiencing an unsettling emptiness. It's making me feel queasy and off-balance, roughly like the car sickness I can be prone to, and it's intensified with each step. I try to identify the cause. Discomfort about being so out of place? Apprehension about Theresa? Plaintiveness for generations no longer alive? Whatever it is, I do know this: compared to Hal's enthusiasm, it is contrary to reason.

Hal, looking at me, says, "I know, it's hard to concentrate on all this right now."

"Yeah."

"I can't say everything's going to work out," he says. "But whatever happens, I'll be here." He takes my hand and we walk down the stairs.

Maybe it's just fear of change.

That's what I tell myself three days later, when I drive to see my father and Theresa, and, as always when I head to that part of

Pennsylvania, Beth. I haven't mentioned the unsettled feeling to Hal, but it hasn't taken leave of me, and in fact it sits more heavily inside me now. It even reminds me so much of car sickness that I've named it house sickness. But I tell myself as I cruise through the hilly country-side that if it *is* only fear of change, everything will be all right. Not that I welcome change any more than anyone else, but all I have to do is look at the people I'm about to visit and I've got proof that change isn't synonymous with misery.

For a long time, for instance, there was tension between Theresa and me. A childless English professor as in love with my father as he was with her, Theresa had neither expected nor wanted to live with children. But when my mother melted down, Theresa's romantic din-ners with my father became family disputes at the dinner table. This wasn't because I, or any of us kids, resented her for not being our mother—our feelings about our mother were too tangled for that. We just felt no affinity for her churchgoing, gourmet-cooking, and re-served nature, and she seemed to find our juvenile worldviews, love of pretzels, and adolescent self-discoveries inexplicable. For years we kept spearing ourselves on the edges of one another's personalities, even after we left the house for adulthood.

My relationship with Theresa changed maybe twenty years later. I wish it could have happened sooner, but the key to this change, com-passion, was a latecomer in my life. It arrived only after my choice to forgive my mother, when I realized that compassion was the fruit that sustained forgiveness. Even then, however, it did not come easily, or consistently. Then Hal and I broke up, and when we got back together, we often found ourselves talking about compassion, and what he'd learned about it through Buddhism—how it was both the opening of one's heart toward others and the selfless desire to alleviate their suf-fering, and how it was important to have a "soft heart" toward all. He'd even say, "Have compassion for yourself." Slowly then, I tried to be compassionate with Theresa. I stitched together enough scraps of her past to grasp her own disappointments and needs. I asked her about her present-day life. I opened myself to appreciating her interests. And in time our tension dismantled—but even better, in its place came something else: the love for which I'd waited twenty years. It is not the heart-thumping admiration I've always felt for my father, nor the guarded love I now feel for my mother, nor the chummy love I have for my stepfather, Gordon. My love for Theresa is a respectful and conscious love. But it is love all the same.

I spot my exit, the one that will take me to Beth—whose relationship with me also attests to the rewards of change. When Beth lived with my father and Theresa, I used to visit everyone at the same time. This was seldom a jolly occasion because, aside from the conflicts we all felt when together, Beth and I often locked horns. In Beth's late twenties, she moved into a group home half an hour from their house, so although my trips then consisted of two separate visits, they became easier. Not that she and I were spared friction. In fact, things actually worsened between us five years later when she moved to her own apartment and developed her fascination with bus riding, a lifestyle choice with which I could not abide. But when I eventually rode the buses, my judgment of her gave way to acceptance, and the proud, playful love I'd always felt for her surged anew. I can't say that we've achieved perfection in our relationship, but I need only think of Beth—and the chest-swelling affection I've always felt in her presence—to remember that while change can bring little to mind but subtraction, it can also transform into addition.

If my house sickness is arising from fear of change, I can handle that. I just hope that's all it is.

Minutes later, I pull up to the bus station. I still feel heavy-hearted, but then Beth bursts out and hustles over to my car, talking about her current favorite driver and asking me to take her to Target. *Nothing's changed here,* I laugh to myself, because now that I'm no longer riding her buses, we often go shopping, and she carpets our time together with stories about her drivers. Today, Cool Beth, as she calls herself, wants to hunt for a DVD of *Scooby-Doo*. By the time we park at Target, I expect a copy of all our past expeditions: she'll rocket across the lot, fly through the store, and leave me wandering the aisles searching for her.

But as Beth is dashing across the lot, everything about this ordinary visit ends.

A hundred yards away, an older woman collapses on the sidewalk and tumbles off the curb. "What's happening?" Beth says, stopping. "I don't know," I say, catching up to her as a younger woman cries out, drops to her knees, and takes the older woman in her arms.

Beth and I hurry over. The young woman is saying, "Oh, Mom, oh, Mom." Her mother remains where she fell, eyes glassy, her shorts stained with blood.

I ask, "Do you have a cell phone?"

The distraught young woman shakes her head no.

"You can use mine," I say.

"Iz in your car," Beth reminds me.

I turn to retrieve it. Beth needn't accompany me, but I get exasperated by losing track of her in stores, and I'd really like her to offer solace while I rush off. However, Beth is generally as given to helping strangers as the drivers and pedestrians roaring past us right now, so I keep my mouth shut and race across the lot.

By the time I return, a passerby is calling an ambulance from his own phone, rendering my trek unnecessary. Beth is, of course, gone. I could run into the store, but I feel more needed here, so I lower myself to my knees beside these women and use my body to block traffic.

Medical help comes quickly and unexpectedly. A shopper with a cart laden with curtains: "I'm a nurse," she says. A woman about to enter the store: "Do you need help?" and adds, "I'm a nurse." Soon four out-of-uniform nurses are working on the fallen woman. "Do we have something for a splint?" "I'll get ice." "Anyone have rubber gloves?"

I remain at their side, wishing I knew what to do like everyone else. But I can receive the daughter's regret without judgment, pay silent witness to their suffering. So I do, and get caught up in caring, and my house sickness fades.

Through that afternoon, as I am sitting at the old family dinner table, and my father is munching on a matzah, and Theresa is paging through a catalog, I feel it return. I am answering their questions about the state of the renovation when it happens, and I immediately decide not to say anything about house sickness. When I said I'd be coming to visit, my father asked me not to bring up the appointment tomorrow—when they'll find out if a new growth in Theresa's breast requires a biopsy. Talking about my own enigmatic affliction, not to mention the strokelike event I just encountered at Target, only seems cruel.

"How's the place you're renting?" my father asks, keeping the conversation going.

"It does the job, though it doesn't feel like we really live there." A minor observation, but to indulge him, I go on about the sense of dislocation, sounding more dramatic than I feel, until, hoping to show that I haven't lost my perspective, I blurt out the first thing that comes to mind—which is, regrettably, "But it's nothing compared to what you're facing tomorrow."

My father shoots me a look.

Theresa glances up from her catalog. "I'm sure it's still unpleasant," she says.

I'm blushing. I can't believe I said that—but I also can't seem to stop. "Yeah, but it's a really trivial concern, given what you're dealing with."

"I'm not dealing with anything," Theresa says, flipping the catalog page with a snap. "All I'm doing is seeing the oncologist. I honestly don't think it's anything."

"I hope not," I say, stealing a glance at my father, who has dread in his eyes.

"You two are making much more out of this than you need to," she says, kindly but sharply. "I really am not worried." She closes the catalog and reaches for another.

A few hours later, my father walks me to my car. To my eyes, he still looks to be in his mid-twenties, his age when I first held him in my gaze and he lifted me from my crib and danced me around on the top of his shoes. Teacher of American history, champion of unions and civil rights, possessor of a hearty laugh, he could tell stories like nobody else, and whenever I was with him, I felt a rushing between us of giddiness and trust and enchantment. He was, as fathers can be for daughters, my first love, and despite all the mistaken turns he took as parent and I as child, I still feel that love today. But as I look at him now, his face taken over by vulnerability, I see him as he is: a bald seventy-five-year-old with white eyebrows and pleats in his neck. How much longer will he have with Theresa? How much longer will we have with him?

He stares at me, frightened in a way I've never seen, and says, "I've been thinking."

I wait. Then I understand that he's not intending to state *what* he's been thinking, though I know it's some jumble of thoughts about mortality.

I wish I knew the right thing to say, but I feel as unsure of myself as I felt beside the fallen woman and her daughter. All I can think to do is say, "Call me, will you?"

"She's always around. I can't talk with her right there."

"Call me when she's at work, like you've been doing."

Theresa comes out the front door then, her spirits no different than two hours ago. My father's eyes bulge with worry. I hug him, I hug her. "Let me know how the test goes, okay?"

I wave as I back out, and look in the rearview mirror. She is smiling; he is not. I want to be there when they fall, I think. Yet I know that even if we pull through this time, someday—maybe far too soon—Theresa will be gone. Then, his heart crushed, my father will be gone. Eventually, my mother and Gordon will be gone, too. Just like all the generations that once inhabited my house. And when they are all gone, what will I do with all my love? I cannot mourn my parents while hugging my children. I cannot immortalize my parents by raising my children. I cannot even look into the backseat and console my children.

I do not have children.

Where did *that* come from? I snap at myself. I thought I came to terms with that one long ago.

I force my eyes toward the road, the house sickness swelling like a cobra.

When I get back to the rented house that night, Hal's saying with glee, "They've started taking down the pantry!" He's shaking turmeric into a pan, moving breezily along to Tal Farlow on the stereo. "It's happening, man!"

Gee, I think. I don't feel the way he does at all. I feel like I could cry.

Over a late dinner, he fills me in on what they've been doing, but I'm barely able to hear. Maybe this creepy emptiness started because of the disappearing house, along with the coincidence of Theresa's situation and thoughts of deceased people I never knew. Maybe that's where it would have stayed, one big psychic mush that amounted to fear of change. But then I came upon the suffering of a desperate daughter, and listened to the suffering of an anxious father, and this house sickness advanced to a whole new stage.

I don't want to admit what it's becoming. I've never felt it before. But I know what it is.

The next morning, a Saturday, with Hal sleeping late and the workers off for the weekend, I go to the house. I can't say why, except that when I lay awake all night, tormenting myself, I thought I might be able to blunt this feeling if I return to the scene of the crime.

Alone in the demolition, I close the door behind me. The living room floor is now talcumed with dust, the air smells of wood and plaster. It's so quiet that I hear myself breathing. I step forward, unconcerned about nails and splinters, unclear on what I'm seeking, feeling ridiculous. Hal was right—the dining room pantry has been torn down, exposing dingy wallpaper. In the kitchen, the cabinets, sink, and stove have been carted off, their silhouettes remaining like photo negatives on the floor. I go upstairs. Nothing has changed in the hall or my old study, except that the mantle mirror is now mummified in plastic and marked with the grandiosely misspelled "FAGILE." A large mirror, it leans against the back of the closet and reflects my entire body. With so much plastic, I can make out only a generic womanly shape staring back at me. Perhaps that is why, as I confront her, I let the house sickness finally speak.

The first voice I hear is my old belly-dancing friend Amina. She is in a memory where we are changing into our costumes for a class, and she turns and asks, "Do you want children?"

I am in my early twenties, on the verge of living with Hal, and I give her the only answer I have. "I don't know."

"I always wanted kids," Amina says. Then she looks at me, and sees something—confusion, doubt, maybe fear. "Haven't you felt that way?"

"Not really."

"But you like kids. My kids like you. And you've got a great boyfriend. He'll want kids."

"Actually, he hasn't said that."

"What has he said?"

"It hasn't really come up."

"Maybe he's afraid. That's typical of men. Once you're ready, he'll go along."

"What makes you so sure I'll be ready?"

"Do your parents bug you about giving them grandchildren?"

"They don't even expect me to be married. They have a liberal view of adulthood."

"So wait. Someday you'll just feel you're ready, and then you'll do it."

That's a relief, I think, as we take our places in the dance studio and fix our eyes on our veiled images in the mirror. I feel too young and unknowing even to think about children. None of my siblings has begun doing so, either. Only Hal's sister has had a child, a gorgeous boy who is endlessly entertaining. But he'd been colicky, and Hal's sister spent every night of his first months driving him all over town, the rumble of the car quieting him. How could I handle *that*? Or bullies? Puberty? College tuition? I have enough trouble believing in myself and making ends meet. Besides, there are all those Beth issues. I assume that any child of mine will have a disability, not because Beth's condition is genetic, but because, as her sister, I know that things don't always go as planned. Also, my parents have always expected that Beth will live with one of us, a fate that has come to feel like a prison sentence when compared with my friends' freewheeling ways. Why, if I can possibly get a pardon, would I volunteer for lifelong duty?

My question ushers in the next memory.

This time I'm with my friend Ethan from college, and we are having lunch together. We're nearing our mid-thirties, and he and his wife have recently had a little girl. "Having kids is great," he says.

I guess it might be, if you're not, as I am, on the verge of breaking up with your boyfriend. I say, "You're lucky. You're just a natural dad."

"For the record, I think you'd make a wonderful mother."

"I don't know."

"It's not like your mother was such a good role model."

"I don't blame her. I don't blame anyone. I just don't really, really want a kid, and it seems you should really, really want a kid if you're going to have one."

"And for what it's worth, I think Hal would make a wonderful father."

"He says he doesn't want kids."

"He can't be set on that. Have you pressed the issue?"

"What would be the point? I can't even decide to stay with him."

"Well, sometimes people just wake up one day, and they know they want to have kids."

We go on with lunch, and I think, Wouldn't it be nice to wake up with certainty? That's apparently what happened to Max. He'd never even talked about parenthood, but here he is with a wife and two kids. Of course, I could go the other way, and wake up committed to *not* being a parent, which is what Laura's always felt, even during the time when she was married. Though there's also being like Beth, attracted to the idea of kids until she got serious with Jesse, then deciding against parenthood. All these options seem appealing. All of them terrify me.

Which takes me to an evening in my mid-thirties, right after I broke up with Hal. Roberto, a journalist and notorious skirt chaser, is driving me toward what I see as an interesting dinner and he sees as a date, when he asks, "Do you want kids?"

"I've been ambivalent a long time. Now I'm alone and I have no savings and I'm renting a room in a house and I'm working in a bookstore and I'm about to start teaching, too, so if I ever make up my mind, it sure won't be anytime soon."

"You know," Roberto says in a thoughtful tone, "I keep meeting women like you. Bright, good-looking, educated women who don't want kids. And I have to say that it's the most selfish thing I've ever heard."

I lose the ability to see for a moment. When I gather myself together, I point out that Roberto doesn't have kids, either.

"I will."

"You have several careers going at the same time, you travel constantly, you seem to have nothing but flings. How would you take care of kids?"

"There are always nannies, and when the kids get older, there's boarding school."

"Why do you even want kids if someone else would be raising them?"

"So I can have someone around to look after my papers."

He isn't kidding. Nor is another man I date briefly during the years away from Hal, a perennially unemployed ne'er-do-well whose idea of fatherhood consists entirely of being able to loaf around while living off his wife's salary. Then there's the ponytailed guy who derides his sister's tendency to "pop out" kids. As I turn thirty-eight, thirty-nine, forty, and sift through this kind of chaff, I start asking myself, If I met the right man, could I be nudged into taking the leap?

Around the time I give up looking for the right, or any, man, I receive a letter from my friend Sandy in which she brings up babies. It's a small moment in a long letter, but it imprints itself so strongly that I hear her speak the words now. "You know what I do when I'm feeling stressed out? On my way home from work, I go to the hospital nursery and I look at the babies. I still don't know if I'll ever want any of my own. But just looking at them makes me feel great!"

When I first receive that letter, I smile, knowing, if only vaguely, what she means. A year after Hal and I parted, I started teaching creative writing. I loved it immediately, and as one semester has spilled into the next, I've found myself becoming more patient, more bar-raising, more selfless, more inventive, more joyful at another's triumph. Meaning now courses through my days because every day flows toward someone's tomorrow. Teaching is not parenthood, and I don't confuse the two. But I feel a kind of love toward my students—an I-will-hold-the-lantern-through-your-forest-and-never-blow-it-out kind of love. And I wonder, as my students move into their lives, becoming teachers and editors and journalists and psychologists and librarians, some still turning to me for guidance that I'm delighted to give, would I be as dedicated to them if I had children?

Then comes a dinner with Hal at a Ruby Tuesday. It's six years after we split up, our friendship is now romance, and as we're laughing at a joke, he says, "We should get married."

"Is that another joke?"

"What if it weren't?"

"I . . . I . . ."

Hal's eyes tear up. "It would be wonderful."

"I wasn't expecting this at all."

Hal collects himself, then says, "Tell me what would get in the way."

"Well, I've never been someone who dreamed about being a bride."

"So we'll have a really simple wedding."

"We know too many people who don't get along."

"We'll go to a justice of the peace."

"But my bookstore job's too far away. I'll have to keep my apartment if I keep that job, and we'd live separately half the week. That's not what a marriage is supposed to look like."

"Why do we need to be in anyone else's marriage? Why can't we create our own?"

Now I'm tearing up. "You're giving pretty good answers."

"Say yes."

"One more question." I take a breath. "What about children?"

"What *about* children?"

"What have you thought about having children?"

"Oh. I don't want any."

"Boom—no kids. That's it?"

"I'm forty-nine. I don't want to hit sixty-five with a teenager."

"People do it all the time."

"I know. But I see what my friends deal with. They don't have time for their wives or their own interests. Some of them have to work at horrible jobs just so there's enough money for a kid. Some of them have kids with nightmare problems. I like my quiet life."

"But what if I decide I want kids?"

"Then I'm not the guy for you."

"But you're so easygoing about everything else. Why not this?"

"Why are you surprised? I never said I wanted kids. I always said I didn't."

"I never took that seriously."

"Why not?"

Good question. "Maybe because we never really talked about it?"

"Which, I'll remind you, was because you were up in the air yourself."

"I guess I thought that if I changed my mind, you would, too."

"Whatever made you think such a thing?"

"Everyone told me that's how men are?"

"And every woman is absolutely certain that she wants a baby, right?"

"Are we fighting about this?"

"There's nothing to fight about, unless you've made a decision about kids. Have you?"

"Uh . . ."

"You might not know if you've changed your mind. But I can tell you that I haven't."

Now I avert my gaze from this plastic-wrapped mirror. Of course, I know how I ended up making my peace with Hal's feelings—it is a story of Beth and a hospital and a blue light. But I will not latch on to *that* memory now. I cannot. Because four years after I thought I'd settled the matter, four years after I opted out of ambivalence to choose the man I would marry, four years after I thought I would never feel the longing that so much of the world feels, I am suffering from a house sickness so profound it is making me dizzy.

I will never fill this house with the burble of toddlers and the chatter of schoolchildren and the giggles of teens; no one will ever dance on Hal's feet. And when my parents and stepparents slip away from me, and, assuming I don't go first, Hal passes into memory, these rooms will be silent.

Trembling with an unbearable sorrow, disoriented with irreversible regret, I make my way to the front door, finally understanding what has been obvious. It wasn't just the fallen woman and the possible biopsy that made my house sickness acute. It was the falling walls, the finality of choice, the kindred spirit of an empty home whispering of barrenness to me.

The oncologist orders a biopsy. My father and Theresa decide to keep their vacation plans at the shore and return just for the morning next week when she'll get the procedure. Then they purchase their first cell phone ever so they can return to their beach house afterward and the oncologist can call with the results. "But I have no idea how to use the thing," Theresa tells me when she calls to announce their plans.

"Go back to the store and have them explain it."

"We did, but it didn't do any good. And the manual's impossible."

There's no point discussing the phone with my father—he lets Theresa handle all feats of engineering, like fixing the chain in the back of the toilet. But I speak with him anyway.

"How can I reach you while you're away?"

"If we can get this damn phone to work—"

"Will you just call me collect if anything happens?"

"Nothing's going to happen until the test."

I pause. "And how are you doing?"

"I'll know after the test how I'm doing."

I try to imagine scenarios, but decide to stop *thinking*.

So it's a good thing that Hal tells me that we need to start shopping. Needless to say, I balk at first, since selecting things like doorknobs and wall sconces, which Hal properly calls "fittings," is even further from my mind than usual. "Why now?" I say, as Hal removes eco-friendly linoleum samples from his bag the next night. "I thought we were in the demolition phase."

"We are. But there's a lead time for obtaining materials, and you also have to account for the time to select them. You just have to work backward from when they're going to be needed on the site and then you know when you have to start thinking about them. Which is now."

That night we easily agree on the color of the floors for the bathroom and kitchen. The next day, at a specialty hardware store, we both like the crystal doorknobs. There's a great deal to recommend shopping right now, I think, as we start paging through catalogs. By reminding me that Hal and I have always been good at give-and-take, it's affirming why, after that night at Ruby Tuesday, I made the choice that I did.

Then we go to a tile store. Hal makes a beeline to tiles with marine motifs, but my eye is caught by a display of glass tiles, emerald and azure and teal, and he is quickly won over. Since they're too costly for the whole bathroom, he pulls out some paper and sketches a pattern that will combine these glass tiles and a more traditional white. Then we take the sketch to the owner for pricing, and as he and Hal discuss measurements, I notice another employee showing customers around. Wouldn't you know. She's pregnant.

I look away, but wonder what kind of conversations she and her husband had before now. A few nights ago I asked Hal—"just out of curiosity"—to tell me how he came to feel the way he does about having children. He reminded me that he'd told me long ago: after the demise of a brief, childless first marriage to a high school sweetheart, he watched friends who were starting families, and quietly, without inner strife, concluded that parenthood would prevent him from having the freedom to pursue his creative passions and structure his time. I then remembered him saying this on the rare occasions when the topic arose during our first thirteen years. But I'd assumed that since he's generally so agreeable, he could be persuaded to change his mind, if I ever felt determined to do so. Only I never did.

When we get in the car at the tile store, I say, "Do you ever wonder if we should have had kids?"

He looks at me. "Why are you thinking about this?"

"The pregnant woman. Just, you know, it made me think."

He pauses. "No. I don't."

"Would you ever, well, reconsider?"

He takes a deep breath, then lets it out. "No. I'm sorry." His tone is both sensitive to the distress he must see on my face, and resolved that, whatever I am contending with, it is my battle to fight on my own. I fold his sketch on my lap over and over, and silently we drive home.

. . .

Hal has started holding weekly job meetings on mornings before work, then calling me from the office to tell me what happened. A few days after Theresa has the biopsy, Hal has his next meeting. "You just have to see it," he says when he calls. "Let's meet at the house tonight."

I won't let it get to me any further, I tell myself as I drive to Teacher's Lane. I need to suck in my emotions. I need to pretend I'm a regular person who feels regular things.

When he meets me at the front door, he's grinning broadly. He walks me into the living room, which is fleeced with dust. "Keep your eyes on your feet," he says, flicking on the overhead lightbulb, taking my hand. I follow Sherpa style, stepping in clearings left by his shoes. We pass out of the living room into the dining room. Then he says, "Look."

I lift my eyes and gasp. The wall between the dining room and kitchen is gone. We are standing in one astonishingly spacious room. "It'll be even bigger when we finish," he says.

"Because they'll be demoing that back wall, too?"

"That's right."

It's really something, though I'm dismayed to feel no less morose than I have for weeks. I just continue after him, now up the stairs. On the landing I spy one yellow rubber glove—from a pair, I remember, that I lazily left in the bathroom cabinet. Why is it on the floor?

At the top of the stairs, I see. The bathroom's been gutted—toilet, sink, tub, cabinet, tile, and ceiling are gone, wood exposed to the roof. This room of bright light is dark as a cave. But that's not the only change. The two bedrooms beyond the bathroom are now one, the demo team having torn down the separating wall as well as the corridor wall. My study-to-be has appeared.

"Won't this be great?" Hal says, pointing to where I'll put my desk, how the southern light will gild my books' spines.

I wish excitement would replace this lump in my throat. I wish I could meet the emotional specifications. "So," I say, just to say something, "is the demo almost done?"

"There's still the back wall in the kitchen, but before it gets removed they have to hand-dig the new foundation in the backyard so we can extend the first floor by five feet. Then they have to get a new back beam in place—and *then* they can take down the wall."

"You haven't mentioned a back beam before."

"The existing back wall's a bearing wall, so we have to replace the bearing. The new beam will rest on posts and support the joists in the ceiling."

"Is that how it works? If you trash a bearing wall, you compensate in a major way?"

"I wouldn't call it compensation. The bearing's just happening in a different way."

During the time when Dan is working on the beam, I don't go to the house. Instead, I talk with friends who have children, asking them how they feel about their choice. Some are rhapsodic. Others say, "It's not all it's cracked up to be." Some surmise my dilemma. Maybe, one says, Hal will have a change of heart, or I could arrange to have an "accident." Another says that by never having made up my mind, I made up my mind. I listen to everyone and have no response. Incredibly, after so much house sickness, I feel no more decisive than I did before the demolition began—and I still feel low. Will this awful feeling ever go away?

And then I go to the lighting store.

I've always been a pushover for glass and light, so I arrive before I'm supposed to meet Hal. I tell myself that this is so I can narrow down our choices, but as soon as I see the Tiffanies and chandeliers and torchères glowing like an orchard of incandescent trees, I am drawn deep inside the aisles. There, bathed in heat, I ignore my duties as a shopper, and lift the seal on the pivotal memory. At last I am in the hospital with Beth, moving toward another kind of light.

The memory is from four years ago—a month before Hal and I are set to get married. For a long time, Beth's doctors have been expressing concern about her worsening medical conditions. Her eye doctor, who performed two surgeries for a rare malady, says she needs one more. Her dentist says she needs serious work, though her insurance won't cover the anesthesia. Her gynecologist says that Beth's uterine fibroids are nearing the point where a laparoscopic hysterectomy is in order. Since I've become the family member most involved with Beth's medical care, I make a flurry of calls—and learn that if we can coordinate the doctors, Beth can have triple surgery. Yes, three surgeries in one day. Not only will this take care of the dental anesthesia, but Beth loves the idea of getting it all over with. But the prospect of three surgeries is daunting. I ask, "Will it help if I stay in a bed in your hospital room?" "Yes!" she says. Thus, a month before Hal and I will stand before the justice of the peace—after I've said yes but am still wondering if I'll ever resolve my ambivalence about children—Beth and I check in to the hospital.

At first I give little thought to where they put us, which is the maternity ward. I have too much else to think about as I sit in the waiting room, conferring with one doctor after another throughout the day. Each surgery is successful, but I am tense. I spend the day calling Hal and my father, buying lunch for Beth's boyfriend, Jesse, and trying to concentrate on my students' papers. The sun is beginning to set as Beth is wheeled back into the room.

It is hard to see her. She has bandages over her eyes, cotton in her mouth. She's woozy, and I stand over her and whisper, "It'll be okay." She mumbles something about not wanting to wear these stupid bandages, but soon she sleeps. Jesse leaves when visiting hours end, and then nurses come in to check on her. I get into my pajamas, turn off the light, and climb into my bed.

But I can't sleep. I'm too anxious, and my feelings for her are pushing hard against my chest. Plus, she's on some machine that keeps clicking and wheezing, and I can hear voices down the hall. After a few hours I give up on sleeping and get up and go into the hallway.

It is the middle of the night, and all the patient rooms are dark. The hallway is dim, but a peculiar light of some kind is glowing around a bend in the corridor. It isn't an ordinary light—it almost seems like a light from an aquarium. I can't imagine what it could be, but since it also seems to be where the voices are, I shuffle that way, and when I turn the corner, I see the nurses' station, positioned near a glass wall. The strange light is coming from this wall. It is blue.

The two nurses at the desk look up. They're friendly nurses whom I already met in Beth's room. I ask them about the light beyond the glass. "That's for the preemies," one of them says. She walks me over, and I look into a room that's decorated like a nursery at home, except for a few incubators. A nurse is in a rocking chair holding a baby smaller than her hand, and I remember what Sandy wrote me in her letter years before. She still hasn't had children, and although she's beginning to get her life together, she doesn't think she'll change her mind. But at last I know how she felt when she stood at the nursery window and looked in. My breath just stops at the sight of such fragility, of such miniscule heads and quivering hands, of a person who could be anyone but is already, in ways yet to be revealed, someone. I stand here, my heart soft. *I can still change my mind about marrying Hal.* Yet moments later, when I return down the hall and look at my sister, who is also fragile, and who I have nurtured and fought and accepted, and who has become a someone who will, I hope, prevail every day of her life, I feel just as moved as I did with the babies—though in a different way. In a lifelong, frustrated, dedicated, chest-melting Beth way. As the night drags on and I read my students' stories, and chat with the nurses, and think about my father and Theresa and Hal and Jesse, and watch the preemies, I feel moved again and again. The truth, as I come to see in the blue light, is that I feel many kinds of love in this world, and I enjoy them all. There is one love I cannot call my own, but over the course of that night, I do not ache to do so. By morning I know I can marry a man who does not want the one love I am missing.

Now, in the lighting store, I hear my name. Hal has just walked through the entrance, and he's waving across the shimmering lamps at me. I look at him and feel the same longing and respect and even, despite my house sickness, merriment that I always feel. And I know that I will not blame Hal for what I still haven't felt in myself.

Amazingly, this realization does not pitch me deeper into sorrow, because it occurs to me that as a passerby without a child at her side, I felt no need to rush past the fallen woman and her daughter, and that as a woman whose first loyalty is not to her children, I can be available for Beth, and my students, and my parents, and even nurses in the middle of the night. Of course, maybe I'd have been a better passerby or sister or teacher if I'd had children. I'll never know. But I do know, as I wind my way through the lamps toward Hal—who once told me, "Have compassion for yourself"—that I will go back to the house and look at the woman in the mirror, and try to soften my heart toward her. Because I now understand that my house sickness hasn't been about the desire to have a child. It's been about the long-delayed grief that I won't.

Two days later, my phone rings. An electronic voice says, "Collect call from Theresa."

I accept the charges. "What happened?"

Theresa says, "It's benign."

I put my hand to my chest. "Thank God." I hear my father on the boardwalk beside her, his relief filling the ocean.

At my next visit to Beth, the day after the demolition is done, I do not tell her about Theresa's ordeal. Nor do I tell her about the lump in my throat, or that it disappeared yesterday, when I had a transcendent moment during a trip to the house.

Instead, after we go shopping for a DVD of *The Little Mermaid,* we get ice cream. Our visit is easy and fun, with nothing memorable except the absence of anyone falling. I don't even feel a twang when she tells me about a bus driver who's having a baby. Having survived the upheaval of demolition, I've come to suspect that I might never feel closure about being childless, but since yesterday, I also know something else, something I think about now, as Beth spoons up her chocolate chip mint beside me, and we hear a song we both like on the car radio. "Turn it up," she says, and I do. In the end, I will have loved no one like a child. But I will have loved many someones, and maybe someone will still love me. When the woman fell at Target, she was ringed by nurses. When numerous teenagers have felt unrecognized or adrift, they took a class with me. I remember something an older friend told me over the last few days. "My son died young. My daughter is crazy. But you never stop making friends. The people who go through life with you are the ones who want to be with you."

Yesterday Hal and I drove to the house. Demolition was over, he said—the back kitchen wall had at last been taken down. At first, standing in the living room, seeing the single space of the dining room and kitchen expand beneath the new beam, into the backyard, out to the neighbor's lot beyond, and on into the sky, I could barely move. "And check this out," Hal said, leading me to the back edge of the first floor. Just beyond our feet was the new plywood subfloor, over what used to be five feet of our backyard.

This is the moment that I will not tell Beth—or my father and Theresa, or even Hal, but that in some way I will share with them all, and with every student I ever teach and every friend I ever make: with Hal watching, I placed one toe carefully on the plywood, testing out this new floor that I had failed to see from the spot where I'd just been standing. It was the same spot where I'd once washed dishes at the sink. The sink that was now gone. Below a window that was no more. Next to a back porch that had been deleted from the face of the earth. I lowered my weight onto a floor that had not existed until now and drew the other foot up to meet its companion. Eyes on my feet, I planted myself firmly. Then I lifted my head, and my chest surged with fullness, and a view that I'd never seen in quite this way opened up right before me.

Brothers and Sisters

The next Saturday, when I'm returning from a walk and Hal is backing his car out of the driveway, he says out of the window in his Cookie Monster best, "Coffee. Need coffee."

"See you when you get back."

"Need wife to get coffee."

"I know you'll be checking out the old house afterward, so I'll skip the whole thing."

Returning to Hal-speak, he says, "A lot's changed since you saw it. You might like it."

"Anyway, I have that call in a few hours. The one with Craig."

"Ah, yes. Dr. Craig, Sibling Whisperer."

"He doesn't call himself that. He's not even a doctor. He's a social worker."

"Just come. We'll be efficient. You'll get back in time. Plus"—and Hal breaks into Cheapo Commercial Voiceover—"if you take advantage of this special offer, you won't need to go back for weeks."

"Why would that be?"

"Can't tell you. But the sale ends today."

"I don't know," I say, but I'm beginning to smile.

"Ah! Got you to smile again."

"Again? I haven't been smiling for this whole dumb conversation."

"You haven't smiled for weeks."

I look at him. "I haven't?"

"Not since the demo started."

I kick at a pebble on the ground. "I didn't think you knew."

"Sure I did. I don't know what bugged you about it, but I can promise you that this phase will be a lot better." He reaches out the window and touches my hand. "So come."

I'm still tentative when I get in the car. He looks over at me with his most caring smile. "I'm sorry I've been too wrapped up to be available. Let me be your wife whisperer again."

By the time we leave the café for Teacher's Lane, I feel less alone, having shared my descent into house sickness. I also feel less resistant, because Hal assured me that this new phase will have no overlap with my personal struggles. In fact, he said, although it's an exacting time for builders, it will be imperceptibly dramatic for me. "Your risk of psychic turmoil is zilch."

But as I walk inside, the change couldn't seem more dramatic. "Wow. This is lovely."

I'm not referring to the living room, which hasn't altered at all, nor the open back of the first floor, now covered with plywood. I mean the other walls in the dining room–kitchen: shorn of their plaster, they're now exposed brick, granting the house a timeless, earthen elegance.

"I hate to break this to you," Hal says, "but it won't be staying like this."

"Why not?"

"None of these is a party wall. If you take the plaster down on a wall that you don't share with your neighbors, where are you going to put the insulation?"

"Hmm. Good point. Then why remove the plaster?"

"For the roughing-in. That's the phase in the job when all the individual trades converge on the house to install the inner workings— the plumbing, the electrical, the ductwork for heating and air-conditioning. What you're seeing here is the masonry that was beneath the plaster—the inner wythe. It'll get covered by drywall later."

"Too bad."

"I understand that an interior brick wall has a certain charm. But insulation's more important. Though I suppose there *is* a small disadvantage."

"What?"

"I'll show you." He leads me upstairs. I'm relieved to feel no trace of my previous despondency. I can pass the hollowed-out bathroom without a glance, and when I see that my new study—as spacious as the dining room–kitchen immediately below—also has exposed brick, I'm free to feel chic and sophisticated.

But the room isn't quite the same as the one beneath. Parallel to each of the walls stand structures made of lumber. Hal, predicting my question, says, "That's the framing."

"Oh. That's what you see"—and I flash back to being eight and goofing around with my brother and sisters in the development to which we'd just moved, where we watched construction underway for the first time—"when a house is going up."

"Well, the framing for a tract house, like what you played around in as a kid"—I smile at how quickly he grabbed on to my unspoken memory—"is both the structure of the house and space for utilities and insulation. This framing is *just* for the utilities and insulation. And that's the disadvantage. We'll lose a bit of square footage."

"Our tiny house will get tinier?"

"You have to give up something to get something." When I frown, he adds, "But remember—one of the cost-saving measures was not to do this in the front rooms on both floors. We're keeping those plaster walls, so those rooms won't shrink. When we do the insulation, we'll just use a hose to spray behind the plaster."

I look around. Even though the finished house won't retain this trendy appearance, I'm impressed by how it looks.

"Roughing-in takes time," Hal adds. "There'll be a good stretch ahead when you won't see a difference. If you don't want to come back for a while, you won't be missing much."

This is convenient, because I have a heavy schedule of talks over the next few months. I've taken off the semester to limit my stress, but I'll still be flying all over the country. "In case I take you up on that, tell me in advance what sea monsters we might encounter in this phase."

His smile gives way to seriousness. He holds up three fingers.

"One: unforeseen conditions. Two: poor coordination by the general contractor. Three: people not getting along."

"Yikes. Them's serious perils."

"Well, unforeseen conditions are part and parcel of working with existing construction, so that's the one that seems most likely. Poor coordination is less so, since Dan seems like a good general contractor, and part of a good g.c. is his coordination of the work."

"What about people not getting along?"

"This is definitely a major time in a job when people have to co-operate. Everybody's got to stay out of everybody's way while considering everybody else. Like if the mechanical guy installs ductwork without thinking about the other trades, then the plumber comes in and says, 'The toilet goes here, the drain here, and I have nowhere to put it,' you're in trouble."

I feel my face get tight. "So one sub's self-absorption could mess us up?"

"Self-absorption, arrogance, irresponsibility, frustration with life, you name it. Construction is just another theater in which the human condition with all its nonsense can strut about on the stage."

"Doesn't that worry you?"

"No. I think even with all their foibles, most people get along most of the time." When my expression apparently doesn't change, he adds, "Look, this is how I think most people see it. Whether they're electricians, plumbers, or mechanical guys, every job works a whole lot better if we act like family when we're on the job."

I say, sarcastically, "So you mean everyone should just behave like brothers and sisters when they're under the same roof?"

"Yeah, you could say that," he says with a shrug.

Could he possibly have said something that would have given me more anxiety?

I don't say this as we drive back to the house so I can call Craig—a social worker who has, in a series of phone sessions over the last few months, helped me address recent problems in my relationship with Beth. After all, I hear similar phrasing all the time about the importance of acting like family—or, more specifically, brothers and sisters—

as politicians, pastors, union leaders, social justice groups, and others make appeals for some kind of unity. But as everyone who's actually had a sibling must know—and as my own experience has shown me over and over—flesh-and-blood brothers and sisters, no matter how hard they try, and no matter how much they remember that they're family—can be rather far from united.

It's not that my relationships with my brother and sisters didn't start out well. Raised under one roof, Laura, Beth, Max, and I were one another's earliest and most frequent playmates, entertaining ourselves from sandboxes to school blacktops, sharing games and witticisms and eye-rolling irritations and, as we still find out by uttering identical words with identical inflections at the same moment, mental circuitry. Most important, we loved as well as liked one another. For instance, the year we lived in a development under construction, the four of us would roam in full camaraderie along our street, watching backhoes digging and foundations getting poured, and then, when the workers left for the day, we'd clamber up to a just-framed house, dart through the ribs of wood, and scramble from one nascent room to the next, giggling with familiar jokes and secret language. I can still see us then: high-spirited, enjoying one another. With the hindsight of adulthood, I can also see, well, the inner workings that my eight-year-old eyes, unskilled in discerning the sources of mood changes or distinguishing bravado from insecurity, failed to detect: Laura, alternating between giddy and pensive, feeling an approval-starved loneliness and spunk-crushing responsibility; me, cheerful with siblings and schoolmates and newly minted pen pals, but cut to the quick by my parents' ill-expressed agonies; Beth, gleeful with us and bored when alone, relishing the spotlight of my mother's scant energies while puzzling over my father's departure; wise guy Max, disguising his lost-in-the-crowd distress with constant sardonic humor. In my child-scopic world, I did not miss that we were distinct, but I did miss my siblings' inner strife. Perhaps this was due to my youthful self-absorption, which didn't permit me to see behind the walls we were all carefully erecting. Perhaps, though, it was because we had, at least in my mind, a playscape so engaging that our aches mattered less than our fellowship. Certainly we fought, but our resentments perished quickly. One babysitter seemed almost annoyed at how immediately we got on after fights.

If only that were the way siblings remained as they progressed through the slow, muddy currents of time. But as almost anyone who's been a brother or a sister knows, sometimes the bonds between siblings weaken. With us, our parents' struggles, both between each other and within themselves, might have initiated the process. We were not unaware of this as it was occurring. We knew that, as their divorce molted into finger-jabbing, decibel-shattering showdowns when our father came to see us, our parents' antipathy toward each other was instructing us in the ways of polarity and provocation, along with the impermanence of truce. But we did not understand that by the time our parents were no longer able to set foot in the same building, their feelings toward each other had seeped into their actions with us. My father expressed dismay when our habits reminded him of our mother's less favorable qualities. My mother expressed despair that our presence frustrated her pursuit of a new man. Watching this, we would hunker down in each other's rooms, trying to make sense of what was happening. But even as we sought to console one another, even as we observed the pain on the others' faces and felt it in our own, even as we shared fears about the larger world of which we were uneasily becoming a part, we could not resist a pull toward competitiveness, mistrust, rash acts wrought by misaimed anger. Soon we developed into ever-shifting factions. We defined ourselves in opposition to the others. Our love ceased walking with our like.

Even among siblings who are spared such chaos, difficulties might still arise in their relationships, and the reasons are not hard to understand. Due to many details that vary right at each sibling's birth, from order of arrival to time in a parent's emotional life to the family's fortunes, none of us *is* raised under the same roof. Each of us grows up in a house so unique it might as well have been designed by a different architect. Thus, as I framed my own rooms where I retreated with friends, so did Laura and Beth and Max, and there, whether our friends were school buddies or teenybopper magazines, solitary book-reading or lone bicycle-riding, ambition for careers or numbness about tomorrow, we grew into adulthood.

And that, as Hal and I have concluded many times, is why siblings—the very people who might be expected to be like-minded—don't always get along. Despite all the overlaps that brothers and sisters have with each other, we also have such complicated affections and such separate histories that the most essential parts of ourselves—why we do what we do, how we believe people ought to behave, and what we want most out of life—might not overlap at all.

I wonder: what does it take for brothers and sisters to get along? Not just in the years soon after the cradle, but through all the decades that follow?

Barely a week after the rough-in begins, I find out that the first of our sea monsters has appeared.

Hal breaks the news when we're in a discount warehouse for large appliances. As we amble up and down aisles looking for a stove, he happens to let slip something he's failed to mention until now: we have encountered the infamous "unforeseen conditions."

Two, actually. "Someone years ago cut a channel into the brickwork on the eastern wall of the dining room to run the drain line from the bathroom and ductwork to the second floor, and the remaining masonry crumbled a bit around those utilities. So that section of wall needs to be rebuilt. Plus, the bottoms of the joists above the dining room—kitchen aren't level, so we have to fur them down to create a level plane for the installation of the ceiling."

"Will this cost us anything?"

"A few extra thousand."

"Geez."

"That's fair. None of this is Dan's fault."

"It isn't ours, either."

"I'm just glad we caught it. An uneven ceiling is an eyesore, but a major wall with a hole in the masonry might make the house structurally unsound."

"We've been living in a place that could have fallen down around us?"

"People live with all kinds of things they don't know about until they renovate."

"This worries me."

"You wouldn't be you if it didn't."

"But I don't only mean about the wall. I mean—"

"They might be the only problems we encounter."

"I hope they are."

"I won't be surprised if they are."

"That's good to know."

"But I won't be surprised if they're not."

I shouldn't worry, but life is well-stocked with surprises, as I'm reminded when I head out for a walk the next morning. Sometimes, of course, they're pleasing, such as what happened soon after we moved last month to the rented house, when, knowing that we'd be leaving in four to six months, I was content to remain detached from our surroundings. But soon neighbors began crossing their lawns to initiate welcoming chats. I learned that this has long been a friendly corner of Delaware, a place where people settled in for decades and looked after one another, and before I knew it, I was coming to enjoy exchanging hellos. This, in turn, made a second and less heartening surprise easier to bear. A little after we arrived, two other households also moved onto the block, both of whom began indulging in behavior that the established residents, and Hal and I, found distressing: letting their dogs bark endlessly, parking cars on the lawn, blasting music. All of this rattled me, but because I was feeling a warm association with the old-timers, I felt hopeful that harmony would return to the street. It hasn't yet, but here's one more nice surprise. A few days ago, I found myself falling into a lengthy conversation with Ginny, who lives across the street, and discovered that we had much in common. She teaches special education. She and her five-year-old love books and the arts. Despite challenges in the past, she's close to her family. And I started to make a real friend.

So stop worrying about the renovation, I tell myself, as my walk carries me into an adjoining neighborhood. Not all surprises are miserable, and the bad ones might be offset by the good. Besides, with Hal on the lookout, nothing truly terrible is going to happen.

Yet it's hard to believe that fully. I know all too well that sometimes surprises of knee-buckling magnitude come bursting out of no-where. I think about the conversation I had just last night with Ginny, when we were hanging out in her living room, her daughter Eliza drawing pictures, us eating snacks. Ginny asked me about Beth, and I told her that if I'd been asked as a young adult to peer into the future and describe my relationships with my siblings, I would have said that I'd be close to Max, distant from Laura, and besieged by guilt about my discord with Beth. That's how things were then, so that's how I imagined they'd stay. I sure did have it wrong with Max and Laura. Beth, too, actually, because in my late thirties I rode the buses and we came together.

This is where my discussions about Beth have concluded for years: at the plateau where she knows she can call whenever she wants, I em-brace her right to make choices, and we enjoy a guilt-free, easygoing rapport. But last night I risked telling Ginny a bit more. I wasn't sure I should, but with one troubling neighbor to her left and another to her right, our conversation kept returning to the topic of people not getting along, so it didn't seem out of place. Not that I was detailed. I just joked, "But sometimes sibling relationships encounter unforeseen conditions," and then I gave only the broad sweep. It's not that I didn't want to say more, but I knew I'd get overwrought if I did.

When I rode the buses with Beth, I came to feel a tender admira-tion for her boyfriend, Jesse, so after I stopped riding, I was happy to comply with Beth's wishes to turn our visits with each other into visits with the two of them. I found him to be a soft-spoken, gentle-souled man, one who would talk about watching deer in the woods, riding his bike around town, staying up late to see the news about the war. Some-times he would tell me stories from his childhood: wrenching tales of family troubles, an accident that left him blind in one eye, living for a while on the streets. I knew that a beloved uncle had been murdered when Jesse was a boy. Recently, a brother with whom he was close also died under suspicious circumstances. I knew as well that Jesse had never received grief counseling for these losses, and that when I sug-gested that he might benefit from talking to someone, he would agree, but then a few days later do an about-face. I could hardly insist that he get help, so I just listened when he wanted to talk, which was usually while Beth ran around Wal-Mart and he and I stood in an aisle, my heart going out to him.

Then about a year ago I noticed a change. Was it untreated post-traumatic stress? Did he have some condition that I lacked the knowledge to understand? Was he mimicking the behavior of someone he knew at some time in his life, or disclosing a part of himself that he had kept from me? All I knew was that an unfamiliar pattern emerged: whenever I drove to see them, Jesse wouldn't be waiting with Beth at the bus station, as he'd said he would. He'd show up ten minutes later, or a half hour, and then he'd be surly, cursing, belligerent. Sometimes he'd even eye us from a distance; then, as we headed down the sidewalk toward him, he'd jump on his bike and ride away. It was as if he'd become a different person. One day I actually saw the transformation happen: as he sat in the back of my car, his face switched in a second from the tranquil, kind face I knew to one filled with meanness. I didn't recognize him. Nor was I feeling my earlier trust, or any pleasure in my visits.

It didn't help that Beth insisted at each no-show that we drive around looking for Jesse, and then, when we came upon him, simply ignore his foul mood. I would tell her I was getting way too frazzled and plead with her to just turn the visit into a time with me, but her mind was on a single track. I would also ask him before every visit if he really wanted to join us. He would say yes, yet the problem would recur. Then I started asking if he would consider talking to his aide, a doctor, anyone, about why he'd changed so suddenly. He'd promise he would—and then be even more extreme when I came by again. I felt completely over my head.

Then around the time when I was packing up the house to move, I had lunch with a professional who works with Beth, and poured out my frustration. She suggested that I might benefit from speaking with her former colleague, Craig, a social worker with expertise in helping people who haven't responded to traditional therapeutic treatments. People who might, in some ways, be like Jesse. I contacted Craig, and, since he lives far away, we began to meet over the phone.

In our conversations, he's been telling me that there are several important things to keep in mind when interacting with Beth. One is to give her unconditional positive regard, which is to indicate at all times that I care about her, and that there is nothing she can do to make that caring go away—a suggestion that's useful for interaction with any loved one. The same is true for the second tip he's been giving me: that my time is as valuable as hers, and if I'm not enjoying myself, I need to address that with her—in a way that won't be bossy or leave me feeling guilty. Most of our conversations have concentrated on the specific approach I can take to doing this, but at the heart of it lies my own understanding of what I want when I see my sister—which is, I now know, to see *her*. My responsibility is to Beth, not, as much as I care for him, Jesse. So, Craig said, I have a right to tell her that "Jesse isn't being the kind of person that I want to be with right now. When he can show me that he is, I'll want to spend time with him again. But for now, I need to see you without him around."

When Craig first gave me this advice, I worried that Beth might just choose not to see me anymore. But that was a risk I had to take. I called Beth and told her, and it turned out that she had expected something like this. In fact, she did not argue with me at all. She just asked what we would do together if we weren't with Jesse. I said we could still visit her favorite drivers, and we could go shopping, and I could take her for ice cream or to the movies. Immediately our visits became as peaceful and fun they used to be. Yes, I was sad not to have my almost-brother-in-law still in my life. But I was also relieved. It's like what Hal said in the old house: you have to give something up to get something else.

Back on our street after my walk, I see Ginny sitting on her front porch, watching Eliza ride her bicycle in small circles. I go over, and we pick up where we left off last night. The dog belonging to one of the unruly neighbors is barking away, but when I sit down on the porch beside my new friend, I completely forget to hear it.

Some days later, when I meet Hal after work for our weekly grocery shopping, he greets me in the produce aisle by saying, "Well. We've just hit Problem Number Two."

He discovered it, he tells me, at the job meeting this morning. His drawings called for conduits to be installed through the new foundation so that lines could later be run into the backyard for lighting and the HVAC unit. At every meeting he'd asked the job supervisor, Henry, when the conduits would be installed. Henry had said the equivalent of, "Uh, we'll get around to it." This morning, when Hal saw that the footings had been poured and the area under the slab filled in with stone, he asked if the conduits were there. "And Henry's jaw dropped and a fly popped out."

"You mean he screwed up."

"That's right."

"So is this poor coordination?"

"Yeah. Sometimes poor coordination equals dumb forgetfulness."

"I thought you said Dan was good."

"Dan delegated it to Henry, and Henry messed up. But they'll fix it."

"Who pays for this?"

"They will."

"Is this bugging you? It's bugging me."

"I'll subcontract the being bugged to you."

"Please don't be blasé. This is our house. It's a ton of money. Our lives are in limbo."

"But what's the point of worrying? So far our problems are minor. None of them is worth getting bent out of shape about. If I ever thought it was worth worrying about this kind of stuff on a job, experience has taught me otherwise. Anyway, I have a good feeling about this. No one's acting devious or manipulative. No one's drinking or not showing up. Dan's totally on the ball. Okay, Henry's a bit of an issue, but I can work with that."

"So I should just relax? Trust that we won't get to Problem Number Three?"

"I can't tell you that for certain. But it just doesn't seem as if it's going to go that way."

I look away. A middle-aged woman is examining a grapefruit. An elderly couple is picking through string beans. Maybe a plumber once flooded their kitchen, but you'd never know it to look at them.

"So?" he says, brushing my hair aside and looking into my face. "Not to worry?"

"Maybe this isn't a dramatic phase, but that doesn't mean there's no drama playing out in me."

"Yeah," he says. "It's always a little weird when your inner wife begins to crumble."

"Save me, please," I say, smiling and pushing him away.

"Got you to laugh," he says, pulling me back. "My lovely inner wife. Now, can we get on with our shopping?"

So, okay. I won't worry about the job. I'll distract myself by obsessing about something else, which, wouldn't you know, requires no effort. Whereas I spent the demolition thinking about children, it turns out that I'm spending the roughing-in having more sessions with Craig, visiting with Beth, talking on the phone with Laura, flying around the country to speak to groups and families who are cohesive or fractious, and coming home to a troubled neighborhood. People getting along, or not getting along, is simply what's in the air. Plus, it's the stuff of my conversation, even when I'm not with Hal: more and more often I find myself crossing the street in the evenings to hang out with warmhearted, hospitable Ginny. There, as Eliza draws pictures, we indulge in long discussions about our families, teaching, the conflict on our street. We still don't know what we can do about the difficult neighbors. But, as I tell Ginny, I often haven't been able to figure that out with people I know a whole lot better, the siblings with whom I once shared a roof.

Actually, I tell Ginny, I finally understand some things about Laura. Like Beth and me, Laura and I remained distant for many years of our adulthood. We still called each other and visited when she made her annual return east from Arizona. But I was self-conscious about everything I said, because often I inadvertently offended her. Then when she'd express her annoyance, I'd despair that we were clashing again. Neither of us would know how to turn the conversation around, and the resulting strain would last until one of us, usually me, would send a card or make a call. How could this be? We thought so much alike, we loved each other, we were both trying, yet the bond between us was so twisted, it's a wonder we held together at all.

But a few years ago, the pattern changed. It became evident that Laura was no longer taking offense as easily as she once had, nor did she seem to hold on to anger toward me. When I eventually asked what happened, she admitted that she'd felt so lonely and burdened and unattended to in her childhood that she'd long had difficulty trusting anyone in the family. She told me, too, about a few incidents from our early adulthood that loomed large for her but that I had forgotten, moments when I had let her down, thus reinforcing her mistrust. She'd never said anything at those times, so neither the apology that might have lightened her pain nor the self-reflection that she might have inspired in me came to pass. Ten years went by. Twenty-five. Finally, she dated some men who, for all their flaws, loved her with the wholeheartedness she deserved. She also saw a counselor who offered her specific guidance. And she began to value those cards and calls from me. Little by little, her mistrust ceased, which in turn made the sparks between us cease. We began speaking more often—to offer support, give each other reality checks about our family, celebrate each other's victories, comfort each other's pain. Whatever liking we'd lost over the years fell back into step with our love.

Max, on the other hand, has become inscrutable to me. Sometime, maybe after he got married, maybe after his children were born, he grew inconsistent about responding to my calls and e-mails. He seemed disinclined to see me, too, and the few times we did felt awkward. I tried to understand what had soured him, but he insisted that nothing had. For several years now, I almost never hear from him, and since he seldom responds to my efforts, it appears that our relationship is simply fading to black. I agonize over this. Did I do something that was searing to him, but that, as with Laura, I've forgotten? Is his pain from the family just so great that he cannot bear to be around us, or at least me? Does his silence have nothing to do with me? "You can't know," Hal has said more times than I can enumerate. "Any more than you could with Laura, or Beth, or Jesse. Until he tells you, you just can't know."

I don't want to tell Ginny about Max—it hurts too much. So I'm even gladder than I would otherwise be when Eliza interrupts our conversation to show us her artwork, and then sing us a song, and then demonstrate her gymnastic moves on the floor. By the time I remember that I'm avoiding saying something, I'm crossing the street back to the rented house.

I stop at my curb and look at the houses along this cul-de-sac, some with neighbors who open their hearts and lives to me, some with neighbors who appear not to care that they live beside other people. If actual brothers and sisters can't sustain a relationship, and neighbors fail to value harmony, then what's the likelihood that the workers in our house will get along? The sky hovers over the street, cloud-smudged and gray, and I let myself inside with no answer.

Then one afternoon in mid-October, Hal and I go for a walk, and a very different kind of surprise occurs.

In a way, the walk itself is a surprise. Despite the effort we made at the beginning of the roughing-in to be fully back with each other, Hal and I are finding it harder and harder to spend time together. I'm traveling, and he's working full-time at his job, then going to meetings with Henry and Dan, or doing drawings for the kitchen cabinets, or researching online options for energy-efficient dishwashers. So this walk would have been notable anyway, simply because we've been taking so few.

Perhaps that's why, when we leave the subdivision, we head in a direction I haven't taken before. Because this part of the state is very established, we expect to see only fifty-year-old subdivisions, so we're taken aback when our wanderings lead us to a tucked-away plot of land where new houses are under construction. Unlike the houses going up when I was eight, these are close to finished. In fact, as we stroll along, we notice that a few are already occupied. One door is ajar, and when we glance toward it, we see two little girls framed by the storm door, playing in the front hallway. They're seated on some oversized balls and are bouncing around, so caught up with each other that they don't see us.

What a funny switch. Here I am, out in the construction, looking inside to children. I flash again to the image of myself with my siblings when we were little, playing around the just-framed houses. It makes me smile, remembering that time. Even if we've all grown up now, and might never play together again.

"So," I say to Hal, "have we hit Problem Number Three yet? People not getting along?"

He smiles. "Actually, I think we've just had a shining example of people getting along splendidly."

"Are you kidding?"

"Do you remember that my drawings weren't highly detailed about the ductwork? Well, everybody just came together so we could figure out what to do. The mechanical contractor had ideas about the ductwork, so did the engineers I brought in; Dan brought ideas about how to frame things, so did I. And we're making it happen."

"Wow. What did you do right?"

"We persevered."

"Is that it?"

He thinks about this. "We were imaginative. We were flexible. Everyone pitched in. We trusted that we could work it out, and then we put our attention to doing so."

"Do you think that's what it takes for people to get along?"

He smiles. "I'm not sure about that. But it gets a house built."

We laugh as we look back at the kids in the doorway. They're peering out at us now, and when they see us looking, they wave. I wish I could share this insight with them. I wish I could tell them that when they get older and fight and misunderstand and grow apart, they should remember this moment, when a silly older woman on their sidewalk told them a small story about what it takes for people to get along. Then they might be spared a bus ride, or twenty-five years of tense conversation, or a slow fade to black. But I can only smile across the sidewalk, and the construction, and the generations, and raise my hand and wave back.

"Oh, come on," I say to Hal at sunset on Halloween. "It'll be fun."

"But who'll hand out the candy at our house?"

"Ginny says the tradition here is that you just leave it in a bowl on your front porch, turn on your light, and then kids know to take it when they come to the door."

When the sun descends beyond the horizon, we come onto our lawn. From throughout our subdivision, children and parents have gathered at Ginny's house, and as the children, all in costume, surge down the street, we join the adults meandering behind. "Do we go to every house?" I ask, knowing that I did when I was a child. Ginny says, "Only houses where the light is on. That's the sign that they want to participate." That accounts for about half of the neighborhood, Hal and I notice. We notice too that adults don't accompany their children to the doors unless it's to sneak a look inside, usually to see household improvements. Were we on Teacher's Lane tonight, handing out candy in the big block party that our neighborhood makes of Halloween, and the chaperoning parents wanted to peek inside our house, they still wouldn't see much besides wires and framing—but soon that will change, Hal says now, because the roughing-in is just about behind us. Hearing this, I find that I'm a little sad that the job is moving along, because the adults flanking us are chatting about their own homes, and families, and careers, and hopes—and I feel so welcomed into the fold that I realize I will miss them when our house is done. From what I hear as we traipse from door to door, the neighbors here are caring toward the children and respectful toward one another. It is, despite the two difficult households, a lovely place to live. Hal and I look at each other and squeeze our hands together. We like being in this community. We like keeping the lights on.

After we complete the subdivision, we gather on a neighbor's lawn, where she's set up chairs and is roasting marshmallows over a portable fireplace. The children, using the front porch as a stage, dance and sing as if in a variety show. Everyone laughs and eats and applauds, and I think, Yes, there have been periods in my life when I've been apart from each one of my siblings, and only when there has been mutual perseverance, imagination, and flexibility have we come together again. And yes, the human condition with all its nonsense might never be easy to understand, no matter the job site or neighborhood or bloodline. But there are also playful, enveloping moments like these, moments that happen when we aren't expecting them, with people who share no roof with us besides the ceiling of the sky. Then even if we're hurting from losing someone we love, we might remember belonging. I do now, standing here with Ginny and Eliza and so many other new neighbors, the cold air between us growing warm with laughter, the darkness of the night feeling luminous with hope.

Kindred Spirits

"How would you define design?" I ask Hal on my cell phone.
"What kind of question is that?" he says with a laugh.
"Humor me."
"Just look it up."
"I'm in a car in Detroit on my way to the airport." I glance at the board member who's driving me, then back at the highway. "I can't look it up."
"Why are you asking?"
"Because when I told someone after my talk last night that we're renovating our house and you're the architect, she asked about your design sensibility. I didn't have an answer, aside from you being into sustainable design. And it made me wonder what 'design' really means."
"That's it? You called me at eight thirty in the morning to ask that?"
"Well, no. Because then the conversation turned around to the story of how we met—"
"—a-*huh*, I get it now—"
"—and after I told her about how we were total strangers—"
"—and ended up getting *married*—"
"Right. So of course she got a starry look in her eyes, and she said, 'It kind of makes you wonder whether life's all one big design.'"
"The implication being that there's some Grand Pooh-Bah designing the universe?"

"Sure. And, well, what I'm wondering is: what do *you* think?"

"I think we need to deal with the kitchen cabinets."

"That's not the right answer. That's not any answer."

"But that's the question. Will you be ready to go to the store to look at kitchen cabinets when you get home tonight?"

"Can't you just wax poetic for one tiny minute about design?"

"I can define design, but as for how we met, I'm perfectly content not to ascribe it to some master planner in the sky. But we need to pick out the kitchen cabinets."

"Isn't the roughing-in just ending? We're not ready to put in the cabinets *now*, are we?"

"No. We need to *order* them now."

My silent and accommodating driver indicates that we're nearing the airport.

"Fine," I say. "I'll go to the store under one condition. Tell me how you define design."

"Blackmail."

"That's right."

"Well, your scheme has an inherent flaw. I can't answer you now—I'm at work."

"I'm patient. A Buddhist blackmailer, you might even say. Answer me tonight."

"Aye, aye, Cap'n Rachie. Your crew'll be reporting for duty, unless we mutiny first."

Laughing, I hang up. My kindly companion gives me a weird look.

But I can deal with weird looks, I think as I check in at the airport. I might have received an even weirder one if I'd disclosed why I'd asked to get here so far ahead of my flight. I didn't even reveal it to Hal, though he'd have understood the merits of allowing extra time to savor an architectural experience. But given Hal's design sensibility, why say anything that would get him groaning about gigantic carbon footprints?

It takes me a moment to get my bearings after I pass through security. Then I see the crowd surging toward a down escalator. I remember it from yesterday, when I flew into this airport and found myself ushered into an extraordinary place. This is why I've arrived early today—so I could see it again without being in a rush. I grab the handrail, and begin my descent.

Within moments, I am enveloped by the same electronic melody I heard yesterday, which is sailing up the escalator to greet me. Soon I see the same colored lights reflecting on the polished floor. Then I reach the ground, and the eight-hundred-foot-long pedestrian tunnel that dazzled me yesterday becomes visible again, and as I step off the escalator, I am in this phantasmagoric world once more, with LED displays of violet and magenta and emerald and turquoise pulsing down the curved glass walls, vaulting across the rounded ceiling, and encasing, like the body of a wildly oversized airplane, the hundreds of travelers who are walking within.

The trance that overcame me before, but that I'd had to wrest myself out of so I could get to my talk, returns. Now, with a premeditated half hour in which to indulge myself, I back up against a column, away from the river of strangers, and do something I never would have contemplated before knowing Hal: I surrender myself to a physical space.

Entering a designed world, I learned from him, can be like entering another person's dream. I did not realize this as a child, when I mounted the steps to my schoolhouse or passed through revolving doors into my father's office building. I was simply going somewhere to do something. Yet I was also aware, on a level deeper than my own heartbeat, that when my eighth grade class passed into the shadowed embrace of the Lincoln Memorial in Washington, D.C., I felt possessed by a word-stilling reverence for human dignity. When my mother took us to the Guggenheim Museum in New York City and we spiraled down the long ramp leading from the sky-brightened ceiling to the ground, I felt unbound from gravity and expectation. But not until Hal took me by the hand and walked me through the streets of Philadelphia did I permit myself to acknowledge the mood-sculpting, thought-revising power of design.

I was twenty-three when my awareness began. My new boyfriend Hal was walking me to dinner, both of us unspooling stories about our lives, when—"Oh," he said, as a modern-looking house came into view. "I just love this place." We stopped and looked, and I did not understand. Weren't buildings just old, which meant they were attractive, or modern, which meant they were ugly? But something about him— perhaps the same mysterious something that had drawn me to this one person out of so many—made me feel respected and safe. So when he prodded to find out what I thought, I mumbled that I didn't think anything, because, though I'd passed that house before, I hadn't actually *seen* it. We walked on, and I realized aloud that most of the towns where I'd grown up had consisted of houses so dull and homogeneous, and public planning so senseless or nonexistent, that I'd been living in a state of not-seeing. Could he tell me what appealed to him about that building? Or the others that had taken his breath away in the blocks we'd traversed since? Evincing none of the condescension that I'd previously accepted as a requisite of romance, Hal pointed to buildings around us, describing such elements as scale, proportion, materials, relation to the site, ornament, and features for which I'd never known there were words: pilasters, dormers, corbels, turrets, cupolas, cornices, gables, Flemish bond, Palladian windows. As we moved on to the next block, and the next dinner, and the next week, we prowled around historic neighborhoods like Society Hill and Rittenhouse Square, entered the structures of famous architects like Frank Furness and landmark achievements like the PSFS Building, and marveled at the success of William Penn's eighteenth-century plan for the city. Gazing at what I'd ignored, I now admired more than I'd known existed. So we kept walking, month after month, my hand fitting perfectly into his, Eve learning from Adam about the garden.

Thus did I come to understand that Henry Bacon had designed the Lincoln Memorial precisely to usher me into a dream of nobility and honor. Frank Lloyd Wright had designed the Guggenheim to create, as he once wrote, "an uninterrupted, beautiful symphony such as never existed in the World of Art before." Even the basic school, office building—or house—had evolved into designs that fostered a sense of order and authority, or austerity and commerce, or domesticity and privacy. Although the creators of every space I'd ever encountered hadn't known me, and although often their ideas were constrained by economic reality, their work on what I now knew to call "the built environment" was intended to evoke a certain reaction in me, regardless of whether I was just going about my business in a state of oblivion.

Yet even the basic idea that I lived within the creations of others took another seven years to stick, and then it hit me in a single moment. I was thirty then, and on a month's retreat at an artist's colony. Coincidentally, Hal's first professional position had been at this same artist's colony ten years earlier, where he'd redesigned a barn for an artist's studio, and, despite his inexperience, supervised an unskilled construction crew ("of louts and criminals," he added). I'd obtained no more detail from him before I boarded the train for my stay at the colony, where I spent the next two weeks writing, not being conscious of the built environment, even to register a frequent annoyance: every time I reached for a particular door handle in the residence hall, I'd lose my grip. *Why am I such an oaf?* I would unconsciously castigate myself. *I can't even open a door!* Then Hal drove down from Philadelphia for a visit. I ran from my studio to the residential hall and threw myself into his arms. We walked toward my room, quickly catching up, and soon reached the door with the hateful handle. Hal watched as I lifted and, of course, lost my grip. And as I cursed myself, Hal muttered, "I can't believe they still haven't fixed this." "What are you talking about?" I asked. He said, "They installed that darned door handle upside down." I looked. He was right. Here I'd been blaming myself for my own clumsiness instead of considering that I was in a space created by someone, and built by others—whose goals, or execution, might sometimes be, as he put it, "really stinking bad." *Pay attention,* I told myself then. *Look around. See all that you don't let yourself see.*

So it is that I arrived at the airport early to see this tunnel—where the light show I saw yesterday is now changing into something else. Shades of peach are rising along the walls, blushing into rose, then melting into gold. It is a rendering of a day, with hues mimicking morning, afternoon, twilight, and, to the thrum of crickets, night. Then the tunnel takes on the cacophony of a thunderstorm, complete with indigo and black and flashes of lightning. Then I'm in a rain forest, percussion synchronized to bursting reds and greens.

I'd thought yesterday that this tunnel displayed a single, vibrant show of colors. But now I see that it contains a procession of displays. Had I not granted myself the time in which to simply watch, I would have missed that the tunnel possesses a pattern meant to induce multiple experiences, perhaps to symbolize the multiple lands to be visited by the travelers within.

I start laughing. This space is even more cleverly designed than I'd thought. How I wish Hal were beside me, piecing this together at the same moment as I. But he's in his office, making calls about that most banal of topics: kitchen cabinets. I turn around, hoping to lock eyes with an equally captivated stranger. That's when I notice that no one is standing back along with me. Everyone is running or trudging along the moving walkways toward the escalator at the other end, and, with their cell phones in hand, or candy bars, or strollers, or iPods, few are even glancing at the aurora borealis that surrounds us. Certainly no one is glancing toward me.

A loneliness rears up inside. I'm sure I'll still be able to savor the twenty minutes before I have to leave, but as I learned with Hal, design is more moving when we experience it in the company of another. Those William Penns and Frank Lloyd Wrights didn't design for isolated souls, since human beings don't live, work, and play in isolation. They designed for every way that individuals use a space—alone, in a throng, with just one other person.

And in this case, that one other doesn't have to be a husband. It doesn't have to be friend or family member. It could simply be a stranger. A person I've never seen before, and will never see again, but who was once taught, as was I, the simple willingness to see.

The crowds keep moving. No one is noticing. The tunnel has begun to feel chilly.

Though I'm hardly an expert in seeing. There are things I still miss entirely, as I remembered only two nights ago, when Hal threw himself to the bed in despair.

"But I thought you had the kitchen cabinets under control," I said, my suitcase open as I packed for this trip. "I remember you doing the design. I FedExed the drawings."

"Yeah, well, stuff happened."

He explained what I hadn't been seeing. For months he'd put in major time to ensure that we'd have environmentally responsible cabinets. This is not a simple matter, because most store-bought cabinets have, in the eyes of someone trained to understand sustainability, multiple strikes against them. So Hal designed them himself; tracked down a board product that, unlike standard products, doesn't come from a clear-cut forest and doesn't off-gas the carcinogen formaldehyde; and hired a cabinetmaker who'd worked with it before. With few such products in production, this all took ages. But finally everything was in place. I FedExed the drawings. Prices were set. Then he found out that the manufacturer had discontinued the product.

"What does this mean for us?"

"That we've hit a dead end with the cabinets just when we need to order them."

"What are we going to do?"

"I don't know." He made a disheartened chuckle. "Maybe pray."

"Right." Hal, a lapsed-Methodist-turned-Buddhist agnostic, is not one to take entreaties to the divine seriously, and, although I've been known to pray, as a non-practicing-endlessly-ambivalent Jew, I've never felt certain that anyone's listening. If I did, I'd take Hal up on his suggestion. But instead I just said, "Maybe we should go to a store and buy some."

He looked at me, then turned away. Though as I learned this morning, now he agrees.

So it's hardly surprising that, as the tunnel show continues, my thoughts have moved away from the search for a sympathetic stranger to the search for suitable cabinets. However, this isn't only because we're going shopping tonight. It's also because if Hal really does dispense with his plan, it will be yet another blow in his long, frustrating journey to design.

As we kept walking through those early years together and he kept explaining architecture, Hal also informed me that because of the way architecture is practiced, many architects have limited opportunities to design buildings. "Do you want to?" I asked, as we meandered along the streets. "Most architects long to design buildings," he said. But at the small firm where he was serving his apprenticeship, he drew door details and window schedules, parts of unexceptional buildings designed by someone else to please subdivision developers. "I might get a chance later on. Architecture is called the old man's profession." "Well, if you do—*when* you do—what kind of design style appeals to you most?" "Style isn't the issue," he said. "The important thing is letting form arise from listening to the client, the place, and the context."

As the years passed, Hal worked in a succession of firms and sometimes did get the chance to design—furniture for a residence, a chapel for a retirement community, parts of a juvenile detention center, a building conversion at a university. But opportunities were intermittent, and although he reveled in them, he became increasingly disappointed about other aspects of the field. Architecture is intimately tethered to the economy, so architects have little control over whether the scope of their projects will wither, or even whether they'll remain employed, as we discovered one sad day when Hal, working at a firm that was having trouble rustling up jobs, got laid off. And in many firms, like the one that hired him after the layoff, preposterous deadlines are sometimes imposed. There were times when he'd spend weeks working in the office until midnight and returning at 5 a.m. He began to sour on his career.

I tried to console him, but he began steeping himself in his music whenever he was home, and his career disenchantment curdled to cynicism. So whenever I wasn't writing, I walked around our suburb alone, obsessing about the notion of true love and failing to get interested in architectural features I could now name. One night, trying to make conversation, I asked him to list his job titles over the years. He said, "Bum, Bum, Assistant Bum, Associate Bum, Project Bum." We laughed, but he had come to feel such emptiness about his life—as I did with mine, and therefore we did with each other—that no humor could fill us. Then we broke up.

But this is also when he revived an old but neglected interest.

Hal had long been alarmed by environmental problems. When we parted ways and he had time to fill, as well as a hole in his heart, he began studying green, or sustainable, design. This rekindled his affec-

tion for architecture, particularly how it could, even in a limited capacity, influence the world. He still does very little design in his current
position as a project manager overseeing design and construction at a
state university. But he's become the campus advocate for a greener
way of building, and that's helped him make his peace with his field.

So I was glad when, in the planning stage of our renovation, we
thought Hal would not just have a chance to design our house, but
have multiple opportunities to employ green strategies. Unfortunately,
since we had to tailor the job to our budget, some of his ambitions fell
by the wayside. But eco-friendly kitchen cabinets, with his simple,
functional design, were one of the primary features that survived the
final cut.

Until now.

Though, of course, Hal's career disappointments are not the only
reason I'm thinking of the cabinets as I watch the light show. I am also
ogling an entirely unnecessary orgy of energy, and I can easily imagine
that if he were here, he'd be saying the same kind of things he says when
we see gleaming glass skyscrapers that were built without any consider-
ation about solar load, or subdivisions for which long-established for-
ests were mowed down to the last tree. "I just can't see this as attractive.
All I can see is gross irresponsibility." Having picked up a reasonable
amount of knowledge from him, I tend not to disagree. Yet this tunnel
is just so sublime that I'm willing to make an exception—and keep it
to myself when I get home.

But it's still lonely, watching the next light show begin without anyone to whom I can say "Wow." It's like being alone at New Year's Eve
fireworks. If only I could find just one person with whom I could share
it. I'm not greedy. Just one other traveler who would pull aside the flap
of privacy and ask me to enter, or be willing to step inside mine. Not
only would this take my mind off my green guilt and the saga of the cabinets, but it would enhance my delight, as happens when the dream of
one person widens to encompass two.

Of all the lessons I learned when I met Hal, this might be the
most important of all: that none of us is truly alone. It might seem that
we are for long stretches of time. But there are others out there who,
though we do not know it at first glance, have something deeply in

common with us. Who are, in effect, our rhymes. All we need is some tiny connection that brings us together. It can be as small as a meeting of the eyes in a bustling public space, and then, if circumstances are right and hearts willing, it can progress to a hello, then a conversation, then—well, then to a story shared with a woman in Michigan twenty-three years later. And to wondering how we find our rhymes among strangers. Is it only happenstance? Or are we somehow meant to meet?

That was what the woman last night was implying when we sat in her SUV in front of the hotel, sharing the stories of our lives, finding how much we ourselves had in common. Not in an obvious way—as a mother and corporate professional who sat on the board of the disability-related organization for whom I'd just given a talk, she had a résumé of life that bore little resemblance to mine. Yet something clicked between us on the ride from the banquet hall to the hotel, and so we sat in the parking lot, one story spilling into the next, her dashboard clock turning from p.m. to a.m., and as we were marveling over the many twists of fate that had occurred in our lives, the conversation shifted, as it often does at such moments, to the question of whether life is part of some cosmic design. This is what I'd alluded to in my call with Hal, as he knows all too well. He also knows that, as an inconsistent believer in the Listener of Prayers, I've never made up my mind about my answer. But last night, having been through this tunnel just hours before I sat in that SUV, freshly reminded of how the designs of unknown people have shaped my moods and thoughts through my life, I found myself nodding when the woman said, "Just because we can't see it doesn't mean it might not be there."

All night, I kept wondering. I'll admit it: I did a little praying, too.

Of course, I did not wake up to an answer delivered by room service. No prophet has crossed my path this morning and said anything profound, either. All I have is this tunnel, and the parade of strangers passing me. And the story I told my late-night buddy last night—of a time when I was twenty-two, and had never met an architect, and was still not-seeing design.

. . .

That spring morning as I dressed for work, I had a secret plan. It was a very small plan, but I'd decided, as I'd formulated it over the previous weeks, to keep it to myself. I'd said nothing to the two friends with whom I was renting a Philadelphia row house. Not that they'd have laughed at me, but the plan had been giving me something to look forward to, and since I had precious little of that in my life, secrecy seemed a way to preserve that feeling. Plus, if my plan amounted to naught, which seemed highly likely, I wouldn't have anyone to report back to.

Like my roommates, now eating breakfast as I grabbed my jacket, I'd graduated from college the year before. Unlike them, I felt miserable in my job. I was a paralegal, a position for which I was terribly mismatched. I also felt lonely and aimless when I returned to the house at night. My only pleasure was my brisk half-hour walk into the downtown every morning to reach my office, but at all other times I despaired that my life, which mattered to no one and was accomplishing nothing, lacked the tiniest semblance of meaning. Sometimes one roommate and I even debated meaning. Sitting on the green shag wall-to-wall carpet, I argued that meaning could be found through love—soul-merging, time-transcending, misery-busting love. My roommate scoffed that love was a Hollywood construct. Maybe meaning could be found, maybe it could not. But each of us, she said, was alone in the universe.

So I'd kept my plan to myself. Why emphasize any more than I already had that I harbored a fanciful view of reality?

As I'd hoped, when I stepped outside that morning onto my residential street, I felt uncommonly energetic. Yes, my little plan was foolhardy, but it was already elevating the day. This feeling continued, even though I was only tracing the same route I'd walked every weekday morning for the last seven months: down two blocks, make a left, and cross over to my favorite part of the trek: the Benjamin Franklin Parkway.

Anyone familiar with Philadelphia would understand why the Parkway was the highlight of my walk. One of the most photogenic avenues in the city, the tree-lined Parkway was based, as even I knew, on the Champs-Élysées in Paris. With its eight lanes of traffic, generous green medians, world-class museums, larger-than-life fountains, green-domed cathedral, and flags from around the world, the Parkway spans a diagonal stretch from the Philadelphia Museum of Art, two blocks from my house, to the center of the city, City Hall, two blocks from my office. I always felt a spring in my step when I turned onto the Parkway, and that day was no exception. All my senses seemed happy: the air smelled of March seedlings, the cars roaring down the Parkway seemed less noisy than usual. I felt as lithe as a ballerina, despite my sneakers and wraparound skirt. Such is the power of anticipation, I thought, and I was glad I hadn't tinkered with that by hinting of my plan to my roommates.

Of course, they already knew about my quirky habits when it came to my walk every morning. I'd long ago admitted to them that the grandeur of the Parkway so reliably washed away my despair that I'd invented mental amusements to make my thirty minutes even merrier. I memorized the identity of the flags that snapped in the breeze. I timed myself, trying to set new records to reach the Rodin Museum every day, where I'd check my watch against the huge clock on the distant billboard for the Stroehmann Bakery.

Today's secret plan was a new game—which, unlike my other games, required another person. Over the months of forging my routine, I'd noticed that although most of the other walkers I saw proceeded in the same direction as I, a handful of pedestrians walked against the flow, away from downtown rather than toward. There was the bushy-haired man I often saw near the Art Museum, where foot traffic was scant. There was the familiar-looking fair-haired man I'd see blocks later, close to the fountain of Logan Square, where the crowd grew denser. My plan was to arbitrarily select one of these salmon swimmers and start saying, "Good morning." With luck the stranger would say it back, and I'd have one more early-morning treat to enliven my life-deadening day.

And lo! Everything *was* going according to plan: as soon as I passed the Art Museum, I saw the bushy-haired man. As always, he was walking toward me. As always, no one was on the sidewalk but us. He also looked exactly as he had for months: he wore jeans, a brown jacket, and a stern expression. His arms moved stiffly, as if he was disinclined to reach his destination.

I strolled toward him. I glanced at him. I opened my mouth. His eyes glared ahead.

I walked by.

Chicken, I scolded myself. *Good thing you didn't tell anyone your plan.*

The blocks passed. The flow of pedestrians picked up. I engaged in my usual pastimes—acknowledging the flags of Spain, Nigeria, Finland, Chile. I timed myself at the Rodin Museum. I watched the pigeons roost at the Free Library. I crossed to the south side of the Parkway at the Franklin Institute, and looked up to the majestic, three-statue fountain in the center of Logan Square.

Then I entered a catwalk around a large construction site. Eventually a four-star hotel would rise at this location, but at the moment it was a hole in the ground, and a throng of pedestrians was passing along the walkway, just wide enough for a single file in each direction. In among the crowd surging toward me, I saw the fair-haired man. As always, he wore more professional clothes than the other one, and as always he also possessed a hint of humor and originality: his tie was unusual, he carried a shoulder bag rather than a briefcase, and his face was boyishly cute. The aura of familiarity I'd always felt when I passed him had convinced me that he must have been in one of my college classes. How else could I be so well-versed in his face? This was why, I suddenly understood, I had initially selected the bushy-haired man. The rules of the game were, apparently, that I speak only to a stranger. Yet I had not been able to address the first man, and I now understood why. He had looked uninviting, perhaps even hostile. The fair-haired man wore openness on his face, and carried tenderness in his eyes.

We reached each other on the catwalk, me on the right, him on the left. His eyes were ahead. My eyes were on him.

"Good morning," I said brightly.

He glanced at me, startled. For a moment he stopped, then gave a small smile. "Good morning," he mumbled back, and we walked on.

I felt triumphant. I had a new game for my mornings! It would be my little secret. Mine, and the fair-haired man's.

For seven months, the good mornings continued. I grew accustomed to knowing I'd see him, though sometimes we missed each other if I left early, or he passed on the south side of the Parkway before I'd crossed over from the north. But always, when I caught sight of him, I called out a boisterous, "Good morning!" He replied in kind, his tone matching my own. Every so often I'd add, "That's a fine tie." Sometimes he'd say, "That's a fine skirt." We always smiled broadly as soon as we saw each other. But we exchanged no other words than that.

At last I was offered a new job. I was not excited about becoming a secretary, but I accepted the offer, knowing that it would remove me from the void of purpose I felt at the law firm. There was, though, one significant problem: my soon-to-be employer was located in my neighborhood, so my morning walks down the Parkway were about to come to an end.

For the two weeks before I left the law firm, I grieved all that I would lose: the distinguished museums, the towering trees, the man with the tender eyes. Though we'd never said more than hello, I had long since accepted that we'd never met before. He looked familiar, but there was no logical reason why. I did not even know his name.

On the morning of my second to last day at the law firm, I stopped him. In the middle of the sidewalk, as crowds flowed past, I told him that tomorrow was my final day at that office, and I asked his name. Hal, he said. I told him mine. Then, mindful of our time sheets, we thanked each other for adding a lift to our mornings, and continued on our separate ways.

The entire day I kicked myself. How could I not have asked for his phone number?

The next morning—my final morning at that job—I timed everything carefully to ensure that I'd see him. I walked at just the right pace. I crossed early to the Hal-side of the Parkway.

Then, just as I was passing the Art Museum, something happened that had never happened before: a car pulled up beside me. I looked over at the smiling woman inside. It was a friend from college! Exactly the sort of connection I'd been longing for seven months ago, but which now felt very much in the way. "Hey, want a ride?" she asked.

Not wanting to be rude, I got into her car. But as she pulled into traffic and cruised down the Parkway—"I'll take you right to your office"—I felt I was betraying myself. So I finally, and hastily, revealed my secret to another person. As she looked at me in mild horror, I let her know that today was my last opportunity to do more with this Hal than have a sweet little memory. She started filling me in on her life, but my eyes were on the sidewalks. At last, near the heart of the downtown, I saw my good morning man at the far end of a block. I seized her steering wheel and yelled out, "Stop here!" and almost stomped over the gear shift to the brake.

I jumped out of her car, and she roared off. Hal approached from the far end of the block, a broad smile on his face. *How will I ask him?* I thought. *How can I just say, Hey, who are you?* As he neared he whipped out a little black book. "May I be so brazen as to take your phone number?" he asked.

Now, after I return from Detroit, with Hal as my husband of four years, we stride into a home improvement store. I am still thinking about whether there is a grand architect who brought us together. Hal is still thinking about acceptable kitchen cabinets.

"I can't imagine that the cabinets here are sustainable," I say.

"They aren't."

"Then why are we doing this?"

"You were right when you said we should go shopping. We just can't wait."

Still, he winces as we walk around the displays. Not only will these cabinets off-gas formaldehyde, and not only is the wood probably from a clear-cut forest, but they're ugly. Also, when Hal opens some drawers to see how they're constructed, he says, "Man, this is really cheap. It's butt-jointed, see? It won't last. Also, the hinges are weak." He pulls out a shelf. "Look at this—the underside is unfinished. That's really the sign of junk."

"All of these cabinets? Even the ones Dan recommended?"

"Yup. Plus, they're all costing way more than they're worth."

I lean against a display stove. "It would be stupid to buy these."

"But the Woodstalk's been discontinued."

"Was that the only option?"

"There *is* a similar product, Primeboard. But look how long it took to set everything up with the Woodstalk. There's not enough time for all that before Dan needs the cabinets."

"So we buy something that we consider inadequate—and that doesn't have your careful, made-for-us design—just to accommodate the calendar?"

"It's that, or we finish the house without kitchen cabinets."

"So?"

He pauses. "So?"

I realize from the look on his face that I'm saying something completely outlandish. I guess it's almost as weird as going to an airport early just to stand in a pedestrian tunnel, or finding your husband in a mass of strangers on a city street.

I say, "So what if we finish the house without the kitchen cabinets?"

He blinks, then smiles. "As long as we have a place for the dishes, a cardboard box or something, then the cabinets *could* be installed later. We could do it."

"Then we could use your design," I say.

"That would be so nice," he says, his eyes gleaming.

"Then let's," I say.

"I'll call Dan in the morning and tell him to take the cabinets out of the job."

We walk outside, holding hands, swinging our arms. The sun is setting, and Hal's inventing some pirate skit on the spot, and I'm laughing at his bad jokes. It's the kind of love I longed for in the house with the shag carpet. The kind of love that, in all those years of watching him sink into despair about his career, I never believed we could have. The kind of love that makes me wonder if there is a Listener of Prayers.

The next day my sister Laura says, "I can't think of anyone who would agree to move into an unfinished kitchen and use cardboard boxes for their dishes."

"It's not really a big deal," I say.

"It would be to most people. You two are lucky you found each other," she says.

. . .

I am just about to leave the tunnel for my plane when I see her: a woman, positioned hundreds of feet away, her back to a column. She is fiftyish and wearing an opal pendant and earth-toned scarf, and she, too, is doing nothing but watching the colorful cascade. Thousands of pedestrians have passed through the tunnel in the time I had been here, and except for a few snaps of cell phone cameras, not one person has stopped. But she has settled in.

It's too late for me to approach her—I have a plane to catch. I grab my carry-on and roll it toward the escalator, and as I do, I notice that she is hoisting her bag to her shoulder and moving toward the escalator as well. I step on, and then she gets right behind me, and as we begin our ascent, I turn. She isn't staring into space, or preoccupied with an iPod. She's looking at me.

Should I say something? Should I find out if we were in the trance together?

I gesture behind us to the tunnel. "Isn't it beautiful?" I say.

"I love it," she says—the words I've wanted to hear. "I travel through this airport just to see this tunnel. I think it's the most extraordinary work of public art that I've ever seen."

We are beaming now, strangers brought together by design.

I say, "I've been watching, and I'm amazed that no one else seems to notice."

"I saw you when I came down. I went back to the other end of the tunnel and returned, just to see if you were still there, and when you were, and you were watching so intently and happily, I knew you had to be a kindred spirit. So I was waiting to talk to you."

"I'm so glad."

"It's nice to know you're not alone," she says. "I think that's important. To know someone else is looking, too."

After Hal and I return to the rented house from the store, aglow in a feeling of closeness, I decide to take the risk. I say, "Can I show you something online?"

As we sit at my desk and I type possibilities into Google, he says, "You probably want my definition, right? Of design?"

"Sure," I say, clicking on Web sites.

"It's matching to human need or desire the function of objects and the means of production, and doing so as economically and elegantly as possible. For instance, the design for a drinking glass is about fitting it to a hand *and* having it make sense for manufacturing *and* making sure it's durable *and* making it pleasing to the eye *and* taking the production of the materials and end use of the product into account. All of that's important, though each designer might emphasize one of those aspects over the others."

I look from the screen to him. "Users might emphasize one aspect, too, right? Like, you might drink from that glass while thinking of whether it was made from recycled materials. I might think about my friends with mobility impairments and if they'd find the surface slippery."

"Right. But ideally, the designer wants all the aspects of design to work, even the ones the user isn't noticing."

"It could go the other way, too. The user might perceive some aspect of design that isn't actually there."

"What do you mean?"

I sit back. "It's very romantic, thinking that you and I were somehow brought together by a grand architect in the sky. A lot of people who hear the story think they see divine intent. I often do, too. I mean, it was such a miracle. But at the same time, it's a mystery. How much does design rule our lives, and how much do we design our lives ourselves?"

"It's impossible to answer."

"I know."

"Also, there's evidence that our meeting might have been influenced by a human kind of design, the kind you *can* measure. Look at the field of environmental behavioral research."

"What's that?"

"People like Jane Jacobs and William Whyte actually watched interactions in public spaces and discovered basic principles of how the built environment affects social interaction. Like Whyte found that on city sidewalks, people tend to stop and talk in the busiest places."

"The way we met on the catwalk."

"Yes. They also looked at the metrics of human interaction—the distance where you can clearly see another person. That's why, say, four hundred feet is the ideal width of a plaza."

That's about how far away, I think, the woman in the tunnel was when she spotted me.

I reach for the mouse and scroll down the screen. "But where's the mystery in that?"

"Just because our behavior might have been influenced by the built environment so we would meet didn't mean that we'd be right for each other."

"Ah. So *there's* the mystery."

"There's nineteen *years* of mystery."

"What kind of design would you call that?"

"Really bad design."

"Really *stinking* bad design," I add.

I finally find a link and click. The screen fills with a video of the tunnel in the Detroit Metropolitan Airport. It actually has a name: the McNamara Tunnel. I say, "This is where I was today."

I flick off the desk lamp, and in my dark study, the colors flash onto Hal's face. He says nothing for a long time, so, bracing myself, I say, "I know, I know, it uses a ton of energy."

"I'm sure it does," he says. "But it's also beautiful."

I almost fall off my chair. "You think so?"

"If we can't build a few things like this, it would really be a shame."

I turn to him and smile.

"Maybe someday we should fly to Detroit," he says, "just to visit the airport together."

That night, lying in bed, gazing at my husband as he sleeps, I ask myself again about how kindred spirits come together. Do we just observe something in each other—tenderness in the eyes, an attraction to the same sights—and then say hello? I'd like to think that's all it is, but it seems there must be more to it, because if either person feels encumbered by disapproval, or constrained by a schedule, or too mistrustful to think, Hey, who are you?, greetings will not be offered, or heard. So what gets us to recognize *and* speak to others who rhyme with us? Hal refuses to speculate one way or another. I have spent a lifetime unable to make up my mind.

Though tonight, as I think back to the woman in the SUV, and the woman in the airport, and so many dream-sharing strangers I have met in so many unlikely ways over the course of my life, I wonder: do I actually *need* to make up my mind? I might wish I could. But the fact that each of us, no matter who we are, can find kindred spirits in the vastness of humanity—and therefore know that none of us really *is* alone in the universe—feels almost as important. It's not a fact that answers my question. It's an answer to a different question. But on days when I long to know if anyone is listening, it might be the answer that I need.

Hal smiles in his sleep, and I remember him walking toward me on that spring morning, now so long ago. There we were, the two of us, drunk from the taste of something larger. I will probably never decide what that something was. I might never really understand the forces that orchestrate love. But as I look at his face in the dark of our bedroom, starlight pouring through the window, I know that, no matter how lonely I might get, no matter how meaningless my life might feel, there is always one thing I can do. *Just keep paying attention. Look around. See all that you don't let yourself see.*

Mothers

"I've been meaning to tell you," Hal says as we're out for a walk in early November. "I'm going to build a wall."

"A *what?*"

"Not a wall wall."

"What other kind of wall is there?"

"You're thinking of exterior walls and interior walls, like our masonry outside, or the plaster finishes inside. What I'm talking about is"—he clears his throat—"our garden wall."

"We don't *have* a garden wall."

"We will. In the backyard. A nice dry stone retaining wall."

"May I kindly suggest that you tack this nice stone wall onto Dan's schedule?"

"May I kindly ask you to remember how unforeseen conditions have added to our costs?"

"And when are you planning to build this nice garden wall?"

"Any day now."

"But it's November. It might be warm today, but it rains in November. It gets cold."

"So I'll get wet and cold. Look, farmers in this part of the country built walls for centuries, using stones from their fields. Their walls ran the length of huge properties."

"Farmers," I say under my breath, "no doubt recruited their wives."

"This farmer can do it himself."

"It'll be backbreaking work. I'm sure you'll need help."

"The Buddha does say that there is an interdependence of all things."

"Yeah, well, what did he say to depend on when you don't have stones in your field?"

"I went to a quarry. They'll be delivering three and a half tons right to our front curb."

"Excuse me, but it takes serious strength to lay a stone wall. How much do you weigh?"

"One thirty-five."

"When's the last time you buffed up those pecs in a weight room?"

"Ye of little faith."

"And I'm even more of a weakling than you. This'll be an interesting episode," I say.

It's also going to happen concurrently with two other episodes: the next phase of the renovation, when we'll be getting insulation, windows, and drywall; and, far more notably, the moment when I become definite that my mother has crossed into a terrible frontier. I realize it seemed as if I were facing a similar passage when Theresa was awaiting her biopsy results, but when it was benign, we were able to turn back. This time, despite the word the doctors have not yet said, I feel certain that there will be no retreat.

When Hal and I return from our walk, I plunge right in and dial my sister Laura. Days away from flying across the country to visit our mother so one of us can see the situation firsthand, Laura has been far more decisive about what clothing she should pack than what emotions she will need. We know it would be wise if she could wedge patience, kindness, and acceptance into her suitcase, though we're aware that space will be limited, given the well-worn disappointments and annoyances, and so many still-in-the-package fears.

As soon as Laura picks up, she says, "She keeps asking why I'm bothering to come."

"She knows why you're coming."

"As far as she and Gordon are concerned, nothing's wrong."

"Denial," we both say at the same moment, and then we sigh in stereo.

Last spring, our mother, who we've long called by her first name, Rosalie, began to behave differently. For lack of a better word, and for fear of what, for a retiree of seventy-one, that word would almost certainly be, we called her new behavior "forgetful," though not because we'd never thought that it—that years-long, progressively-mind-obliterating It—could happen in our family. We'd always known that brain cells could be degenerating inside a relative for ages before symptoms revealed themselves, but we'd assumed that the relative would be our father, since his father had become, as we used to put it, "senile." So actually saying the word would be to admit we'd been duped by an awful stage trick: look while I juggle the green balls over here, the magician says, thus deceiving us into ignoring the orange balls over there.

Laura and I, the two siblings who'd maintained the most contact with Rosalie, wanted to see the situation for ourselves. But Rosalie and Gordon live in Florida, a thousand miles from me and twice as far from Laura in Arizona. With my speaking commitments and the burgeoning costs of our renovation, Laura's work schedule, and Rosalie and Gordon sticking to their usual long vacations, the opportunity for a visit, even if only from one of us, even if only for a weekend, hasn't arrived until now.

"Rosalie and Gordon *know* something's wrong," I say.

"They think we're just being overly protective."

"What did you tell her?"

"I said . . . I said I was coming because I simply wanted to see her."

Since Rosalie has begun these lapses, we've tried not to speak too insistently about our concern, because there have been moments when we've had just enough doubt ourselves. Although Rosalie's career as a librarian required constant interaction with the public, she's always fallen short when it comes to social skills. She's never mastered the conventions of staying on topic, avoiding excruciating detail, picking up cues that a conversation is ending, or gauging the appropriateness of, say, revealing intestinal problems to waiters. So we have indeed wondered if her forgetfulness is just age redrawing character as caricature.

But we don't think so. Neither do other confidants with whom I've been sharing the evidence. Hal says that although we haven't spent our adult years seeing our mother with the regularity that comes from a more favorable history, we've remained in sufficient contact to know that she is indeed stepping beyond the far edge of her personality. My father thinks so, too, though, not having spoken with Rosalie for thirty years, he's basing his assessment on our reports. I could dismiss this confirmation—Hal and my father have excessive proximity to the matter—but I keep hearing the same from my friend Harriet, who's the same age as my mother. For years now, since I met Harriet while we were taking out books at a library, she's offered the nurturing gestures that I might have sought from my own mother on the occasions when I've needed mothering, like when Hal and I broke up and Harriet had me sleep over every week to comfort me. Or when Hal and I got married and Harriet took me shopping for wedding day accessories. Or now, as hints are adding up about my mother. "It sounds like the way things began with the husband of a friend of mine," Harriet said. "But oh, honey, I hope it's not."

I do, too, even though my relationship with my mother is far from a typical mother-child relationship. And even though the likelihood of her decline, while alarming, has yet to kindle the emotions that I only wish I could feel.

Laura shares my wish for those feelings, to the point where our thoughts about Rosalie are interchangeable. Fortunately, Hal, my father, and Harriet also understand why I lack what most children would feel, so they express no disapproval when I give them the latest update and fail to add, "My heart is breaking," or "How will I live without her?" It's possible that other friends could do the same, say, *I do not judge you for having a steamer trunk of emotions that children are not supposed to feel, and for leaving behind a whole house of emotions that you ought to have brought along.* After all, over the years I've learned that a significant number of friends are also members of this secret club, the one into which we were drafted when our mothers strayed far from what a mother is supposed to be. It's a club of adult children who question the concept of maternal instinct, feel no sentimentality toward mom clichés like apple pie, and greet every May with grimness, as the quest for a not-too-honest Mother's Day card rolls around again. But I generally avoid talking about being in that club—it requires too much explanation, and runs the risk that I'll be viewed as callous. So mostly I've revealed Rosalie's forgetfulness to only these intimates, which has proven easy. Everyone knows I'm deep into a renovation. Who'd have thought that one of the virtues of renovation is how conveniently it monopolizes conversation?

"How did Rosalie reply," I ask Laura, "when you said you just wanted to see her? It sounds so . . . like a regular daughter."

"She sounded surprised," Laura says.

I laugh. "That's it?"

"No. She hasn't forgotten that none of us has been there for years."

"That's heartening. At least her long-term memory's intact."

"Yeah, it was a good sign. But the best part is that she was happy that I was coming."

"That's good."

"It helps me not to dread this trip," Laura says. "Just knowing she'll be glad to see me."

That evening, Hal and I attend a party down the street from Teacher's Lane. As soon as we walk in the door and see our old neighbors, my inner chatter about Laura's impending visit subsides to a whisper. I hadn't realized how omnipresent it had become, but as we catch up with friends, I feel a relief I hadn't known I'd needed. So at the end of the night, Hal suggests that we delay our departure by visiting the old house. Then he can show me—and our neighbor Susan, who asks to accompany us—all the recent developments.

The door squeaks as Hal enters, flashlight in hand. Susan says, "I can't see anything," and as I follow her in, I understand why. Since the electricity is off and the demoed back wall is still covered by plywood, there's no illumination except the streetlight coming in the front and side windows. But it's weak, so all we really have is the flashlight's diameter.

"What are those?" Susan asks. She points to the top of a plaster wall in the living room.

Hal holds the flashlight still, and I see a lot of tiny holes. Hal says, "That's where they'll be spraying the insulation in the next couple of days." Then he walks us into the dining room–kitchen and directs the flashlight to the exposed brick. "Here, they'll blow the insulation right between these studs. Then they'll put up the drywall."

"Oh, look at that," Susan says, pointing across the room.

Hal swings the flashlight around. That's right: since our dining room windows face our neighbors', we've replaced them with glass block. Instead of clear views we have grids of refractors. They're like crossword puzzles filled with squiggly letters that no one will ever read.

"That's really nice," Susan says. "You can't see them and they can't see you."

"Yeah," I say. "We still get the light from outside, too. Wow."

"I thought you'd like it," Hal says.

I also like how, as we walk around, there's a lot more framing in preparation for the insulation and drywall. But otherwise, I must admit, things look much as they did at the start of the roughing-in. My house sickness hasn't returned, but I can't say I'm feeling excitement.

"Ooh," Susan says as we continue through, "this is going to be great."

I'm glad it's dark, so she can't see that I don't share her emotions. I know many people feel a bond with their house, a sense of safety and pride in its embrace. But I can't imagine how they get to that feeling. I can only hope that I will.

The next day, I call Laura one last time before her flight. Then I pull out the box of paint samples that Hal brought home from work, and try to put my mind to selecting our colors.

Many possibilities catch my eye as I thumb past dozens of pigment cards, so many that I think I can't possibly narrow things down until Hal is sitting beside me. Then I see that I've actually skipped over a whole color family—orange—and I roll my eyes at myself. Orange is Rosalie's favorite color, and I associate it so strongly with an emotionally ravaged time that I've always avoided orange. I know Hal will respect my disinterest, but just to play it safe, I remove all the samples from Avid Apricot to Organza and set them on the far side of the table.

There was a time when I saw orange as a completely acceptable color, as enticing as the blues and purples and reds to which I'm still drawn as I'm flipping through this box. That was back when I was a little girl, before Rosalie's problems began with my father, and before the unhappiness she'd carried since *she* was a little girl became even harder for her to bear. In those days, I loved her as unreservedly as any child loves any mother. I would, with Laura, play dress-up in Rosalie's clothes. A few years later, I would learn the Dewey Decimal system from her, walk through art galleries with her, sit by her side at Broadway musicals. But she retreated from us as the divorce became final and loneliness and desperation overtook her, and then we found ourselves living with our father and not knowing where in the world she might be. On the occasions when I tried to make sense of my baffling mother during her disappearance, I could find no answers except for one memory: I was six, and watching her fold laundry, when out of the blue she made a great sigh and said, "I never should have had children." So that's it, I told myself. Some people just shouldn't have children, and my mother didn't know that until it was too late. By the time I finished college, my mother had been reduced in my life to an aversion to orange and a phone number in my pocket. Now that she is again an actual presence, I still love her. But it is no longer the love that I think most adult children feel toward their mothers. It is love from behind a barrier. It is love smudged by history. Yet it is also a love that is both chill-resistant and warmth-retaining, sealed as it is by compassion.

This isn't the way I wanted things to be when I called my mother after our six years apart, though I can't say I had any picture of what I *did* want. I just wanted not to feel the hatred I'd been feeling, and then, when we met for the first time, I just wanted to survive dinner with some meager understanding of the woman before me. I hadn't envisioned forgiving her.

But forgiveness, which dims the lights on one story, turns up the spotlight on the next. For us this meant that as I embarked on my new relationship with Rosalie, a trapeze effect began: I realized that I now had to be the mother, because she was still, at heart, a suffering child. I learned about her childhood then. In fact, the distant past was most of what we discussed, except for when we talked about the present—she couldn't, I understood, face the years in between. So I decided to push aside my resentment and longing, learn to live with my irritation and disappointment, and let her, my mother-child, direct the show, and as she told me story after story, I learned much more about her life than she'd revealed when I'd lived with her: how she'd been raised in a first-floor apartment with a spineless father who couldn't figure out a career, a caring mother who couldn't stand up to her own mother, a demeaning uncle with a drinking problem, a grandfather dying of cancer, and both grandmothers, who were at each other's throats. An only child lost in the crowd, Rosalie would look out the window at her neighbors, aching to go on picnics as they did, to be the loving family that she imagined them to be. But knowing that she could, at any moment, become the target of a family member's misery, she committed herself to being inconspicuous. This sense of her own unimportance followed her into adulthood: she made no friends, had no passion to achieve, and was a novice when it came to good judgment. As the first years passed and I came to understand all of this, I acquired a sense of sympathy and forbearance. I did not entirely lose my more disagreeable feelings, but my new awareness made me choose not to give in to them. Thus I ceased hoping for a nurturing mother. Instead, I reached out to grasp the mother I had, and allowed her to hold on to me.

It has been in this spirit of upside-down love that I have kept up with Rosalie. Not that she would refuse any request I might make for motherly offerings like advice or solace—my mother is not hard-hearted or malevolent, and her door has been open to me for many years. But it doesn't seem to cross her mind that she could solicit such requests. Nor has she ever suggested that we speak weekly or monthly, that I visit on holidays, or even, when she and Gordon moved to Florida soon after our reconnection, yearly. It just doesn't appear to occur to her that when they take cross-country vacations, they could visit her kids at least as often as they visit lighthouses. There was a time when this apparent indifference upset me, yet I also felt, during the infrequent calls and visits, that she did love me, so I made yet another decision: I would view her behavior not as a lack of love, but as who she was. So for two decades now, when I call or visit Rosalie, I do so because I care about her, and know that she likes to see me. Unlike some friends in the secret club, I've also come to enjoy my time with my mother, particularly since she retired a few years ago. Her exit from the social pressures of the work world released her from daily awkwardness, and her new free time with Gordon, a cheerful, childless guy who dotes on her, came to make her feel, at long last, cherished. Even though her melancholy remains, it's farther below the surface, and her smiles have become more genuine. I might even say that she has finally recovered, to the extent possible, from a life of pain. Although I came to feel in my early twenties that the name "Mom" conveyed emotions that contradicted the reality of the relationship, and although she welcomed my switching to "Rosalie," we still look forward to our times together, and burst into tears when our visits end.

This is why Laura and I have had a hard time figuring out what's going on. In fact, we didn't realize *anything* was going on until one day last spring, when we were still mending our own relationship, and Laura said to me on the phone, "Have you heard from Rosalie lately?"

"Come to think of it," I said, "it's been way longer than usual."

Laura, annoyed, said, "She never calls anymore. It's like we don't matter to her."

"We don't," I said with a laugh.

Laura said, "I mean, I even sent her a really nice present for her birthday"—two weeks before—"and when I didn't hear anything, I called. You know what she said? 'Oh, what did you send? I must have put it somewhere.'" Laura, whose anger toward Rosalie is sometimes difficult for her to contain, blew out air hard, in disgust.

I then remembered that, also two weeks before, I'd sent Rosalie a videotape of the movie made from my book, weeks in advance of its air date, and I'd heard nothing from her.

I hung up with Laura and called my mother. As always, she was surprised to hear from me, as if any contact from her children came as a shock. We chatted pleasantly for a few minutes, and then I said, "We don't hear much from you anymore."

"Oh, yes," she said, in a meek, apologetic voice.

"Are you annoyed with us?"

"No, no. I just"—her voice trailed off, then returned—"I just never think about it."

I chose not to let this bother me, and said, "Well, Laura was concerned when—"

"I know, I know, she was very annoyed with me for not telling her that I got her present."

"She was worried it got lost in the mail."

"I know. I should have called her."

Then, thinking I was only checking on something else that might have gotten mishandled by the post office, I said, "Actually, did you get something *I* sent recently?"

"You sent something?"

"Yes? A package?" When she said nothing, I added, "The movie of my book?"

She said, "Your book? . . . Oh, a book . . . It was about Beth, wasn't it? Something about her riding buses? . . . It's so nice that you wrote a book about her . . . I wonder where it is . . ."

I got off the phone and stared at the wall in my study. It stared back, blank as a page without words. Yet I knew what I was seeing.

I called Laura back. "I think something's wrong," I said. "I do, too," she said. Immediately dumping any remaining tension between us, Laura and I opened up right then, poured together all the questions we'd begun asking ourselves, and decided on the spot that we had to be united. From that moment on, we've been a team, facing this frontier together.

Now I glance at the orange paint samples, set far away from me in one big fist of color. In the apricots and tangerines I see my mother's face, finally truly smiling, and I think about how she at last has the affection and security that every person deserves. But if Laura's eyes confirm what we already feel—what we already know—then Rosalie is about to lose everything that took her seven decades to gain. "It's not fair!" we used to say when we were little. "Life's not fair," she would reply. It always just seemed like something she said, not a truth with a lifelong echo.

.   .   .

"There they are," Hal says the next day as we get out of our car in front
of the old house, dressed in work clothes. "Pennsylvania fieldstone.
Three and a half pallets."

"They look like ordinary gray and tan rock."

"They are, if you're in a field in Pennsylvania."

The pallets, bound with wire netting, contain rocks ranging in
size from oven mitts to dinner trays. They're rectangular, triangular,
and teardrop-shaped—"with ragged edges," I say.

Hal says, "Squared-off edges are used for more formal, mortared
walls."

"Wait—we're not going to have mortar?"

"This is a dry stone wall. If we lay it right, gravity will hold it
together."

"Are you kidding?"

"The dry stone walls throughout the Northeast were built three
hundred years ago, and they're holding up fine."

"I guess my knowledge of walls is a bit limited."

"You just haven't noticed what's out there. But trust me, this'll
work."

"If we survive building it."

"I've already started. Look."

I follow him into the alley, which is so slender it prevents us
from walking abreast, then ascend the two steps to our new concrete
patio. The backyard beyond is filled with a huge pile of dirt. We will,
Hal explains, be laying our wall in the trench he's been digging between the patio and yard, which is where the dirt came from. I'm
impressed, and while I squeeze his biceps and make Arnold Schwar-
zenegger jokes, Hal remains serious. The wall will be three feet high
and eighteen feet long, and will separate the patio from the soon-to-
be-flattened yard. He'll also need to sort the stones by size, since the
largest go on the bottom. He'll also need to measure and lay steps
into the yard as the wall goes up. Though for now he needs to keep
shoveling.

"What am I supposed to do?"

"Cut the wire around the stones." He points to a pair of tools: tin snips, he says. I notice other tools like a level and mallet. "Then get the stones down the alley to me, and I'll sort them."

"They're kind of heavy. They're, like, stones."

"Use the cart in the back of the alley." He points.

I look. It's a rolling cart, but it has no bottom. "Uh, there's nothing to support them."

So while I snip the wire off the pallets at the curb, Hal hauls plywood out of the basement and onto the front porch, sets up a work table on two sawhorses, and power-saws a rectangle of plywood to create a solid bottom to the cart.

"Gee," I say, as we set the wood into place, "you're not letting anything stop you."

"That's just how you have to be," he says, heading down the alley to the backyard.

"Unless you're a natural quitter," I call after him from the curb.

"Just load the stones, Simon," he calls back.

Actually, I think as I start loading the stones, I'm not a natural quitter. Once Laura and I became partners last spring, we e-mailed each other every day, sharing the details of our calls with Rosalie, whom we also began phoning regularly. Laura did research, too, and found out that the sooner Rosalie started medication, the greater the chance that she could slow the development of whatever was happening. Rosalie said we were making a fuss unnecessarily, and we wondered if we were, until one day when I called and she started complaining about Gordon being out while she was home alone, confused. "Confused about what?" I asked. "I'm fine," she said. "I'm just having . . . a dizzy spell . . ." We later learned she was so disoriented that she couldn't leave the house. "Please," Laura said, then I said, then Laura said, "see a doctor."

Finally, in late spring, my mother went to a doctor. "He says I have senile dementia," she reported in a merry voice. "He says I don't need to come back for years."

We looked it up, and saw that, while we'd been worrying about the A-word, there were in fact others that were equally foreboding. Not only that, but this new one, the D-word, was sometimes used as a syn-

onym for the other, or was a precursor. It was already getting complicated, whatever It was, or would become, and she didn't seem to be
taking It seriously.

"Rosalie," we said, "senile dementia is serious stuff. Did the doctor talk to you about how it might progress, or if it will progress? Did
he suggest any treatment?"

". . . I don't know."

"Was Gordon with you?"

"He offered to take me, but I told him not to bother. That wasn't
good, because I couldn't remember how to get home."

"Oh, Rosalie."

"But I asked for directions. I stopped at a library."

"Did you look up more information while you were there about
what the doctor said?"

"No."

"Will you go back to the doctor and ask him these questions?"

"Oh, I hate to bother him."

"Will you go to a specialist, then?"

"There *is* one in his building. I guess I'll do that."

The second doctor said that her memory was better than his.

"The doctors where you live have screws loose," we said. "Please
get another opinion."

"I wouldn't know who to call."

"Get a new referral from your doctor."

"I don't want to be a pest. Maybe after our trip"—a four-month
lighthouse tour—"I will."

So not until *this week*—months after she started writing everything
down so she wouldn't forget, and walked out of the supermarket and
forgot how to get home—did Rosalie see a new doctor. That means
it's also been months since Gordon has driven her everywhere, as well
as taken over the cooking and cleaning. Only this week did that new
doctor weigh in when, after the exam, he told her, "It's not nothing but
it's not yet something."

"What else did he say?"

"He gave me pills for Alzheimer's, just in case. I start them right
before Laura's visit."

So while Laura and I alternate between questioning our perceptions and being furious with the doctors, we've also moved on to practical matters—which are getting us more agitated with every call. How can we help when Rosalie lives so far away? How can we convince Gordon to move them near one of us? How can we get them to admit she's ill? Discuss their insurance? Living wills? Will Max, whose focus is on his wife and children, ever want to get more involved? When should we break the news to Beth? What should we expect of ourselves, given that we don't have a Mom type of relationship? What does she expect—or want—from us? What do we feel? What *should* we feel? How will we keep moving forward?

"You just will," Hal said to me a few weeks ago, after I finished a call with Laura.

"Oh, that's real helpful," I said to him.

"I've been watching you get more and more stressed about this. I know it's been hard."

"I keep looking into the future, and it seems overwhelming. I don't know what to do."

He set his guitar aside and said, "Can I tell you something that happened to me some years ago at a Buddhist retreat? It's kind of mystical-schmystical, but it might help."

I was not in the mood for Zen koans about the merits of change. But he was looking at me with those big eyes of his, and then he reached up and wrapped his fingers around mine, so I sat down on the sofa beside him.

"Buddhism tells you that the body is the great teacher—that everything we need to know is in our bodies. Well, I was on a retreat, and when you sit a long time meditating, you can get severe knee pain, and in the third hour of a four-hour sit, I felt that pain. It was intense—real suffering. But they teach that if you can stay with the pain and observe it without attachment or aversion, you start to see it for something else. You see that it's energy, or a blockage of energy, you see subtle changes in it over time, you watch how it moves in your body. Then you see that it might be possible to get to a point where the pain breaks up, and you experience it as part of a flowing energy, and then there is no suffering. It's gone. That's what happened to me."

"What does that have to do with Rosalie?"

"That experience changed my view of the world. I realized that I didn't need to be bound up in suffering of any kind, if I could just stay with it with equanimity."

"But how can I have equanimity with this?"

"Well," he said, "maybe you can think about something else Buddhism says, which is that there is a fundamental interdependence of all things. Nothing exists in and of itself. Every cause leads to an effect which leads to a cause and on and on."

"What are you saying I should do?"

"I don't know, specifically. But maybe you can just do what you can do, and don't get hung up on what you can't do, and trust that your actions will spur consequences that will go way beyond anything you can see or know." He smiled. "Do you think it's worth a try?"

So I've been trying. Last week, for instance, while visiting Beth, I told her what's been going on. She listened without distress, though she was concerned. Then I bought her a phone card so she could initiate calls to Rosalie from now on. She placed the first one the moment I drove off, then left a message for me to call her the instant I got home.

When we kids fought as children, Rosalie would say, "When you're older, you'll be glad you're not an only child." "No we won't," we'd yell back, but now we see that she was right. Laura has me to talk to, and I have her, and Beth has the assurance that she's not alone.

Now every few days I call Beth and make sure she's okay. Every day Laura and I call each other. Sisters all, we reach across the phone lines, take each other's hand, and squeeze.

By the afternoon, my shoulders are screaming for mercy.

"Want to borrow my wheelbarrow?" asks a neighbor I've never seen before.

"Bless you," I say. The wheelbarrow moves much more smoothly than the cart.

Fortified by this Samaritan's generosity, I heave stones up from the palette with new vigor, deposit them into the wheelbarrow and, with Hal's help, roll them to the back. Incredibly, he has the brawn to empty the wheelbarrow with me, as well as the brains to lay the wall. I feel such love for this person with so many talents. It inspires me to lift rock.

"When does rock become stone?" I ask as we unload several hundred pounds.

"When it leaves the woods and moves into your backyard."

"So 'stone' is what you call 'rock' when it finds civilization?"

"Domestication, really. But take away the name and it could be the same thing."

I finish the first pallet with my quads and deltoids on fire. I knew that building this wall would hurt, but I hadn't anticipated soreness inflaming my every cell. At the same time, I've discovered a pleasing rhythm as I load the stones—bend, lift, pivot, step, bend, release, stand—and that this fun little dance is shoring up my stamina. I'm far from saying that I'm enjoying this labor, but it's nice to have found some satisfaction.

There are other rewards, too, like our quick exchanges when we unload together.

"How did you figure this out?" I ask Hal.

"I read about it, I talked to people about it, and then I just started."

"Aren't you in pain?"

"Sure. But I'm just being fully present in the moment."

"Mindfulness over matter?"

"Mush, Simon, mush."

Most of our conversations are this short, but we don't only converse. We also sing Sam Cooke's "Chain Gang," make jokes about gathering no moss, and name our stone wall Jackson.

Then Susan, walking by, offers to assist me with the next pallet. We have a lively time, and then her husband, Jim, joins Hal in the backyard, helping him set the first two steps into place. After they leave, there are a few hours when, thanks to another neighbor, we hire someone to work with me—"a knucklehead I know." But Knucklehead, a strapping man who appears to make his living doing construction under the table, lifts only the lightest stones, hums loudly to himself, and takes frequent cigarette breaks. I tell myself that what little assistance I'm getting might preserve my energy, though when he takes a break and doesn't return, I decide that there's enough generosity around to keep going.

And keeping going is the priority—because if I stop, I'll start thinking of Laura, who's now with Rosalie in Florida. Then I'll risk sliding into the new feelings I've been having since I went through the paint colors: a chest-thumping regret that Rosalie had so few years of a good life before her decline, and a fist-shaking indignation at injustice. If only she'd had a happier past, maybe my feelings wouldn't pound as hard. But as I bend, lift, pivot, step, bend, release, stand, I run through all my memories of her before her retirement, and almost all of them are sad.

I remember her story of looking out the window at her neighbors when she was a little girl, and I think, as the sun begins to move toward the horizon, about the difference between the way I surely look right now and the actual fact of my agony. I do reveal this fact to some passing neighbors, the ones who are willing to offer encouragement. But Rosalie never shared her agonies with others, nor did she find out if the families she envied were indeed as loving as she believed them to be. I wish that when I swung back toward her in the big tent of our lives together, I'd been able to grab on to her and somersault us back in time and land on the lawn outside her childhood apartment and say to her, *You are not alone, and you are not unloved, and the world is open to you if you want it to be.* But there is nothing I can do to heal my mother from herself. I just have to keep going, stone after stone, until this day at last comes to its end.

When it does, and I finally call Florida, the heart of the conversation is brief.

"She looks good," Laura says in a whisper in the back bedroom. "She's got energy, she seems happy. To see her, you wouldn't know. But she's gotten fuzzier and more forgetful as the day's gone on. She makes little slips, like when we ran into someone she used to work with and she couldn't remember the woman's name. Or when she wanted to print something out of her computer but couldn't remember how to turn it on. You could think she was just being an exaggeration of her usual self if you didn't know. But I know her," she says. "So I know."

I look beside me to Hal. We're sprawled on the bed in the rented house, ice packs all over our bodies. In the silence as I absorb Laura's words I give him a small nod, and he reaches out and touches my hand.

The call continues for an hour as Laura tells me that Rosalie has been a wonderful host. She was prepared with Laura's favorite food, and took them to an art exhibition and dinner in a seaside village. Laura knows that things aren't going to get better, but she's enjoying the trip.

Only at the end of the call do I ask, "How are *you* feeling?"

Laura thinks a moment. Then she says, "It's funny. Before I got here, I couldn't imagine that I wouldn't get annoyed about all the usual things. But now I just tell myself that her behavior is all about her illness. It's like, after all these years, I can finally blame it on something. And that makes it so much easier to be patient and cope with her."

"That's really nice," I say. "Maybe this whole horrible thing has something really good about it."

"I know. I keep thinking that. I feel guilty thinking it, but also so much relief."

I almost tell her about the satisfactions I've been finding today, too, as I've endured the physical torment of the wall: my stone-hauling dance, my benevolent neighbors, my Hercules of a husband. But I'm way too exhausted. I just say, "I'm so glad we're in this together."

"Oh my God," Laura says, and we laugh the same laugh of gratitude. "I am, too."

"Uh," I say the next morning, completely unable to get out of bed.

"Double uh," Hal says. "Zombie uh."

"Can't we just finish a few days from now?"

"It's Sunday, it's still warm out, and I want to get it done."

"But we're both comatose. How can we possibly do it?"

"You don't have to do it. I can finish alone."

"There's still a pallet and a half at the curb."

"I'll be fine. Go back to sleep. I'll see you later."

He gets up, and as he showers I lie there, thinking of Susan and Jim and the wheelbarrow lender. Then I think of Knucklehead. Well, that's another satisfaction that's come from the wall, I think as I set my feet on the floor. I have a better sense of who I really am.

We return to the house. One hour passes, two, three. The pain in my body gets so acute that I go into a state of numbness, which also has the effect of letting my mind fly free. Of course, most of my thoughts concern my mother, only this time I seem able to find the tiny cracks in her long unhappiness, and come upon not only good memories, but good memories that I shared. She is reading to us from picture books. She is showing us art in Manhattan galleries. After our reconnection, she is taking me to see the Salvador Dalí Museum, to tour a college designed by Frank Lloyd Wright, to walk through parks. She is telling me stories about her childhood. I remember now that even though every one of those stories ended with her feeling forlorn, I liked when she told them to me. They made me feel that she was letting me stand beside her old self, at seven or ten or fourteen, and that my listening really mattered. It's too bad that as her memory fades, these oldest stories will probably be the last ones to go.

But now I realize that maybe, by spending all those years listening to her stories, I *have* somersaulted back in time with her. I wasn't able to change the circumstances of her youth. But I was able to be inside that apartment with her, and witness the truth of her life, and maybe just my being there made the truth hurt a little less. I might wish I could repair the deterioration in my mother's mind. I might wish I could give her decades of happiness. But maybe when all that is left are her memories in that apartment, she will feel less pain than she once did.

And thinking this, I finally feel grief about her illness. Here I've been having regret for the life that Rosalie will not live. But now I feel regret for the life that *we* will not live. Our opportunity to keep mending our relationship is coming to an end. Those few good memories of museums and walks might be the only ones I'll get, and the only ones I'll give.

Does anyone, in the secret club or not, know what emotions to pack for this frontier?

I don't think I'll ever know. But around the time the sun begins its arc into midafternoon, as I near the bottom of the third pallet, something of an answer comes to me. To my astonishment, I start to feel my labor getting easier. I'm sure I'm imagining it, or have just grown so used to my scorched muscles that I've ceased feeling them. Yet it really does seem as if the agony, the numbness, all of it, has lifted. Might Hal's mystical-schmystical stuff be true: that by staying with my task and being at one with the pain, I am transcending suffering?

It is in this state, a state that is almost like bliss, that I recall another good memory. It was the one time that we went to a circus, just Rosalie and Laura and me. Laura was in second grade, I in kindergarten, and although we found the circus smelly and dirty, we were awed by the trapeze artists sailing back and forth through the air in their spangled costumes, until one let go of her swing and got caught by the other and they grasped hands and swung back and forth high above the net together. When we got home, I told Rosalie that I wanted to learn how to do what they could do, and she said, "Then let's write them a letter and ask for advice." I was too young to write, so I dictated it to her. Then I waited for their reply, and waited some more. When we moved a few years later, I knew I wouldn't ever hear back. But I think now about the way I reached out for Rosalie when I met her again, about Harriet reaching out for me when I lost Hal, about Laura and me reaching out for each other. That letter from the trapeze artists *did* find its way to me. It just wasn't written in words.

Right before sunset, Hal and I set the last stone step into place, then sit down. Our bodies are wrecked, but we feel light with accomplishment, as gravity holds our new wall together.

"To Jackson," he says, making a toast with bottled juice.

"To bed," I say, clinking his juice against mine.

We drain our libations and he howls, "Ow-wow-wow-owf!" and we slump triumphantly against each other.

"Ta da," Hal says, throwing open the front door of the old house.

"Oh my goodness."

It is two weeks later, and I am delivered into a dazzling new world. The insulation is in, the drywall installed, and sunlight pours through

glorious new floor-to-ceiling windows in the back of the house, setting the rooms aglow. As I walk from one room to the next—the bones
and veins of the walls at last covered by skin—I feel enchanted. I'm finally in a *house*. *My* house. A house that will protect me, and inspire my
pride. Most of the windows, Hal says as I enter my study, are now new,
with the rest to be installed in the next few days. Soon the hardwood
floor throughout the house will get sanded and sealed; appliances, fixtures, linoleum, and tile will appear in the bathroom and kitchen; trim
and doors will return; and paint will adorn our walls. I turn around
and around, envisioning a real room. Thanksgiving is four days off; by
Christmas, he says, we should be back in. Yesterday our landlady, Natalie, found a buyer for the rented house. Tonight Hal and I will finish
selecting our paint colors. So the timing is perfect. I feel myself rise as
high as the walls, higher than the ceiling—finally savoring the pleasure
of change.

But we haven't come to the house just so I could see the walls and
the windows.

We go outside, and I help Hal lift the potted baby tree out of the
car. It's called a fringe tree because of its feathery blossoms, though
since it's late November, its blossoms are long gone and its leaves have
browned. "People sometimes think their fringe trees have died over
the winter," Hal told me when we went to the nursery this morning,
"because it's always the last to leaf." At five feet tall—the same height
as my mother, the same height as me—our baby fringe tree is heavy,
and together we carry it down the alley to the backyard. Then we dig a
hole beyond the new stone wall. "It might grow as tall as twenty-five
feet," Hal says, lowering the tree into the hole. I watch it go in, shaking
my head at the metamorphosis. "It's amazing," I say over and over.
"It's a real backyard now." Then I remember something my mother
told me long ago, when we looked out my childhood window at the
tall trees in our backyard, and she said that it wasn't our family who
had planted them. "You don't plant a tree for yourself. You plant it for
the people who come later. Someone else did this for us." Hal presses
the soles of his shoes on the dirt around the tree, tamping down the
soil. We step back and admire our new tree, our new wall, our new
yard, our new windows, our new house. Tonight, a fraction of an inch

of tree growth from now, I will get a call from Laura, and the news will be no better. My mother will surely be gone in twenty-five feet. Hal and I might be, too. But I think I can already feel them now: the tree's roots reaching deep inside the soil, opening their grasp toward the future.

THE JOB STOPS

D·I·S·A·S·T·E·R

Students

We are not in the house when the explosion occurs.
     It is a windy, slate-colored November afternoon, two days
before Thanksgiving, two days after we planted our tree. On site are a
couple of HVAC mechanics, who are installing our new heating and
air-conditioning system in the basement; a team of drywallers, who are
taping up seams on the second floor; and a carpenter, who has just returned from lunch. There is no reason to think that our job will not
continue flowing toward completion—until, at an indeterminate moment before 12:20 p.m., someone opens a valve on the natural gas line.

     Days will pass before we ferret out the details. All we know at first
is that once the valve has been opened, the gas line—a slender silver
pipe running behind the new drywall in the kitchen, which possesses
an end point that resembles the sneering face of a snake—begins to
leak natural gas. For a period that might last minutes or mere seconds,
gas climbs up the western wall, prowling skyward under the house's
skin, then rolls across the kitchen ceiling, and then descends within
the soffits on the eastern wall, unfurling along the entire length of the
dining room–kitchen. But gas, a wily intruder, cannot be contained by
anything porous, so it escapes the sheathing of the drywall through the
minute cracks common in all walls and enters the oxygen-rich room.
Natural gas reaches an explosive mixture when it becomes five to fifteen percent of the air, and as the gas envelopes the room, it achieves
that mixture. The only missing element is a source of ignition.

And at 12:20 p.m., one of the mechanics prepares to solder a line in the basement. He pulls out his welding torch, and turns it on.

"It felt like an earthquake!" a neighbor tells us later.

Susan and Jim add, "Our dishes fell right off the wall!"

The lady with the wheelbarrow says, "I saw a guy blow out of the back of the house!"

The explosion tears the new drywall off the walls and ceiling in the dining room–kitchen, shoving the eastern wall until it bulges into the alley. It bursts through the new floor-to-ceiling windows along the back wall. It ruptures the wooden floor above, propelling huge nails backward into my new study. As it continues on, ripping up drywall and plaster on the second floor, it sends concussive waves across the entire house, hurling cracks through the front rooms, shattering windows too young to have lived a week, rattling masonry outside. In the backyard, our baby tree gets buried beneath debris.

Soon fire trucks are screaming toward the house. Evacuation orders are put in place. The street is roped off. The mechanics are whisked to the hospital.

Two hours later and a hundred miles away, I'm running across a concrete plaza, hurrying toward the high-rise where I have a meeting five minutes from now, when I pull out my cell phone to check my voice mail. "It's me," Hal says, his voice distressed. I stop moving the instant I hear his tone and as wind lashes through my hair I listen to him say, "There was a gas explosion at our house." I stop breathing. "Nobody's clear on what happened. I don't know how much damage has been done. I'm headed over there now."

Desperately, I dial him, but like me, Hal keeps his cell phone off when he's not making a call. I'm dumped into his voice mail, where I beg him to call me right away.

I hang up and look at the gloom-stained sky. The timing could not be worse. I spin toward the parking garage, debating a leap back to my car, then I one-eighty back toward the high-rise. Then I just reel around and around, a weather vane in a tornado. How can I decide what to do? In a matter of seconds, our carefully set plans have been swept off the table, taking rhyme and reason tumbling down with them.

Go home now. How can I not fly back down the highway to Delaware, screech up to the remains—whatever they are; Hal didn't say—of our house, rocket out of my car, throw my arms around my husband, console him as he sobs about the collapse of his proud job, and then weep into his arms if he tells me that anyone was hurt?

Go to this meeting. And how can I not do that? Beth is bouncing on a bus seat only blocks from here, telling the driver that she's having dinner with me tonight. That's why I'm in this plaza in the first place: I'm meeting Beth's new case manager, after which I'll pick her up for dinner. I can't let her down. Yet I can't let my husband down. I thought I'd worked out the balance between all of my loyalties ages ago. I thought I'd mastered how to make rudimentary decisions like these with aplomb. But both choices are right, and everything else has gone wrong. Isn't there someone out there who can tell me what to do?

Finally I conclude that since I can't reach Hal *or* Beth, I should just carry on with the responsibility in front of me. So I pivot toward the building, set one foot in front of the other, and get through that meeting, then dinner. It's hard to keep this disaster sealed inside myself, but I have no desire to introduce worry into my sister's life, especially since my mind is its own scramble. What could have gone wrong? How much of our house was destroyed? Was anyone injured? Where will we find the bars of gold to cover the damages? And—oh, no—Natalie's house just sold! We told her we'd be out by Christmas! How can we wedge ourselves, two cats, and a houseful of boxes inside two compact cars? Will we be homeless? Has this torpedoed Hal's Buddhist serenity? Sense of humor? His deliciously infectious joie de vivre?

By the time I take Beth home, my panic is full-throttle. I drive down dark roads, sticking to my arrangement to spend the night at my father's, pulling over every two minutes to try Hal. But he doesn't pick up. So I just drive, looking out to bare trees. In the gust of the night they are flailing about, a class crying out for a teacher.

As soon as I reach my father's, Theresa says, "Hal just called. His cell phone is on."

I run to a room where I can be alone.

When he picks up, he tells me that he's walking the streets of Philadelphia. Although he sometimes jaunts the twenty-five miles north to that city, he never does so spontaneously, and never on cold nights. His voice sounds pained, and compassion aches in my chest.

"Are you okay?" I ask.

"Well, we still have a house."

"How much of a house?"

"The rooms are all there. But the more I looked, the more damage I could see."

"Oh, no."

"But no one was seriously hurt. The mechanics had singed hair, but the hospital's released them."

"Thank goodness."

"There's a lot to be thankful for. The first thing Dan said when I got to the house was 'I'm going to take care of everything. This is all on me.' "

"What did he mean?"

"He's fully insured, and he said he'll make up anything they don't cover."

"That's incredible. That's a huge reason for gratitude."

"We're lucky."

"But what's going to happen to the house?"

"We don't know how bad the damage is, and the job's shut down until we do. Tomorrow the insurance adjuster and a structural engineer are coming by to make decisions."

"We were going to move back in less than four weeks."

"That's not going to happen."

"But Natalie's house just sold."

"Well, until we know more, let's not worry. Let's just say we're in limbo."

"How did this happen? Who's responsible?"

"The fire marshal will be investigating. We just have to wait to learn more."

He sounds matter-of-fact, but his voice seems small—so small, I have no interest in saying that the anxiety I've felt throughout the renovation now seems like premonition. He knows that anyway, and really, only one thing matters now: I say, "I'm worried about you."

"You know, there're some miracles about all this," he says, conspicuously taking the focus off himself, and he elaborates. The carpenter smelled the gas as it began to leak. To play it safe he opened the front and back doors of the house, which meant that the concussive waves had voids in their pathways, which spared many lives. Coincidentally, no one was in the kitchen, where the blast was worst, thus minimizing injuries. The timing was favorable in other respects: the carpenter was ten minutes away from climbing a ladder on the patio, so he wasn't on the front line of bursting windows, and because we'd just repaired the crumbling brick inside the dining room wall, it remained standing—thus keeping the house upright, too.

"As disasters go," I say, "I guess we're not doing so badly."

"That's true."

"But are you okay?"

"Are you?"

I hesitate, and realize that my pulse isn't beating nearly as wildly as it was when I was with Beth. This conversation has nudged away quite a bit of the panic, if not the shock. "You know, I'm all right," I say, and hear the surprise in my voice. But I know from *his* voice that he's not all right at all. "Please, tell me how *you* are."

He says, "It was my job, and everything was going well, and that felt great. Now . . ."

I hear the chatter of shoppers as he enters a store to get warm. I want to say something comforting, but can't think of what. So I just listen to us both breathe. Finally, he breaks the silence with, "Look, there's nothing more to say. We can talk tomorrow."

"Take care, all right?"

"Yeah," he says, his voice half-hearted, and adds, "You too, Baboo," and at that word, I tear up. But by the time I think to ask if I should drive home tonight, he's turned off his phone.

It is a night of no sleep.

After a sober review of the facts with my father and Theresa, who are as stunned as they are sympathetic, I make up their extra bed, though I already know that a stubborn awakeness will light my path all the way to morning. Yes, Hal relayed much about luck and miracles, and that has provided a measure of relief. But I feel as defenseless and needy as a child, and the riot of thoughts that began this afternoon has grown more cacophonous and plentiful.

Of course, I'm still castigating myself for not being on the road to Delaware. However, the storm that lurked all day is now battering the windows, and Beth is expecting to see me again tomorrow, and I know that Hal wouldn't want me to scythe through this downfall, let alone stand my sister up. Our imminent housing quandary is also firing through my brain. Might my father let us live here? He might, but it wouldn't matter. This place is too far from Hal's job, as well as, once my semester off ends in January, the college where I teach. What about cheap hotels? We don't have the money. Someone's living room? How could we do that to a friend? My body tightens as I browse through all the options and see that we don't have any.

But flickering among these regrets and dreads is a disturbing new concern. As I look out to the days, weeks, or, heaven help us, months of disarray that lie ahead, I know that this disaster will, in some way, change me—and I worry about what that change will look like. Will I come to incubate an anger I don't yet feel, but that will run so deeply through my veins that it will blacken my disposition? If so, will it lead me to travel such a separate emotional journey from Hal that we will fall out of sync? Will I come to cast Dan, the workers, even the entire building industry, as enemies worthy of rancor? Will I dive into the bog of attorneys and paranoia and monitoring everything I say about every business transaction to the end of time? Right now, I can't say I feel anything other than dazed. But I've seen other people forever changed in just these ways after fate dealt them a blow. Who, after I make it to the end of this misfortune, will I be?

I shouldn't add to my insomnia, but the possibility of hardening my heart worries me. As rain drums against the glass and I watch sparkling shadows on the wall, I remember how, when Rosalie disappeared, it took me six years of aiming my rage and pain at her before I understood that my emotions had been curving back to strike me. That was one of the most important lessons I learned in the long educational process that I've come to call my life: although other people might create havoc for me, the more I seethe toward them, the more I make myself suffer. Since that realization, I've tried to resist acid feelings. The problem is that I haven't always succeeded. I've griped about inexplicable colleagues, used caustic names for imperious physicians, and wished harm on politicians who peddled poorly thought-out policies. Each time I'll try to hold myself to my own standard, but thinking ill of others can, unfortunately, give a rush of pleasure. Also, anger, judgment, and their ilk roam through so much of American culture that sometimes when I take a charitable approach toward someone who's done me, or others, a bad turn, I wonder if I'm just unsophisticated. Were I more worldly, I'll think, especially after seeing ads and hearing radio shows and watching movies and reading books that portray the mind-boggling stupidity and shallowness of other people, I would finally come to my senses.

And it is this pull—between lessons I've already learned and lessons I hope to avoid—that is really to blame for me lying awake all night. I keep considering who I might become, and if I'd really want to know that person.

Late the next day, when I get back to Delaware, I decide to visit the wreckage first.

I park in the gathering dusk, and as soon as I see the house, my heart feels heavy in my chest. Yellow police tape seals off the front steps, and the windows—new only a few days ago—are boarded up. I walk carefully down the unlit alley, unable to see my footing. The backyard is heaped high with empty window frames, which are further squashing our fringe tree. The floor-to-ceiling windows are boarded up and roped off. But the new glass door, which was open at the moment of the blast, survived. I slip under the tape and peek through.

What a sight. The dining room—kitchen is knee-high in the drywall and plaster and insulation that blew off the walls, exposing chunks of framing and brick. Higher up, the ceiling is ripped in half like paper. Apparently, the whole back two-thirds of the house was ravaged. Only two days ago, I felt so happy at how alive the house was. Now I just want to cry.

I gape at the sight, shivering. *Turn around and get out of here,* I tell myself. *No. Give in to this sorrow and grieve.* I try to figure out what to do in the brittle November twilight, but before the answer presents itself, a memory that has nothing to do with explosions or anger returns to me. It is a memory of a lesson different from the one I learned about Rosalie, and I often call it to mind when something seems impossibly bleak.

It happened during the summer after Hal and I broke up. I was living in a friend's attic—depressed, jobless, and destitute. All that sustained me were sleepover visits I kept paying to friends like Harriet or Sandy, where late-night conversations helped distract me from my hopelessness. One night I stayed with Lisa, a friend with a deeply spiritual core who made her living translating the writings of the seventeenth-century mystic Emanuel Swedenborg. For hours, I asked Lisa over and over what possible reason there could be for why things had gone so wrong in my life. Just before I curled up on her sofa to fall asleep, she said, "Maybe there is no reason," which made me feel even more dismal. But in the morning, after Lisa drove me back to the house where I was living, just as I was leaving her car, she said, "Actually, Swedenborg does address what you were asking about, but he doesn't say that things happen for a reason." Then, paraphrasing Swedenborg, she said, "There is nothing that happens out of which good cannot occur." I stood beside her car in the summer sun. Some lessons take their time to seep in, but this one struck suddenly and fully with the force of a revelation: what mattered was not what had gone wrong in my life, or even how horribly wrong it had gone, but that something had delivered me to a new shore, and now I had a choice about whether I would embrace the new land or stay right where I was, resenting the ferry that had carried me.

That morning was the first time I began to feel that something meaningful might lie beyond the agony of my breakup with Hal. Although good did not appear immediately in my life, and did not take any shape I could possibly have envisioned on that sunny morning, eventually, as I stepped into the next day and the next opportunity, it did.

It is a cliché to say that as we walk through life we enter a succession of classrooms, and that each one offers us new lessons. Yet I've gone down many unplanned corridors that have led, after much darkness, to precious truths, either because, as with Rosalie, I've been forced to counsel myself, or because I've had the good fortune to encounter someone like Lisa, who became my teacher at just the moment I needed one. So as I look in the glass door at the ruined kitchen, I tell myself that as freak an accident as this was, and as displaced and glum as I feel, maybe the best approach I can take is to see myself as a student again. Whether I'm now going to be reevaluating my attitude toward others, or trying to weave something good from so much that's bad, I don't know. I also don't know whether I'll be lucky enough to find someone like Lisa, who will say something that will light my way. After all, part of the definition of a student is someone who does not know what she does not know. But I do know that like my own students, I can enter this new classroom with humility or hostility. I can press on or give up. I can allow myself to transform or smolder that my time has been wasted.

I slip back under the police tape. Yes, I know: an exploded house is a pitiful classroom, and this is the time for me to be a wife and sister and, soon, a teacher. How can I also be a student? But a misfortune came to pass and here I am, groping down the alley in the dark.

When I finally get back to the rented house, Hal and I throw our arms around each other and don't let go for what seems like hours. Then, since we're keeping the heat down to funnel all our money toward the renovation, we get under the covers and keep on holding.

"The situation isn't good," Hal says, and proceeds to tell me about visiting the house today to assess the damage. Dan will have to take down much of what remains inside, layer by layer, stopping only when he reaches a layer untouched by the explosion. Only then will we know the extent of the repairs.

"It's a sorry sight," I say, my teeth chattering in the chilly bedroom.

"It is," he says. "For a while last night I kept asking myself, 'Why me?' "

"I was so worried about you. You sounded so bereft when I finally reached you."

"I'd gone to Philly to calm myself by going to record stores. But I couldn't concentrate. My mind was all over the place. I'd been feeling so good about the job, and then . . ."

"I guess no one's immune from bad things happening."

"Yeah. Not even a fool like me."

"A fool? What makes you a fool?"

" 'Cause when I did the drawings, I didn't say, 'Don't open gas line and light torch.' "

We let a laugh slip out, and our muscles loosen. He says, "But talking to you helped."

"It did?"

"I was concerned that you'd say, Oh, my God! But you were level-headed, and you were there for me. Standing in that cold, hearing your voice in my ear. That helped a lot."

"I didn't know I did anything."

"Well, you did. You were okay, and that helped me regain my perspective. Our house is still standing. No one was seriously hurt. And you're with me."

"Two fools together."

"Why are *you* a fool?"

"Because I've entertained the idea of getting angry about this. You could even say that I *want* to be angry about this. As soon as I figure out who to be angry with."

"Maybe that's only human."

"But you're not angry."

"No. I'm sad."

"I am, too."

"But we're sad together. That's what matters. We'll get through this."

"Even if I do get angry?"

"Whatever you feel—whatever *I* feel—as long as we feel it to-gether, we'll be okay."

His words are so comforting, I stop wanting to feel angry, at least for now. But anticipating that I'll have this same desire for anger again, I ask, "Did you come to an answer for 'Why me?' "

He's quiet for a minute. "I think there's only one answer, and that's, 'Why *not* me?' None of us is so special that we can avoid suffering."

The house is still a wreck and our future uncertain, but here, under the covers, students together, this cold night has come to feel warm.

For the next several days, we both go about doing what needs to be done. Hal attends meetings with the insurance adjuster, the structural engineer, and Dan. I review my syllabus for my return to teaching. Hal does not mope, and I stay level-headed.

Fortunately, none of this is difficult because good things are already occurring. The insurance adjuster does not haggle. Nor does he deny compensation to neighbors whose masonry was cracked by the explosion. Dan lets his job supervisor, Henry, go, seeing a connection between the disaster and Henry's inattentiveness to detail, and starts running the job himself. Also, one day at the rented house, I happen to mention to a couple of our neighbors that we're apprehensive about what to do after Natalie finalizes the sale, and one of them replies, "Did you know that the new owner is my cousin?"

I say, "You're joking."

"She might not need the place immediately. I'll talk to her for you."

"We'd like it if you could stay longer," the other neighbor adds.

"I'd love it," Ginny says that day when I stop off at her house for a visit.

I really like these people, I think, as Ginny and I watch a video and eat pretzels. Now, because of the explosion, I might have more time with them. Swedenborg was a wise man.

Perhaps this is why I feel none of the indignation I'd have expected when, the next day, Hal pieces together what happened. It was the two mechanics who opened the valve to the gas line. They hadn't known that the valve was for the gas line, nor that the line hadn't been capped. Why they turned it on is unclear, as is why the line, which fed the oven until it was removed at demolition, was never capped. But it seems that the fault lay in a series of poor decisions, and the culprits, one of whom was blown out the back when the explosion occurred, must have been scared out of their wits.

Both of us feel bad for them, but when Hal adds that Dan's crew has nicknamed these guys Sparky and Torch, we indulge in a long laugh. If there's any lesson to be learned from this, I don't think we've found it yet.

A week and a half after the explosion, on a Sunday whitened by the first snowfall of the season, Hal and I lift the police tape for my first walk-through the house since the disaster.

It's freezing in here, and as I take in the living room, I feel cold inside, too. The wall between the stairs and dining room is nothing but framing. Plywood still substitutes for windows. Drywall and plaster have been stripped away from almost all the walls as well as the ceilings. Insulation hangs loose, vents have worked free of ductwork, joists are split.

"Would you believe," Hal says, as we move toward the back of the kitchen, "that this is the only evidence of flame?" He points to the snake-face of the gas pipe, which I see for the first time. The insulation that surrounds it isn't the beige of the rest of the house, but orange. I later learn that in a natural gas explosion, there's only a quick blast of fire and heat. It is the concussive waves that cause the damage. Typically, the roof rises and the walls either bulge out or fall in. Gasoline explosions can create total destruction. Natural gas explosions end in rubble.

"I want to show you something else," Hal says, leading me up to my study.

As with downstairs, the room is shorn of its drywall and plaster, and the insulation is exposed. The windows are still intact, but the wooden floor has split as if it were the bottom of a boat impaled by— and I don't laugh as I think this—a sea monster. We walk carefully around the long hole, with me gaping at everything. The worst has happened, I'm at last letting myself think. If there were a time when anger would be justified, this is it. For a moment I want to indulge, but then tell myself to resist the temptation. This isn't hard—the sight before me is so desolate, I almost feel numb.

Then Hal asks, "Do you see what I was talking about?"

"No," I say.

"Look at the back wall."

I turn to the southern wall, which overlooks the backyard. "What am I looking at?"

"You can see directly to the studs that were behind the plaster."

"Yes, that's what I'm seeing."

"You shouldn't be able to do that."

"Why not?"

"They insulated the house, remember?"

Sure enough, on the other walls, there's insulation. Above our heads, there's insulation. But not on the southern wall. "Why isn't it here?"

He says with a laugh, "Because the insulators didn't install it like they were supposed to."

"*What?*"

He looks at me with a wry smile. "And we would never have found out had there been no explosion. Only because the plaster came down have we seen the places they missed."

"Or skipped."

"Whichever."

And blam: all the anger that I haven't been feeling erupts. "So you're saying they were trying to *rip us off?*"

"What's the point in being angry about it?"

"Aren't *you?*"

"Nah."

"Why *aren't* you?"

"I learned long ago that a temper is a liability in this field."

"But we paid them to do something that they didn't do!"

"Right. But this is *nothing* compared to the enormity of the work to be done. This is a reason to be glad. Something good came out of this. Now we can make sure they do it right."

"Are you kidding me?" I stare at him. "How can you not be angry at such greed?"

"You know what someone in my office says? 'Never ascribe to malevolence what you can just as easily chalk up to incompetence.' I don't know if this happened because of greed. People in construction are the same as all of us—they can be greedy, lazy, careless, distracted, arrogant."

I want to say something back, but before I can find any words in my boiling anger—which suddenly isn't boiling as intensely—he walks toward the window, then turns around and, leaning against the sill, says, "I've always seen the construction process as a microcosm of the larger human experience. This is a human endeavor, where people are motivated by the same things that motivate humans everywhere, good, bad, and indifferent. You can guess, but you rarely *know* what those motivations are.

"In this case," he continues, "the insulation guys thought they were going to be here for one day, and it became four. By the fourth day, they were probably in a hurry, and because this was one of the plaster walls, they couldn't see if the work had been done. Maybe they just forgot about it, or thought no one would notice if they skipped it. I don't know, and I don't care."

Now I'm more startled than angry. "You don't *care?*"

"After twenty-five years in this field, I know that construction is not something where perfection is easy to achieve. Hey, if you're an architect and you think you can do a flawless set of drawings, you've got another thing coming. It's virtually inevitable that something will go wrong somewhere in the construction process, or compromises will be made. I'm just glad we found out about the insulation. Now it can be fixed."

I look down at the hole in the floor. I feel so sad, seeing the fragility of this house. But amazingly, I don't feel angry anymore. I wait a moment for it to rear up again, but it seems as if it flashed high inside me and then, doused by Hal's logic, dissipated.

I walk over to him and say, my voice back to normal, "I've been wondering if I might learn something from this disaster. I didn't think I would. But I think I just did."

He says, "You know, I've learned something, too." He pauses. "I learned that I was wrong about you."

"About *me?*"

"If I'd had to predict how you'd take something like this, I would have imagined the reaction you just had to the insulation, only times a hundred. But you've been very calm and thoughtful through the whole thing. You just accepted it, and dealt with it, and were there for me. And that helped get me back on my feet right away."

I smile, already forgetting the tension that just gripped my face. "But we still have a long way to go. The new owner hasn't said whether we can stay in the house past Christmas. Dan hasn't gotten to the bottom of the damage. There are still other chances for me to lose my cool."

"I know," he says. "But I think we're over the worst."

We put our arms around each other and look out the window. The yard has been cleared, but it is not empty. There still stands our baby tree.

The next day, Hal sends me an e-mail from work:

> Just talked to the structural engineer. He and I are on the same page about how to do the repairs ... and that does NOT involve whole-sale replacement of any masonry walls. The SE corner needs to be anchored to the joists. Sections of that wythe need to be taken apart and put back together in line with the surrounding wall. But the scope of repair is sufficiently small that we can have high hopes that they'll go quickly.

I shut off my computer and look outside. It is the second snowfall of the year, and I was planning to go to the library. But with Hal's message fresh in my head, when I get in my car, that is not where I go.

I still feel like a student, I think as I drive, struggling to learn what I can from this mess. But I know something now that I didn't before I checked my voice mail as I ran across the windy plaza ten days ago. This new classroom—and maybe every classroom that I'll ever be in—isn't only a classroom for me. Classrooms, even those that lack teachers, even those where we lack the wisdom to instruct ourselves, contain other students, and we can turn toward one another, and we can help one another—even without knowing we're doing so.

And that, I suppose, is how, along with being wives and husbands, sisters and brothers, teachers and architects, we can, when called to do so, become students—and, indeed, welcome the chance. Because a student is not only someone who does not know what she does not know. She might also be someone who knows more than she realizes, and can make more of a difference than she can know.

I park at the house. It is dusk again, and nothing has changed in the front. But as I hurry down the alley and snowflakes whiten the narrow walk in front of me, I can finally see my feet.

Then I go into the yard.

"I thought the fringe tree had died," I said to Hal when we stood looking out the window yesterday. I was surprised to see the little tree, now free of the smashed window frames and shattered glass, still pointing toward the sky.

Hal said, "When the windows blew out, some of the bark got stripped."

"But look. It's standing."

"I know. But it needs the bark to protect it through the winter. Whether it can survive with damage to its bark, we'll find out."

That was a whole day ago. Snow is still falling, and the tree is still here. I climb above our stone wall and come as close as I can to the tree. It is bent from its injuries, but my breath coats its branches. We just might make it until spring.

R·E·P·A·I·R

Allies

A nd then, a series of awakenings start happening within me. The first makes itself known one morning in early December, as Hal is getting ready to leave for a job meeting and I find these words leaving my mouth: "Can I come with you?"

He puts his hands on my head and says in a Captain Kirk voice, "Bones, can you get over here right away? An alien life force is invading my crew."

Laughing, I throw his hands off, despite being as surprised as he, and keep talking. "Well, you said the house looks really different with them peeling so much back for repairs."

He raises an eyebrow Spock-style, and says in his Vulcan best, "I fail to see the logic, Captain. We could easily visit the house tonight."

"I, you know, just figured I could go now, with you driving there anyway."

Making a determined Scottie face, he says, "I'll get us there, Captain. But you just got to tell me—why in the blazes are you changing course now?"

I try to puzzle it out. At a job meeting I could watch Hal doing on-site work, which I've never observed. Come to think of it, I don't actually know what happens in a job meeting—and, well, I've never wanted to find out firsthand, lest I reveal my ignorance to someone less forgiving than my husband. And right here over my morning tea, I have my first awakening: that my time-honored indifference has actually been unease—and that the explosion has finally blown it off, exposing the curiosity underneath. "I guess," I say, "I want to know your world."

His comic impulse flees, and in its place I just see him, no longer amused, but moved.

Though when we park on Teacher's Lane, which is dominated by a purple Dumpster where Dan and his crew are disposing of our tattered house, I go tense. I'm crossing the border into a land of the rugged and muscular, where I'm so clumsy with the customs that I shouldn't even speak.

"Not to worry," Hal says as he lifts the police tape for me. "We'll just be going through a list of things to be done. Dan and I had a good working relationship before and now it's even better." He pauses as we mount the porch steps. "Of course, he *might* react when I ask him to check if there's insulation behind the plaster walls that haven't come down."

"Why would that be an issue?"

"It's extra work for him, and that means extra money. But I'm justified in asking him."

I suddenly remember that when we were signing the agreement with Dan, Hal mentioned that the relationship between the contractor and architect—and contractor and client—is set up to be adversarial. But before I can panic, we're entering the house.

Immediately I feel worse. Standing in the living room, looking directly at us, is a slim, fair-haired guy who, in his brown jacket and jeans, makes me think of a clean-cut Marlboro Man—and I have no idea who he is. But I don't want to say anything inane, so I say nothing, and Hal, forgetting that we've walked separate paths through this renovation, doesn't provide introductions. Only after he retrieves his notebook to start the meeting does the man say, "Hi?"

"You don't know each other?" Hal asks.

"It's been a while." The man extends his hand. "I'm Dan."

"I just thought I'd come along," I say, feeling klutzy and meek.

His grip is firm but not bone-breaking, and his voice is courteous, not robust. He says, "I told Hal that I'm going to take care of you, and I will. My reputation is everything."

I want to reply that I'm not here because I'm doubting him, though I'm so afraid of putting my foot in my mouth that I retreat to silence. Fortunately, as our hands part, we hear voices in the dining room–kitchen. Hal follows the sound into that room and Dan and I follow him, and then we realize that they're coming from high above. All three of us gaze up.

The difference from our visit only a week ago surpasses my imagining.

Gone is the ripped-in-half ceiling. Gone is the second story wooden floor, except for a tiny catwalk. Gone is the ceiling above *it.* We are peering directly up through the branches of the joists, past two workers on the catwalk, through my study, and into the cumulous insulation just beneath the roof. Due to the stripping-away that's preceding repair, the back two-thirds of the house has become one gigantic room, its guts hanging out for all to see.

I put my hand to my heart, taken aback at the extent of the injuries. It makes me think of people who've broken every bone in their bodies, or suffered complete emotional breakdowns. The difference, I suppose, is that if I were visiting someone whose body or personal life had ruptured, I'd be able to sit with her, give hugs, listen to her speak. Here all I can do is be present.

And feel awkward. As some machine begins whirring, I look back into the kitchen and see Hal moving toward a worker who's atop a ladder, screwing a bolt on a joist.

Hal looks up at the man's handiwork and smiles. "Hey, you're scabbing on a sister."

"Yeah," Dan says. "We've got a lot of sisters already."

With the machine so noisy and my discomfort so acute, I can't have heard them right. "He's *what?*" I yell.

"A sister." Hal points up. "They're doubling up the joists to make them stronger. That's called sistering. When a joist is damaged, you reinforce it by scabbing on a sister."

Oh, no, I think, as we move toward the stairs. I am way over my head.

We walk up the stairs, the wall beside us still naked to its frame, the steps powdered with plaster. With no furnace or electricity, the house feels wintery and our breath shows. I pull my wool hat down but it doesn't help, and only makes everything feel more alien when, at the top of the stairs, I step into my study—or, really, my mezzanine. For a moment I just stare down into the kitchen, distressed at being a stranger in this strange land. But I also start to feel sympathy—not toward the two gangly men on the catwalk before me, or Hal and Dan behind me, but the house itself. *I know how you feel,* I think. I feel absurd thinking it, and if the house were a hurting friend I would hardly say it. But there have been many times after love has dropped out of my life when *I* have felt like what I'm seeing: dismantled, forlorn, vulnerable. It's striking, actually, how similar the feeling was. Whether the love had been for a romantic partner, parent, sibling, or, even on a few occasions, friend, I felt so raw, I couldn't believe I would ever recover.

I turn to look for Hal and Dan. They've moved on to the front bedroom, where they've begun the meeting. At least I guess it's the meeting, though when I go in they're just standing here, speaking as if this were any conversation.

Hal says, "When might we expect the insulators?"

Dan, similarly nonchalant, replies, "I want to do it before Christmas."

"Do you know when the replacement windows are due to arrive?"

"January 13."

"I've got an update on the kitchen cabinets."

"Good news?"

"Remember me mentioning Primeboard?" Dan nods, and I remember, too: it's the product that was just as green as the one that was discontinued. "The job stoppage is giving me time to move forward on the research." Now Hal acknowledges me. "We might get the cabinets in the house after all."

"That'd be great," I say, as surprised at this possible perk from our explosion as I am to hear my own voice.

Then, with the mood perhaps strategically lightened, Hal continues right into his contentious item, saying to Dan, "What about the walls that haven't been removed?"

"What?" Dan asks—maybe stalling, maybe not hearing, I can't tell.

"What about checking behind the remaining plaster walls for any missing insulation?" In an easygoing voice, he adds, "It blows my mind that there wasn't any in the southern wall."

Equally easygoing, Dan says, "I don't think they did that on purpose."

"I don't either," Hal agrees.

"We'll check behind the plaster walls next week," Dan says pleasantly.

Just like that, we're over the hump. How deftly Hal introduced the one item that might have cast a pall on the meeting, and how well Dan received it. I can easily imagine less experienced clients—like me—having an edge to their voice when they made the request to check behind the plaster. Just as easily, I can imagine a contractor feeling provoked, particularly one who's anxious about profits or tends toward unruly temperament. It must take years of practice to conduct a job meeting uneventfully—and a real commitment to not being adversarial.

The meeting ends just as casually as it began, and we all head downstairs. I still feel out of place, but I'm also relieved. I made it through without tipping my hand about my unfamiliarity with construction, and at the same time I gained a regard for Hal and Dan's rapport.

I think that's all I'll get out of the meeting until we're all walking outside and discover that Hal left his notes upstairs. I run back up the unprotected staircase, grab the papers, and then halfway back down I just stop and gaze out at all the wounds and amputations around me—and my second awakening occurs. I find my heart going out to this poor house. It's more than the empathy I felt when I stood on the shredded balcony of my study. It's a sense of responsibility mingled with affection, as if the house were an actual person who once took me in and cared for me, and who now needs me to minister to it. I feel foolish. I'm not sentimental about buildings, and have felt no twinge of loyalty toward this one. Yet apparently it is growing on me.

.   .   .

I think that's all that will happen. But a week later, after I give a talk in New Jersey and stop off on my way home to say hello to someone important, a third awakening occurs.

It is a bright autumn afternoon when I turn off the highway and pull into a picturesque town. I haven't been in this area for quite a while, but came to know it intimately during the years when Hal and I were apart. Actually, I think as I park, this is an interesting coincidence. Although when I came here I felt as bruised as our house, this is the place where I recovered.

I get out of my car, inhale the December air beneath the tall trees, take in the holiday decorations adorning the streets, and remember that time. Shortly after my friend Lisa shared the insight from Swedenborg, when I still couldn't envision any goodness arising from my breakup with Hal, I received a call from an acquaintance. A coordinator of events in a bookstore, Deb had once hosted a reading I'd given, and this call was one of our occasional hellos. Usually our exchanges were light, but this time I opened up and admitted that I was at an abysmal moment in my life. She said, "I think I can help you," and asked if I wanted to interview for a position running events in a different bookstore—in the very town I'm in now. I'd never run events or worked in a bookstore. In the interest of concentrating on my writing, my only employment for years had been odd jobs like artist modeling and temporary secretarial work. But now I was broke and alone and regretful, and although friends like Lisa and Harriet and Sandy were looking after me, I felt as if the entire structure of my life had collapsed. I went to the interview, crying the whole way there. Incredibly, I got the job. Then one friend talked me through the purchase of my first car, another friend advised me on the kind of clothes I'd need as a person with a real job, and other friends helped me move from the attic to this area.

But I hardly began mending right away. As I stroll past university dormitories and the town square and the evergreen tree, encircled with Christmas lights, in front of the historic inn, I remember beginning my new life. I was still so depressed about the ways I'd botched my relationship with Hal—buckled understandings of love, disregard for his talents, indecision clogged with dread—that managing anything more than day-to-day living seemed impossible. I did nurse the hope that eventually I might achieve something I'd come to see as good, but I felt way too ragged for such grand ambitions.

Yet as time passed, I started to realize that every night when I hosted another event, I'd look into the audience and see faces, engrossed and inquisitive, and that when the event wrapped up, many of these customers would linger to chat. Some were at peaceful moments in their lives, but others were in hard times, coping with cancer or divorce, and it became clear that they'd come not just to see authors, but to be around other people, stimulate their thoughts, forget their struggles. As part of that, they wanted to talk about their lives, and I, disinclined to return to my lonely apartment, was happy to listen. So night after night, as we stood in the aisles of books, they shared their stories with me, and soon I understood that simply by giving them the events they desired and then listening to those who wished to speak, I was bringing good into their lives. Even better, I'd found a reason for being that I hadn't known I was missing. A year later my work life expanded, when I added in a part-time position teaching writing at a college a few hours away. Although the skills and role were different, the result was similar: just by delivering the knowledge that others wanted, and being interested in their well-being—that is, becoming their ally as they passed through this time in their lives—I was able to offer something important.

But until a winter afternoon not unlike this one, I didn't see the connection between the two jobs, or to Swedenborg. I needed many discussions on my own, and although I engaged in them with my friends, the person who inspired some of my greatest understandings was a therapist. I found Robin by accident, when an author who was scheduled to appear in the store had to cancel for an illness. Since his book was about recovering from failed love, I worried about disappointing customers who were desperate for his insights. I looked around, found a local therapist who specialized in the same subject, and left a message on her machine: would she be willing to substitute for this author—and, um, would she be willing to speak to me, too? I couldn't believe I'd added that, but when Robin came to the store and ran a discussion in her soft, caring voice and relayed an attitude of patience and understanding, I was glad that I had.

As the years passed and I listened to my customers and guided my students, Robin listened to and guided me. Indeed, because she was *my* ally, I felt freer to be an ally for others. She was, for instance, the person who finally, but gently, persuaded me to see that what I called true love was false. She also addressed one of my most deeply held ancillary beliefs: that I would know I was feeling true love when I felt almost drugged by the perfection of the fit. Actually, she said, since the foundation of healthy long-term relationships is two people caring about each other, it makes less sense to look for intoxication than a partner who is genuinely kind.

Robin helped in other ways, too. She was gleeful at every self-doubt I discarded, every old dream I polished, every regret I replaced with hope. She applauded my concern for my customers and students. She insisted that I mattered. And I began to repair. This is why, on that winter day, it was just after I left her office when I stood on this very sidewalk, looked up at the trees, and finally knew that good *had* occurred from my breakup with Hal. It hadn't been in the form of adoring boyfriends or sumptuous paychecks or any of the possibilities that I had, I'd come to realize, initially desired. It was simply the act of giving to others. That night, and for many nights afterward, when I got into bed, I would lie there in a state of euphoria and think, *I might have failed at love. But my life is filled with so much purpose.*

And now, as I enter Robin's building, going to an appointment I made because I was in the area and wanted to say hello, my third awakening occurs. I began this renovation while searching for some new challenge in my life, some second-act reason for being. Hal and I even gave it a name: The Search for Life Purpose 2.0. Yet I forgot all about it. How is that possible? Only a few seasons ago I was ready to change the world. It seemed a minor impediment that I didn't know how.

But it's obvious why The Search faded. The grief of packing came to pass, and then our movers broke the phone line, and I locked myself out of the bedroom, and demolition dredged up my childlessness, and on it went, one episode after another—and The Search got left in the dust.

When Robin comes out of her office, arms already open for a hug, I understand that I haven't, in fact, just come here to say hello. I've come here to talk about the renovation, and the many ways it keeps shaping my life.

As the days of December begin adding up and our job continues peeling backward, we start getting asked about our plans for Christmas, which, this year, coincides with Hanukkah. Our families are not religious, so our annual debate over a nice meal with Hal's parents in Virginia versus a nice meal with Beth and my father in Pennsylvania usually resolves with us seeing his side on December 25, mine a day earlier. But this year, the whole idea of holidays feels forced. Our lives are on hold. Our finances are spent. Also, Natalie has informed us that she'll be closing on the rented house in February, so we'll need to move out by late January—which seems improbable. The truth is that we've been in this upheaval for so long, and might be for so much longer, that we just want to stay put. We tell everyone that we'll see them at other points in the month, and then we ignore the season.

Still, we're busy. Hal works out the details for our kitchen cabinets, and indulges in his music. As for me, I start acting on each of my awakenings.

First, I look up information on our house. City records show me that the property has had at least nine owners, stretching back to when it was mere land in the nineteenth century. I try to imagine them, Mary Elizabeth Montague and Harry and Rebecca Orenstein and Simon Abramson, but the records are so ornately handwritten or poorly microfilmed that the few details in them are unreadable. I page through books on similar houses, and see numerous features that I've taken for granted—high and detailed baseboards, detailed window surrounds, five-panel wooden doors, beveled glass on the front door, hardwood floors, transoms—and finally acknowledge that they are not just seen as desirable by aficionados of old homes, but also by me. Likewise, my readings on green residences reinforce the merits of our tiny footprint, as well as our energy-efficient alterations. I might never boast about this house, but as I understand that it is a place of history and worth, I come to respect it.

The Search for Life Purpose 2.0 is, as anyone can imagine, a trickier proposition. When I finally worked my way around to it in Robin's office, I didn't get the kind of *Aha* I got when mentioning my feelings about the house and concluding that a few days of research would allow me to cultivate them. I couldn't even speak coherently. I just went on breathlessly, bringing up one possibility after another—doctor, philanthropist, online entrepreneur, multimedia mogul—only to reject each as unattainable, at odds with my personality, or counter to our financial needs. "I thought you loved writing and teaching," Robin said. I told her I did, but what if there was something more I could do, maybe alongside my writing and teaching, that would accomplish something not just good, but great? Wouldn't it make sense to find that out? "Yes," she said, "but there's also a lot to be said for what you're already doing. Maybe for now you can stay with that and see if anything else comes to you." This seems rational, and is underscored when Hal says, "It's not like picking out a dress. You can't just browse in a mall and find your perfect life." Even though that's exactly what I want. So with reluctance, I tell myself to be patient. After all, it's entirely possible that I'll wake up one day and *just know*.

Having decided this, I move on to pursuing my interest in Hal's world. Since I exist in such a construction bubble—the magazines we receive, the books on our shelves, the job meetings we attend, the projects at his office, the conversations about the renovation—this is easy to do. As in our earliest years together, I begin reading and asking questions, only this time there are more opportunities. Hal can now teach me about green design. I can go to see projects done by his architect friends. I can even, if I get up the nerve, talk to Dan.

Looking at me over his guitar, Hal says, "What do you mean, get up the nerve?"

"It took me months to pay attention to him. He might be insulted. Besides, everything I read about contractors focuses on their unscrupulousness. He might have something to hide."

"I have every reason to think he's aboveboard, and I don't think he minded at all that you didn't know his name."

Well, now that I think about it, as I've been at the house more, I *have* seen that the only resemblance Dan has to the Marlboro Man is that he's a person of few words. He also isn't testy, unresponsive, dismissive of Hal's ideas, sloppy with paperwork, given to surprise bills,

erratic about showing up, or anything else I'd associate with unprofes-
sional behavior. He's on time every day and tidies up at night. He
laughs at Hal's jokes and doesn't raise his voice. He wears clean-cut
clothes. His workers aren't the wolf-whistling, bar-bouncer types I
might have expected, either. They're respectful and hard-working.
Several are even middle-aged. I suppose it's my own cluelessness about
Dan's life that, more than anything else, stands in the way of my talking to him.

"If only he'd just let me tag along," I say, "and see what his life is
like."

"Why not just ask if you can do that?" Hal says. "What do you
have to lose?"

So it happens that a little while later, I spend a day at Dan's side.

When I arrive at his office at nine a.m., I think that we might begin
with a cup of caffeine. But Dan's been going since four forty-five, when
he woke to train for his next triathlon, then eat with his wife and kids,
then hurry here, where he's been faxing invoices, writing letters, proof-
reading estimates. It's like any hectic office, except his phone never stops
ringing, and if his receptionist can't answer, Dan has to. All six of his
other employees are skilled workmen out at jobs.

Then we're out to a church he owns. In addition to residential
contracting, he explains, he also does small-scale development. This
can be a lifesaver when the economy drops; for instance, he receives
rent from the day care center that leases this church. Well, not the
whole church. He reserves the basement as storage for his company's
supplies. But the basement ceiling is low, and Dan hits his head every
day. Also, the church roof leaks. That's why we're here, to meet with
the roofer. When the roofer arrives—late, but so are we—we climb
onto the roof, where they trade ideas about how to make the repairs
work. The meeting almost gets tense. But Dan doesn't flinch and the
roofer caves in, sealing their agreement with a shake.

"You have a lot of rough people in this industry," Dan says, driving
to the next appointment, cell phone ringing away. "There are a lot of
anger management issues."

At the next site, the addition for a historic house, Dan checks the foundation just completed by a site contractor. Then a truck with steel beams shows up, though the sub who should be handling them isn't here. Dan mentions that he recently worked with a framing sub who disappeared to work on another job, which set Dan back two weeks. Then he switches to a different frustration. This house belongs to a friend who insisted on using his own kitchen subcontractor, despite Dan saying that such divided work would be a headache. Another friend once got him to price out a deck, then hired a contractor whose use of illegal immigrants allowed for a much lower rate. And finding good employees is problematic as well. Too few people have a strong work ethic, and the best workers are aging out—the average age is forty-eight.

Over the day, as we go from site to site, he maintains his pleasant demeanor, but also expresses no love for his career. When he was growing up with his single-parent father, Dan dreamt of being in finance. But during college, a job in the financial field didn't click, whereas a job painting houses was fun. Soon thereafter his father died, and Dan, having only himself to rely on, opened a painting company, then eventually expanded into general contracting. The work was hard, and he hoped to return to his first dream. He even went to night school to get an MBA. But just as the diploma reached his hands, the market collapsed, his wife had their first child, and Dan elected to stay with what he knew. Construction, however, remains far from what he wanted for his life.

How much does his company bring in? Eight hundred fifty thousand dollars last year. What does he pay himself? "Less than I pay my employees. Forty thousand a year. My wife works, and I know how to invest. Otherwise, I couldn't do it."

I'm amazed that he's never hinted at any dissatisfaction. I didn't even know until today that a worker on our house quit suddenly, then was discovered to have stolen some of Dan's supplies and ended up in jail. Nor did I know that the insurance company didn't cover everything from our explosion—and that Dan made up the fifteen-thousand-dollar difference.

Late in the day, I ask, "Why do you think people get upset with contractors?"

"Ninety percent of the time, homeowners think they know what needs to be done, but there's always something they don't know. They also don't really understand how the business works. And they almost never ask for proof that I'm insured."

"But don't you think people get upset because there are shady contractors?"

"Sure. But there are crooked types in every industry. Look at Enron. Look at chemical companies dumping toxins into streams. But in this business, the public is more aware of it. It's their homes—and their money. A lot of money."

His cell phone rings. At lunch we counted forty-seven calls that had come in since morning. Hours have passed, and he's answered none.

"Hope you don't mind if I take this," Dan says, signaling the end of our day.

"Man," I say to Hal that night, "your industry is really depressing."

"It can be."

"Not to mention that whole adversarial thing. It's all around Dan. He can't escape it."

"Sure he can, at least sometimes."

"Like when?"

"As I keep saying, he and I have worked very well together. That's probably true of some other architects and clients he works with. He has a bunch of good employees and reliable subs, too. I know his two mechanics blew it"—he laughs as I throw a napkin at him for his pun— "but I think he tries to surround himself with people who are really on the same team."

"But it seems the industry is set up for problems."

"In some ways that's true."

"What can be done about it?"

"It would be nice if we could wave a magic wand and change the whole system. But I think even a genius billionaire who devoted his entire life to reforming the industry would fail. I don't think about changing the whole system. It would make me crazy."

"Then how do you deal with it?"

"I think about it on a small scale. In very simple terms, that's what Dan and I have been doing: agreeing that we have a common purpose, and working together to reach it."

"So if you can't change the world, you can still do something in your small corner of it?"

"That's right."

"And relationships are the key."

"Pretty much. When you have a relationship that works, it might not make the rest of the nonsense go away. But it certainly makes it easier to face."

Of course, the importance of relationships has been one of my major preoccupations as we've moved through the renovation. As befitting thoughts inspired by a house, my focus has been on personal rather than professional ones, but even so, it's been clear over and over that strong, mutually helpful relationships can be hard to come by, or fail to last. This unfortunate truth makes each relationship that does cohere, and endure, all the more precious, even if it is with a professional like Dan or Robin. But what I hadn't thought about until our house readies itself for repair is that most of us have a tendency to rank relationships without even knowing we're doing so, placing intimates like family and friends above those who build our houses or counsel us for an hour, or teach our classes or work in our bookstores—even though sometimes our family and friends are not really working with us, walking side by side toward some common purpose. This isn't to say that professionals necessarily do. Goodness knows, we've all had disappointing cashiers or physicians. In this month of not-building, however, I start to think that there is a kind of relationship that transcends all others, whether they are personal or professional. It is a kind of relationship rarely discussed except in terms of warfare, yet it can be found anywhere, and it can get us through anything. Allies.

This is what Hal and I end up talking about on Christmas, an unusually warm day, which we spend going out for a long walk. As we're strolling about the city, looking at buildings, we talk about Dan and Robin—and Deb, who helped me get the job in the store; and the friends who helped me buy a car, select a wardrobe, move my life; and

Laura, who is at my side as we face Rosalie's decline; and Hal himself, now that we are there for each other. Hal has his own memorable allies, too, and as the day goes on, both of us remember more and more.

I hadn't thought we'd feel festive when this day arrived. But it turns out that we have a lot of fun, reminding each other about people who ministered to us, and to whom we did the same. It might not be as celebratory a time as we'd have had with our families. Nor is it as grandiose as figuring out the big question about the meaning of my life. It is, though, a fine way to spend a quiet holiday with my husband, and it does help me figure out one piece of that question: however I try to make a difference, I want to be an ally—and it doesn't have to be, as I'd been thinking, of the whole world. All the allies Hal and I ever had have made a difference just by helping us. There is no need to think in terms of millions. Even one person will do.

Eventually I explore more of the construction industry. During and after our renovation, in our house and at other sites, I ask carpenters and plumbers and electricians and painters about their lives, and when they get to the point in the conversation where they express frustration with the industry, it is relationships they talk about, too—and the forces that can undermine them.

Immature behavior comes up a lot, such as the carpenter who tells me, "The silliest and most childish things can bring on problems. Like a mis-cut of an eighth of an inch. It could actually come to blows. I've seen it—jail time over something like that! Dude, grow up." Another frequent grievance is self-absorption, or, as a different carpenter says, "You got footer people, and all they do is pour footers and they're out of there. They don't care where the dirt got piled, they don't care about no mess they're leaving. The attitude is, 'I ain't never working here no more so whadda I care about anyone else.'" Other common difficulties might be summed up as attitudes that are arrogant or rigid, illustrated by stories about bosses who refuse to listen to ideas from their employees, highly skilled craftsmen who see no point in hiding their impatience with less proficient workers, and plumbers who are so fixed on laying their pipes one way that they hack away at brand-new construction to do the installation. The top lament, though, is rudeness. This covers a lot of ground, from the contractor who's brusque when a client expresses anxiety to the roofer who dumps materials into a neighbor's yard to the temperamental worker who snaps at anyone around him. One painter put it this way: "You need to be courteous to everyone. Corporate employees might object to the fumes and get confrontational. You don't want to talk back to them—they have good reason to feel the way they do. Home-owners don't want anyone scraggly and smelly. Take showers, don't bring your dirty clothes inside. Don't even be rude to a beggar asking for a handout. That's his neighborhood. And you never know. He just might come down the street later and kick the ladder out from under you."

I enjoy listening to the insights of people who work with their hands. Certainly they have a lot to say about how to trowel on plaster or hang a door, but now that I'm really paying attention, I see that they're also perceptive about people. Hal was right. Construction isn't just the act of building—it really *is* a microcosm of the larger human experience.

Right after New Year's, when we return for a job meeting, I see that repairs have begun.

Nothing seems different when we enter the still-unheated living room, holiday cookies in hand. But as we continue into the kitchen, looking for Dan, we pass sawhorses, a power saw, a ladder, a shovel, a work belt. The soffits are now framed. Above our heads, a subfloor has been installed for the second story, and just below it, metal rods run between the west and east walls, a form of repair that will tie them to-gether structurally.

The back door is open. I set the cookies on the ladder, and we continue outside.

In the alley, Dan and Victor, one of his carpenters, are standing on scaffolding. Victor is patching around the metal rods I saw in the kitchen, which extend outside the masonry. Once he's finished, he'll weld metal plates to the ends of the rods. I didn't know this before, but I do now, and the knowledge makes this land feel less strange, and me less of a stranger.

Not that I understand every detail of the meeting, which begins when Dan climbs down from the scaffolding. But I can follow it.

"What's the schedule for the insulation?"

"After the inspection, which is today."

"The replacement windows still on schedule?"

"Yes. And we'll be installing the new floor on the second story next week."

"If kitchen cabinets are here two weeks from now, is that okay?"

"Should be fine."

Then Hal unfolds an oversized sheet on which he's printed a schedule of everything that remains to be done. He says, "So what's your estimate for the move-in date?"

Dan says, "I think we can get the Certificate of Occupancy by the end of February."

Oh, no. We need to be out by late January. No, no, no, no. I try not to look at Hal.

Hal says, "Could we do it any sooner?"

"Well . . ." Dan looks at Hal's schedule. "Friday, February 17," he says.

"You sure?"

"It'll be tight. But we can do it."

I shoot a look at Hal, but he keeps his eyes on Dan and the notebook.

They keep talking, and I tell myself that it's all going to work out. I'm not so sure I believe it, but remembering the good graces of the neighbors who helped when we were building this stone wall, I know that we have people to turn to. Maybe Jim and Susan will know someone in their church with an extra room. Maybe the insurance agent will know of some hotel where we could live for two weeks. I won't worry. We have allies.

As the meeting breaks up, and Dan walks us toward the front door, I think about how Dan's career is not at all his Life Purpose. He never reached the great pinnacle he dreamt of when he was a boy. Yet he is a good man, and he does a good job, and he has been an exemplary ally to Hal.

And at this incredibly banal moment, as Hal and Dan are talking about when we need to pick up our light fixtures from the store, I have my fourth, and final, awakening. Hal has long suggested to me that the whole question of Life Purpose is silly. I still don't want to think that, but I do see, looking at Dan, that just as important as anyone's purpose is his character—and maybe even more.

It's a quiet thought. No trumpets blare, no dancers leap from the walls. In fact, no one notices, because at that very moment, Hal and Dan are having a tiny exchange.

"Hey," Hal says, nodding toward a windowsill in the living room, "nice job with the Dutchman."

"I thought you'd like it," Dan says, smiling.

"What are you talking about?" I ask, no longer afraid to speak up.

"When something's rotted or broken," Hal says, "you cut out the rotted stuff and make an even perimeter, then cut a new piece and patch it in. The patch"—he points to a patch I now see in the windowsill—"is called a Dutchman."

We can't always figure out the big questions, I think, as Hal and I continue out the door. But until we do—and even if we don't—there are still the small things we can do. We can be sisters. We can be Dutchmen. We can give, and receive, repair.

We head down the porch steps, now freed of its police tape. Victor calls after us, "Thanks for the cookies."

I am waking up, and the house is coming back to life. Maybe there is nothing left to fear.

CLOSING IN

I·N·S·U·L·A·T·I·O·N   A·N·D   W·A·L·L·S,   A·G·A·I·N

Time

"By the way," I say to Hal one evening in mid-January, as we stack the dishwasher in the rented house, "you know how we're supposed to move back to the house on February 17?"

He freezes, a dirty plate in his hands. "There's a problem?"

"Well, I kind of have a talk on February 16. At seven in the evening. In Florida."

"*Florida?*"

"Sorry."

"It would be a good idea if you got out of it."

"I tried all day today. But it's for a university. They've already advertised the date."

"So?"

"They made my book required reading for the entire freshman class, which is thousands of students, and they've already secured an amphitheater for a large audience."

"But we're moving the next morning."

"I know. But my publisher set up the event, and the head honcho there called me today and said that it would be really, really bad if I pulled out. Like it could ruin their business account with the university for years."

He lowers the plate to the dishwasher, his motions controlled. "Why did you tell them you could do it *then?*"

"We discussed dates last fall. I asked for one after New Year's, since I thought we'd be back in the house by then, and we settled on February 16. How was I supposed to know it would turn out to be a terrible time for a trip?"

He pours in way too much dishwashing powder. "Well," he says, "that's great."

I decide it would be unwise to indicate that this news is only half of what I want to say. While Hal's demeanor generally vacillates between playfulness and composure, he also has the capacity to grow aloof. I tend to forget this side of him during the long stretches when it vanishes from the scene, which has been the case throughout most of our marriage as well as this entire renovation. But after the last job meeting, I began to detect its return. First came a few tense nights as he strategized about how to ask Natalie to extend our stay until February 17. Fortunately, he found a way to present our case and Natalie has a big heart, but she also emphasized that, come what may, our move-out could be nudged no farther down the calendar. At that point, as I became jittery about whether Dan would be able to get everything done on time, Hal lost his joviality. This was not only because he had to be on-site all the more and step up his efforts with such dreary tasks as pestering the lighting store for still-undelivered fixtures. It was also because it was time to turn his attention toward finishing the third floor—himself. I'd forgotten this, too: one of the compromises Hal made to get Dan's estimate down was that he himself would handle the walls and floor and paint in his studio. And it is this combination of pressures that appears to have darkened his spirit.

It took me many years to accept the variations in the ways we endure stress. I prefer to ponder, and, whenever possible, make light of the situation. Hal usually does, too, which perhaps accounts for my forgetfulness about the occasions when he does not. But every so often, he will instead sink into what I call his moodiness, when he'll engage in little joking, few smiles, no light banter, maybe no conversation at all. When this happened in our first relationship, I took it personally. I'd launch into direct questioning about what he was feeling and why he was feeling it, then get annoyed when he couldn't, or wouldn't, answer—all of which only made matters worse. Time, however, can be love's friend. After Hal and I began our second relationship, I came to see that part of the pact of loving another person is both learning to accept the more mystifying aspects of his character, and finding ways to conduct oneself when they arise. Although I've hardly mastered the latter with Hal, I do know that if I refrain from direct questioning, stay upbeat, and steer conversation toward other things on my mind, he usually resolves whatever prompted his moodiness on his own. It might not happen immediately, but time has also taught me the value of patience. This has been my approach for the past week.

But then, a few days ago, I received an e-mail from the university in Florida, saying how happy they were that I was coming February 16. It had been months since they'd been in touch, which had allowed me to entertain many I-guess-I'm-off-the-hook scenarios—and say nothing about it to Hal. Upon receiving this bombshell, though, I begged them to change the date. I explained the renovation, the explosion, the tight schedule. Unthinkable, they replied. How could they have a thousand students show up at an amphitheater without an author on the stage?

"And Florida *again*," Hal says, throwing the dishwasher on with a hard shove.

"Orlando, even," I add.

I don't laugh, though my sense of absurdity makes me want to. This trip to Orlando is actually the parenthetical mate to another inconvenient talk, also in Orlando, days before the renovation began. I hadn't wanted to do that one, either. I hate steamy heat, and that's what Florida is in July. But when that invitation was extended—before Dan had determined our starting date—I had a very good reason to say yes: my mother lives directly across the state from Orlando, and after months of fretting with Laura about Rosalie's encroaching forgetfulness, an all-paid trip to a city two hours away seemed like a gift. Plus, Rosalie and Gordon had driven to Orlando when I'd had business there years before, and we'd had a nice lunch together. So I'd agreed to that talk, and only then did we learn that we needed to move out four days later. Just as belatedly, I discovered that the whole trip was pointless: Rosalie and Gordon were going to be out of state that month, motor-homing across the country for yet another of their lighthouse tours. Thus, I'd left Hal on his own, packing boxes and breaking Ikea mirrors, while I boiled away in Florida. Now, here we are again—with Hal knowing full well what I'm not yet saying.

"Orlando," he says curtly. "So you'll want to go a day early to visit with Rosalie."

"No." My voice is a squeaky-high lie.

"It would be much better if you were up *here* that day early."

"But now that you mention it"—I recover my regular tone—"it *does* make sense for me to fly down a day early. What if it snows the day I'm due down there and I'm stuck up here?"

He leans against the roaring dishwasher and crosses his arms.

I say, "When we moved in here, the movers did everything—I was useless. I can just come back the afternoon of the 17th. It's not like you'll need me that morning."

I start wiping a counter. There's no need to look up when I can easily envision his face.

"Oh, do what you want," he says. "I know that's what you want, so just do it."

He walks upstairs.

Secretly, waiting until after Hal leaves for the office the next morning, I call Rosalie.

"Oh, hello, dear!" she says in her stunned-to-have-a-daughter way. But she's whispering.

"Why are you whispering?"

"I just went back to bed."

"You're whispering because you're in bed?"

"No, no. We didn't get the birds up yet"—the two cockatiels that she and Gordon have doted on for fifteen years, and the reason they vacation across the country in a motor home and not on airplanes— "and I don't want them to know I'm awake and start making a fuss."

"Are you okay? Why'd you go back to bed?"

"Oh, I'm fine. I'm just lying here to let the eye drops work."

"Eye drops?"

"From the eye surgery."

Yes, that's right. I've been so preoccupied with her waning brain cells, and so thrown by disjointed exchanges like the one we're having right now, that I've forgotten about her recent medical miracle. Since she was a little girl, my mother has worn glasses. I've never even known her to misplace them because, except to shower and sleep, she never takes them off. To me, glasses are simply part of my mother's face. Then a few years ago, her eye doctor detected cataracts and glaucoma. He waited until both conditions had advanced far enough to warrant surgery, then offered to perform an additional service at the same time. "After one operation for the left eye, and another for the right, and then a treatment of eye drops," Rosalie had said, "I shouldn't need glasses at all." "How amazing," I'd replied, though I thought, How strange. It will be like having a different mother.

"How *are* your eyes?" I ask.

"Very good."

"Are you glasses-free yet?"

"My last bottle of drops runs out soon. The doctor says I should be able to throw away my glasses by, well, I guess, mid-February."

The timing startles me, and I almost interpret it as a cosmic confirmation of my scheme to visit her, despite Hal's irritation. Trying to sound nonchalant, I say, "I'm just curious. Where will you be then? In the middle of February?"

"Why? Will you be down here?"

"I, uh, I might. It's a possibility. I'm still working it out."

"Oh! That would be marvelous. When?"

"Well, hmm . . ." Do I commit now? Or stay unresolved until I've found a way to win Hal over? I stall with, "Will you put Gordon on the other line? And ask him to bring a calendar?"

This request, while diversionary, also marks a milestone. When Rosalie's doctor told her a few months ago, "It's not nothing, but it's not yet something," Laura and I debated when we should begin including Gordon in any important discussions with Rosalie. Laura started immediately, but my conversations with my mother have been inconsequential until now.

"Yello," Gordon says as he gets on. A cheerful seventy-five-year-old, Gordon worked two decades in the factory down the street from his childhood home in Pennsylvania until it relocated to France. Then, losing none of his chipper optimism, he went back to school to learn landscaping. He's been retired for years—they both have, which is why they've seen a considerable number of lighthouses by now—and when they're home, he spends his time tending to their yard. Though for the last few weeks, he says now, he's stayed indoors. Rosalie, still on the line, tells me that he's had a head cold since Christmas, so he's taking things easy.

I explain the fantasy logistics of my trip, four weeks from now. I will *try* to work my schedule so I can arrive on February 15, and if they drive to see me, or I rent a car to reach them, we can spend the day together. They, or I, will then go home that night, I'll give my talk on the 16th, fly home the morning of the 17th, and race to Hal's side. Voilà: I can be a good daughter and good wife at the same time. "That sounds wonderful," Rosalie keeps saying, though she slips from one date to another, as if time is becoming fluid. She also keeps thinking that they can stay in the hotel with me, maybe for several days. Gordon calmly corrects her, and we work the specifics out—though I don't tell them everything depends on Hal's reaction.

After Gordon gets off his line to wake the birds for their breakfast, I ask my mother, as offhandedly as possible, how things are going with her memory.

"Fine, fine. Of course, Gordon might not agree." She laughs her short hee-hee laugh, which often seems to convey self-deprecation rather than humor.

"Are you still taking the memory medicine?"

"Yes, but it's not doing anything."

"When will you know more?"

"Gordon, when's that next appointment?"

"He got off the phone, Rosalie."

"Right. I see the doctor in . . . February or March." Then she adds, *sotto voce,* "The doctor won't tell me which kind of dementia it is."

"I thought he said it was senile dementia."

"Now he says there are three possibilities: senile dementia, Alzheimer's, and one other I don't remember. He doesn't want to make a decision about what I have, but at this next visit I want to get it

pinned down. I'm hoping it's senile dementia. I dread Alzheimer's.
Everyone dreads Alzheimer's. And we need to know so we can decide
whether to do the next trip."

"When's that?"

"In the fall. We're going to see lighthouses in Seattle. When is
that trip, Gordon?"

"Gordon's not on the phone."

"Oh, yes. Well, it's sometime this fall." She makes her laugh. "My
memory permitting."

Fall seems a long way off, given the fog in the harbor today.

Late that afternoon, as dusk is falling, I ask Hal if we can make a run to
Teacher's Lane. Things are moving faster now that the missing insulation has been installed, and since tonight is the last night before he'll
begin working on the third floor and I return to the classroom, I'm
hoping I can reel him back to his usual spirits before we both get
absorbed.

"Be careful," Hal says as we mount the porch steps. "They just
poured the concrete to repair the cracks in this landing yesterday, and
it might not be completely dry."

"I didn't know that concrete took that long to set."

"It doesn't, if you use an accelerator. But I didn't want to, because
it creates other problems."

We jump up to the tiled porch. Hal unlocks the door and we
walk in.

Immediately we feel that the heat is finally on. A moment later,
we see that the new drywall is up. I almost feel, once again, as if this
place is actually our house—that we *have* a house—and relief rises in
me, inspiring a confidence that I'll be able to draw Hal out of himself
while we're in here. But the replacement windows encountered a delay,
so plywood still covers the old windows, and when we fail to find the
light switch for the one working bulb in the living room, which is also
the one working bulb in the house, Hal says, "We'll just have to do this
in the dark," and my hopeful feelings fade.

In the almost disappeared light of the day, we walk through the
house, two silhouettes, one behind the other. Specks of streetlight

dapple the drywall, which is shiny between the newly applied joint compound. We feel our way through the dimness, hands on the walls, silent as mimes. The bathroom now has its sink and tub. My study has regained its floor and ceiling. I think we will turn back here, but Hal continues up to the third floor, perhaps to survey it one more time before he launches his labors. I do not ask, as there is no indication that he's interested in conversation. When we reach the third floor, I just follow as he makes his way to the windows on the northern side. Then we stand there, looking out above the rooftops, across the Brandywine Creek Park, and through the dots of streetlights farther beyond.

I want to say something, but not about his mood or my call to Rosalie this morning. In fact, this would be a poor moment to mention anything that might ratchet up the tension. Then I realize that these two concerns—and this whole phase of the renovation—have something in common. Something I never thought about in the halcyon days before now.

"You know," I say, "time scares me these days."

"Now there's a non sequitur."

"Not really."

"Well, what do you mean?"

I pause, trying to find the language. What I want to say is that time has turned from friend to foe. No longer instructing me on such slowly accrued lessons as compassion or patience, the clock is now dominating all the time. When will the concrete set? When will the new windows come in? When will Hal return to himself? When can I persuade him to agree—without resentment—to my going to Orlando early to see my mother? When will my mother find out if she will remain who she is or become a different person? Every concern seems attached to these questions: how can I find enough time—and how much time do I have?

"Time just seems such a big concern right now," I say.

"Or our lack of control over it."

"Yes. That's what it is."

"I know. You think I like spending my lunch hour calling the kitchen cabinet manufacturer to find out when they'll be finished?"

"I know you hate it. I hate it."

"You're not spending half your life on it."

"That's true. But it's making us get short with each other, and I hate that. And you seem unhappy. I haven't seen you dance with the cats in a week."

"It'll pass. It's just a brief period in our lives."

"I know."

"Like our six years apart."

"I know."

Side by side, in our own thoughts, we look out the window. I do not know what he is thinking, but I am remembering a phone call with my mother during those years apart from Hal. I said to her, "There are so many things I miss about my relationship with him. I feel terrible that I might never find them again with another person." She said, "You might not." I said, "That's so painful to consider." "It is," she agreed. "When your father and I got divorced, I felt sick over the things I might never have again, and I never did get them again, and I'm very sad about that. But I got other things, and even though they're different, they turned out to be good, too."

I knew she meant Gordon. He's not the kind of educated, dynamic guy my father is, but he's smart and personable in all the ways she needs. He's devoted to her, and easy to be around, and as soon as I met him, shortly after I re-met her, I liked him. Unlike the catastrophe of her second husband, Gordon does not drink or smoke or exude a surplus of testosterone or suffer from fugues of paranoia or want to gamble away her life savings or encourage her to sever her ties to her children. Gordon is not someone with the kind of charm or magnetism or striking looks that attract admiring hoards at a party, but he's the person you're relieved to spend time with once you happen across him at the punch bowl. Gordon listens well. He has unusual interests, like airplane shows. He's husband, not boyfriend, material. And I knew, as I held the phone, years past my relationship with Hal, that in his all-around good-guyness, Gordon resembled Hal. I said to my mother, "Gordon's so wonderful, but he's so unlike the guys you saw when I was living with you. Do you think you would have given him the time of day if you'd met him back then?" "Not at all," she said. I asked her why not, and the harsh regret in her voice stunned me. "Because I was an ass," she said.

I remember thinking, I don't want to be an ass. But believing my time with Hal was already long over, I hung up the phone feeling worse than before.

"What are you thinking?" Hal says now.

Although I long to tell him about my call with Rosalie this morning, I also make a decision, in that split-second way that's familiar to any spouse who's ever weighed the risks of blurting out what's really on her mind against the benefits of calming the waters, to talk about that *other* call. He's heard my memories, but one of his many virtues, as I've seen over the years, is that he doesn't mind hearing stories over and over, and as he listens now, and I look at him in the streetlight coming through the windows, I can see the strain loosening from his face.

"Your mother sure knows how to pick up your spirits," Hal says, shaking his head.

"You can say that again," I say.

He does not know, and I do not indicate, that my response is not entirely in line with his. Some years into her marriage with Gordon, their lighthouse trips started to last as long as three or four months. I would like to say that I know a lot about these trips, that we spoke often from pay phones (Rosalie, like my father, resists cell phones), and that I charted her adventures at a distance, climbing lighthouses vicariously. But the truth is we seldom spoke during her trips, and when we did, I asked her nothing about the sights she'd taken in. I viewed Rosalie and Gordon's interest in lighthouses as eye-rollingly dull. Counting sheep seemed less tedious than looking at one tall white tower after another. And doing it year after year? To the point where lighthouses came to bear such importance that her trips took precedence over visits with her own children? It's not fun playing second fiddle to a stack of bricks.

But today, as I was on the phone with my mother, acutely concerned with dates for moving and deadlines for diagnoses and how much time we had, I suddenly fathomed that these lighthouse trips must have upset me more than I'd realized. Why else would I have never asked my mother what appeals to her about lighthouses—a question I would have asked anyone else? Why wouldn't I want to know? Didn't I find that when I pushed myself to understand Beth's ardor for riding city buses—a far more unusual indulgence—I also bridged the distance between us? Have I not been trying to do that right now with Hal?

A few years ago, soon after I'd joined Beth on her buses, I attended a lecture by a man named William Stillman, who has the form of autism known as Asperger's Syndrome. For an entire day he shared an insider's understanding of how people with autism experience the world. Among the things he discussed is the tendency of people with autism to have a specific passion, which can range from traffic lights to trains to, in his case, *The Wizard of Oz.* He noted that people who do not have autism often refer to these passions as "obsessions," and sometimes try to put a stop to them. His own parents tried when he was a teenager, sitting him down every night for a "talk," until finally, in tears, he agreed to move his Oz memorabilia into the attic and take up athletics in school. He told the audience, "I would have preferred that they'd cut off my hand." Then he explained that the way to reach a person is to *enter* his passion, not try to kill it off. How much closer he would have been to his parents had they tried to enjoy Oz with him.

At the end of William Stillman's talk, I thought about Beth, and how, although she has not been diagnosed with autism, she has a passion—and that I reached her by entering it. Then I thought about other people, and I saw that almost everyone, with a disability or not, has some kind of passion. William Stillman was speaking a universal truth.

I knew all that. Yet it took me until this renovation to learn about Hal's world. And it took me until today, when my mother mentioned her next lighthouse trip this fall, to question my tendency of looking down my nose at her passion. As I did, it occurred to me that what I've felt is not boredom, but envy. How could she love lighthouses as much as, or even more than, she loves me?

So in the call this morning that I am not telling Hal about, I finally asked Rosalie, "What do you like about lighthouses?"

"Oh, lighthouses are fascinating!" she said, and in a rush, she continued. "They're a living history." She told me how the keepers and their families lived in almost total isolation. The wives grew the food, sewed the clothing, schooled the children. The keeper had to work hard, too: twenty-four hours a day, every day of the year, he had to keep the lantern lit, which often meant dragging coal up many steps to the lantern room. But lighthouses were the only warning system that protected ships from hitting the shoals and sinking. Fishermen, travelers—the family never knew when someone might be out there. "That's what I like. Lighthouses are whole families that protect others from tragedy."

Her voice was animated and assured. She didn't need to check her memory with Gordon as she went on, telling me of the vast numbers of shipwrecks that occurred along the American coastlines prior to the construction of lighthouses, whole crews lost to the seas when their hulls smashed into rocks off the Outer Banks or Long Island or California or the Great Lakes. That's why, she went on, every lighthouse has a story. One that she then mentioned was Ida Lewis, the most famous woman in America in the second half of the nineteenth century. The keeper of the Lime Rock Lighthouse in Newport, Rhode Island, Ida Lewis was renowned for daring rescues, performed whenever she heard the cries of sailors, drunks, and young men who'd capsized. At the sound of their distress, Ida—who inherited the work but not the title of a keeper, after a stroke left her father with too many impairments to carry out his duties—would jump into a small boat, row through wind and waves toward the yells, and haul two, three, even four people inside her boat. She became a celebrity, visited by thousands of fans, including President Ulysses S. Grant. "And she did this," my mother said, "while keeping the lighthouse, taking care of her father, and after they got sick, her mother and sister. She left them only to do her rescues."

Now, beside Hal, gazing out at lights sparking through the darkness of the park, I think about Ida Lewis and her need to choose: stay inside to keep the lantern burning for other ships and look after loved ones? Or bolt out into the world to help strangers immediately in need?

· · ·

Even if I do decide to visit my mother two days before we move, I will not be able to go to a lighthouse with her. None of Florida's lighthouses is in the landlocked city of Orlando, nor anywhere near the town where she and Gordon live.

But at least I can learn more, so the next day I go to the library. I can simply look up information online, but I feel at home in libraries. Rosalie took us to libraries every two weeks, on the dot, when we were children. She got us library cards within days of our moving to new homes. Libraries continued to be important when I was a teenager, even though Rosalie was falling apart and had ceased taking us there regularly. By then I saw them as citadels of knowledge and contemplation, so when each summer rolled around, I asked if I could accompany her to work every day. I can't say I did this to mend the friction between us. I just loved spending my days reading random books, writing letters or stories, giving myself topics for research. But those months in the silence of the library were probably the times when I felt closest to my mother. I would watch her answer reference questions, and she would teach me to use obscure indexes. On her break, she'd also take me downstairs into the vast, locked room where the old magazines and newspapers were stored. I'd sit and read and skip lunch, and at the end of the day, when we drove home, we would not fight.

In the library now, I learn about lighthouses. About six hundred historic lighthouses exist in the United States, and they are far more architecturally varied than I knew; some are the familiar cylindrical tower enshrined on a million bath towels, but others are cone-shaped, octagonal, hexagonal, or even squat and round as hoops, or made to resemble Victorian townhouses. They can come in pairs. They can be made of brick, but also stone, wood, concrete, cast iron, and steel. They can rise up from beaches, cliffs, roofs, underwater platforms, forts. They can be as short as forty feet or as tall as three hundred—the height of the world's most famous lighthouse, the Statue of Liberty. There are at least as many different kinds of lighthouses as there are breeds of dogs. As my mother said, each one tells a story.

But she did not tell me that each one, except for Lady Liberty, is also at risk of dying. Abandoned for more sophisticated navigational technology, not protected by the government that their keepers once served, they fall prey to vandals, beach erosion, lack of interest, wrecking balls, and the elements. I am stunned to discover that there is no reliable public funding to preserve these iconic structures. If their lights, now automated, are needed to help ships, their well-being depends on the Coast Guard. Otherwise, their survival relies on the goodwill of volunteers who raise the funds to keep them from ruin.

I feel an urgency I hadn't felt until now. Hastily, I leaf through more books, searching for a lighthouse I can see near me, while my mother is still the mother I know. She cannot be in person beside me anytime soon, but somehow it seems of utmost importance to get myself into the presence of something that she cares about so much. I can tell her about my trip afterward, I say to myself, and that will be a bright spot in her day. Though I know that what I really want to do is understand my mother's passion.

There are a handful of tours within a few hours of Delaware, at lighthouses in New Jersey and Maryland. But it is January, and the tours are closed. I flip through other books, searching for some light-house where I can at least wander the grounds. Nothing.

I close the books. It's a stupid idea anyway, going on my own to look at a tower to get close to a mother who won't be with me, and who, in many ways, hasn't been with me for a long time. I cannot believe how ridiculous I'm being.

Then I remember an afternoon four years ago, right after we got married, and I realized that time was not just love's friend, but a friend of unimaginable generosity. Hal and I had driven to a town on the Delaware River about fifteen minutes from our house because it seemed like a nice hilly place for a walk. We were about forty-five minutes into our walk when we stopped cold and lifted our gazes high above us, and couldn't believe what we saw.

"I don't understand why we're doing this," Hal says that Tuesday, after we finish a late-afternoon job meeting with Dan and his new job supervisor, Dave, and return to our cars.

"Because it'll be fun," I say.

"But why tonight? Why not in the spring, when it's warmer? I mean, the sun's almost down. I have to get to Home Depot for some joint compound. And it's getting cold."

"Indulge me."

"Can't we just go home?"

"Please? We never saw it in the dark."

I lead in my car. I know how to get there. I found my way earlier this afternoon, after a long search online: north on the highway, take the exit, wind through the small town, and park at the intersection of, appropriately enough, Lighthouse and Lore. I'd gotten out of the car and almost lost my senses when I saw its height and majestic elegance. I was standing on the edge of a neighbor's backyard, and within moments she came outside with her dogs and we fell into a conversation. We looked not at each other, but at the sad, boarded-up keeper's house adjacent to her property, and, in its backyard, where a tool shed might be, the concrete lighthouse, rising a full hundred feet above our heads. "It's the only four-sided lighthouse in the country," she said. We cast our eyes toward the sky, and something about the tower—maybe the strangeness of seeing architectural grandeur in the most ordinary of backyards, maybe simply the feeling that we, so small on the ground, were being tended to with the benevolence of something larger—opened us up. I told her about my mother. The neighbor told me she was an artist, recently divorced, and that when she was looking for a place to live, she saw this property with a lighthouse adjacent to the backyard, and just knew it would set things right. "Have you ever been up in it?" I ask. "No, but it's still in operation. Come back in the dark and you'll see."

In the dark, we park at Lighthouse and Lore. When I emerge from my car, Hal comes up behind me, and, as possessed as I was a few hours ago—and am again—he throws his arms around my shoulders and draws me close. "Look," he says, and in his voice I can hear that his moodiness has left him. I hadn't planned this. It is not why I wanted us to come here. But now I'm even happier that we did. "Look," he repeats. "There's a red light."

Up high, the top window of what I now know is called the Marcus Hook Rear Range Lighthouse glows red, and above that, emerging from a letterbox-shaped opening, streams a red beam. I now know, too, that it is angled toward another lighthouse, also automated, many miles away. From the Internet I learned that its partner, not visible from here, does not look at all the same, but that together they hold hands across the Delaware landscape, one high, one low, one a steady light, one pulsing, their beacons a navigational warning for ships. Not ships in history, but ships today.

"I'm so glad you insisted we come," Hal says. "It's fabulous."

"And to think they might disintegrate in our lifetime," I say.

"Is that why we're here?"

"Not really."

"Then why? Why did you need to come?"

"Because," I say, and my voice almost stops. I want to say that I hadn't understood that my mother loved lighthouses for their history. But the truth is that I hadn't understood lighthouses because of my history with my mother.

"Because," I finally say, "it matters to Rosalie."

For a minute he says nothing, and just holds me in the dark. The red light streams out into the mist of the night.

"I have to see her when I'm down in Florida," I say finally.

I wait for him to stiffen. I think he might walk away. But he just grabs me closer. "I know," he says.

Commitment

But just when it seems as though the rest will be smooth sailing, Hal starts to disintegrate.

I'm slow to catch on. For one thing, I barely see him: I've thrown myself back into teaching, as well as packing up the rented house, and every day after work he drives straight to Teacher's Lane to do carpentry on the third floor until midnight. I'd thought that this relentless labor was purely the result of our financial limitations. But it turns out that Hal has an additional motivation, which I grasp only at the end of January, when he slips in some news during a casual workday call.

"You *what?*" I say.

In a meek voice, Hal says, "I lost my coat."

"Your *winter* coat?"

Very quietly: "Yes."

"How could you possibly lose your *winter coat?* In *January?*"

"I don't know. I guess it's my inner blockhead coming out."

"I can't believe it!"

I know I sound heartless, but my lack of sympathy does not concern his coat, nor does his embarrassment. The coat is merely the summit of a mountain of mishaps.

They began with diminutive losses. Back in November, days after we completed the stone wall, Hal said offhandedly, "Have you seen my glasses?" I hadn't, and I immediately worried, because these were the prescription lenses that allow him to read. "Maybe I set them down while I was laying the stones, and they fell into the yard." We went to the backyard and rooted around. Then we shelled out three hundred fifty dollars for a new pair.

A few weeks ago, when Hal began to put effort into the third floor, he said one day, "Have you seen my notebook?" "What notebook?" "I finally got smart after all these years and have been keeping a notebook with all my notes for this job instead of loose pieces of paper. But I can't find it." He also carried it everywhere, including the Home Depot where he bought joint compound and the Borders where he got coffee. We presented ourselves at both places in person. "Sorry," we were told twice, and returned to the rented house in silence.

The next day, the kitchen cabinets were delivered. When we went over to see the two already in place and to celebrate Hal's success in sustainability, Dan said, "Look at this." He ran a tape measure across a countertop he'd just sprung from its packaging. "Thirty inches." Then he measured the site where that cabinet would be installed. "Thirty-six." Had the manufacturer misread the drawings? We checked. No; Hal had neglected to specify a crucial dimension. "Dan can install it so the extra inches will be hidden by the microwave," Hal said, "and I'll build something to fill up the space." I thought for the first time in ages about the mug handles waiting ten years for glue. But this kind of oversight is uncharacteristic of him. I said, "Okay."

"There's one thing that goes ka-thunk in the bathroom," he said five nights later, when he returned to the rented house. "They installed the medicine cabinet over where the toilet will be, and the bottom starts here"—he held his hand way above my head—"so you'll need a ladder to use it." "How did that happen?" I asked. "Design error," he said, looking away. "Whose design?" "The architect's." He whisked one of the cats aloft and nuzzled her. "And what's the architect planning to do?" "Install it lower, which will mean making it shallower. I'll have to saw off the back." A house of mug handles, I thought.

And, after paint began going up last week, we discovered that Hal's ability to discern which samples would translate best to walls needed some fine-tuning. He'd accurately predicted that some of the unconventional colors we'd liked for our accent walls—the deep iris called Venture Violet in the living room, the scarlet Red Bay in my study, and the aptly named Butterfield in the front bedroom—would look stunning. But a candy-corn yellow on the vestibule door was garish. Hal said, "Dan can paint it over with a different color," and we selected a berry purple instead. That wasn't a big deal, but a few days later, when the accent wall in the dining room–kitchen became a digestively oppositional Pepto-Bismol pink, I pointed out that it would clash with the not-yet-installed red linoleum floor. "Plus," Hal said, "I can't stand it." "Then let's have Dan paint over this, too." Hal shook his head. "With eighteen days until we move in, there's no time." "But this wall looks like it's screaming." "I'll sponge on another color to tone it down." "Along with fixing the kitchen and medicine cabinets, completing the third floor, and packing the rented house?" "Yeah." "O-*kay*," I said.

But until the winter coat, I viewed each of these misplacements and miscalculations as isolated bumps in our progress, overshadowed by towering alps of accomplishments. Dan has expressed admiration for the thoroughness of the plans, and Victor has looked in awe at the southern windows in the kitchen and said, "I never would have thought to have done that." From sustainability to contractor relations, Hal has operated with the attentiveness that clients long for. Yet only people can build a house, and people err, especially when they also have a full-time job.

Now, sitting on the phone during our apparently not-at-all casual call, I understand that some of his time over at the old house has been dedicated to grappling with these slips before anyone—like his wife—would notice. "You're obviously getting worn down by this," I say.

"I'm fine."

"You're barely sleeping. You skip dinner too often. You're so tight on time you're not even ironing your shirts before you go to work."

"So what?"

"I haven't seen you play guitar for weeks. Your meditation's gone out the window, too."

"I've handled this before."

"Yeah, but finishing projects has always been for your job. Now it's your *second* job. Or *third*, since you're now a carpenter, too. You can't expect to be alert with every detail."

"Obviously I'm not."

"What can I do to help you?"

"Find the coat." He laughs ruefully.

"I guess it helps to be able to laugh at yourself."

"I learned that early in this line of work."

"Well, what if I help you with the third floor? You tell me what to do and I'll do it."

"There's nothing you can help with."

"I can paint."

"When's the last time you painted?"

"I was fifteen, helping my mother out. She paid me."

"I remember the story. I also remember you were terrible."

"You need help. And I'll try to be a good painter. Or at least a not-terrible one."

"All right." He sounds relieved. "Can you start tonight?"

That night I find myself, Ms. Non-Third Dimension, reaching for Hal's clothes again. Since I own nothing that I'd sacrifice to paint, I put on a pair of navy corduroys too small for him but sliding off me, and the T-shirt in which he laid the stone wall. Because there's no heat on the third floor—the specs call for a separate wall unit, but it remains inoperative because Sparky and Torch, who knew how to get it working, were released from the job—I also wear a sweatshirt, hood up. Because I don't want to ruin my skin, I pull on yellow Playtex gloves that I grabbed at the last minute. A professional painter would laugh at this parody of an amateur. I look at myself in the mirrored medicine cabinet—now on the floor of the third story, waiting for Hal's saw—and see a Fashion Frankenstein.

"Start with the railing," Hal says, as he changes into work clothes. "There's the primer."

I look at the railing, which separates one end of the room from the staircase. "Which part? The newel post? Spindles? The top rail?"

"Just prime the whole thing."

Priming the railing turns out to be impossible for me to bungle. It's also satisfying—at some point in our house's history, an ancestral homeowner painted this railing the orange of Gulf gas stations, and needless to say, I've been eager to see it go. Hal, in the meantime, rolls primer on the walls. Unlike the rest of the house, they're gray paneling, and have always given the third floor the ambiance of a sixties rec room. His work last week consisted of disguising the paneling with generous applications of joint compound, and with the primer rolling on from ceiling to floor, the paneling might as well have metamorphosed into drywall.

As we labor away, concealing the decorating preferences of people long gone from this house and perhaps this earth, we listen to cassette tapes Hal brought—Neil Finn, Crowded House, Sandy Denny. We chat about our day, and the songs. I finish the railing and start on the baseboards. Hal moves to the next wall. We are painting our house. We are entering the pantheon of the fearlessly handy. We are engaged in the long tradition of the industrious American do-it-yourselfer. I bet there aren't many writing professors who are sitting on a frigid floor right now, dipping a brush into primer and sweeping it across baseboards. Actually, I bet there are. Two thousand Home Depots and fifteen hundred Lowe's don't exist for nothing. I am finally in the know—or as in the know as I can be, given how little I know.

We have a grand time. We catch each other up on his projects at work, my new bevy of students, and the colors he's considering for the railing and accent wall in this room. When we get hungry, he calls in an order for takeout from the Japanese restaurant a few blocks away, then walks to pick it up. I eat while he primes, he eats while I prime. Occasionally I go to warm myself on the lower floors, which the furnace makes cozy, and where I can gaze out the windows, now finally replaced. The rest of the time I prime, musing about our pioneer spirit.

Our architect-assistant team finishes in the Olympic record of four hours, feeling so resourceful and efficient, I'm sure he's forgotten about his recent mistakes. I decide that I have.

But as we're about to leave for the rented house, he pauses on the second floor to shine a work light into the bathroom, saying, "They've finished tiling the walls." I expect to see what we bought during the Cretaceous era of demolition—white tiles punctuated by blue-and-green glass. Partially, this *is* what I see. The white tiles are laid perfectly. But the colored glass on the main wall is sparse where it will be most visible, and dense where it will be hidden by the toilet.

"I can't believe they did that," I say.

"Yeah," he agrees.

"I guess we can't ask them to change it, can we?"

"Not really."

"Well, it seems pretty stupid. How could they set those beautiful glass pieces so a lot of them won't even be seen?"

"I don't know." He turns off the light. "But I'm no one to throw stones."

Driving to the rented house, wet paint on the corduroys staining the lining of my winter coat, Hal in his car behind mine, unsuccessfully warding off the cold with a spring jacket, I feel ashamed of my insensitive comments, and vow not to give in any more to complaint.

Two nights later we return for the first coat of paint. I am wearing Hal's same clothes, which now look worse, smeared as they've been with primer. I am also discomfited to see Dan, but then remember that the job meeting was switched from tomorrow to tonight, and realize that he doesn't care how I look. In his line of work, he sees fashion obliviousness every day.

As we go through the rooms, marking off Hal's new list, I marvel at the changes in just the last two days. It is February 1. We have sixteen days left, so things are moving fast. The crystal doorknobs we selected months ago have appeared. Blue linoleum has been laid in the bathroom, and the toilet will arrive soon. Most impressively, the wooden floors have been sanded throughout the house. They look smooth and golden as a desert landscape, one that will gleam after sealant is applied tomorrow.

"Don't forget that the floor guy comes back tonight, too," Dan says, "to prepare the kitchen for the linoleum."

After the meeting, we hurry upstairs. With time running so short—and all the more so because the floor sealant will take a few days to dry, prohibiting us from entering the house—Hal made his color selections for the third floor on his own today, stopping at a store after work.

As I retrieve the brushes from a closet and he changes out of his office clothes into the work apparel I brought for him—clothes remarkably unslopped by the very same primer that frosts my ensemble—he tells me his color scheme. "All the walls on the third floor will be white except the accent wall. That will be pale lavender—'Breathtaking.'"

"Good choice." We used Breathtaking in the second floor hallway, and I adore it.

"The same color will also cover the top railing and newel post."

"Great. The spindles, too?"

"No, I picked a different color for them."

Aviary Blue? I wonder. Samovar Silver? "What did you pick?"

"Green."

"*Green?*" I look at the can. It's not just green, but a hideous brownish evergreen. I do not look at the name, but I imagine it's called Mildew Toad. "Dark green with *lavender?*"

He pulls his painter's shirt over his head. "Yup."

"I don't think that'll look too good."

"Well, that's what I'm doing."

I say nothing. I'm here to help out. Anyway, the architect knows best, right?

I begin with the top railing, painting Breathtaking, which is as elegant as a Degas tutu. "You could do the whole railing in this color," I say.

"It's been decided," Hal says, rolling Breathtaking along the accent wall.

This time, we're listening to news on the radio. Perhaps this is a mistake. The radio thwarts our efforts at conversation, and the stories are all troubling: the president has just announced that Americans are addicted to oil, although critics say that his efforts fall short of the necessary changes. We've just completed the warmest January on record, though there's no consensus in our country about the cause, let alone cure. There's also a contingent pushing for ethanol, although some scientists say that its production will eat more energy than it makes.

At the end of the news segments, Hal expresses apprehension about the future of the planet, and I indicate dismay at the inability of humanity to come to universal accord about our environment—or anything. "Is it really that hard for people to listen to each other?" I ask. Hal says, "Most people don't want to admit they might be wrong."

While we paint, we hear the floor subcontractor, Kevin, arrive downstairs. He'll be applying a patching substance to the concrete that currently constitutes the kitchen floor, making the surface level in preparation for the linoleum. "With him working," Hal points out, "it might be hard to get to the basement door." This is important, because the basement still contains a rudimentary bathroom, with a working, if unappealing, toilet and sink—which we never used, but which have surely helped Dan's guys, and are essential for our comfort tonight, as well as for rinsing brushes. "Once Kevin gets that stuff down, we might have to go out the front and in the back so we can reach the basement door in the kitchen without stepping on his work."

This circuitous route to the bathroom will certainly be unpleasant with the temperature in the twenties, but the workers have dealt with far worse conditions for months. I can rough it for a night or two. I'm tough. I'm an architect's assistant. I can do what needs to be done.

"Okay," Hal says when I finish the Breathtaking part of my job. "Wash off the brush in the basement and then you can start on the green."

Green, I think, but I just head downstairs. In the dining room–kitchen, I meet Kevin, who is in his forties, with a wrestler's physique and a receding hairline. He's on knee pads, troweling on his mud-colored substance. I say I need to reach the basement—should I just go outside to the back door? No, he says, rising, and then casts about for a way to get me across his patch. "You got a ladder?" he asks. A six-step ladder is folded against the wall. He brings it over, then finds two scraps of wood, which he lays parallel to each other on either side of the mud-colored patch. Then he sets the still-folded ladder horizontally on top of the scraps so the ladder becomes a bridge. "How clever," I say as he helps me walk, each step of the ladder a plank over a gorge. "I'm always figuring out ways to get folks from one side of a room to another," he says.

The basement, on which we saved money by making no improvements at all, is bone-rattlingly cold, as is the water from this tap. I wash the brushes as hastily as possible.

When I return to the third floor, I see that Hal has opened the can of green paint for me. His back is to me as he rolls the first coat of white onto the nonaccent walls.

I look down into Mildew Toad. It reminds me of the dental glue that my orthodontist used for a cast of my teeth when I was ten, and which made me gag. It reminds me of the patch Kevin is troweling onto the kitchen floor now. "This color doesn't seem right," I say.

"Just paint."

I can't believe that he won't even angle his head to see my turned-up lip. I can't believe that with all my help, he won't listen. I've always heard that architects can be imperious, but Hal's gentle ways seemed to refute that stereotype. Have I been wrong all this time?

He knows best, I tell myself.

Maybe he doesn't, I argue in my head.

This is what he does for a living.

But he's not perfect. Look at those recent misjudgments.

Anyway, it's his studio.

It's our house.

Stop being controlling.

Prove it will look bad by starting.

I dip my brush in the can. Feeling like I'm on the brink of overturning a barrel of dioxin, I bring the bristles to the newel post. Eggghhh. It's even worse than I expected.

I say, "Do you want to see how this looks?"

Hal's back is still to me. "No."

I grit my teeth and press on. I give it another ten, twenty strokes. "I have to tell you," I blurt out. "This makes me nauseous."

"Stop it, stop it, stop it, stop it!" Hal says, whirling around.

"How can you talk to me that way?"

"You're just going on and on!"

"That's rude. Don't talk to me like that."

"It's not rude. You asked me if I wanted you to stop and I said no and that's it! Done."

"But this color's awful!"

"You made that perfectly clear."

"So why are you using it?"

"I'm not."

"You're not?"

"Go wash the brush. Just stop."

"You're not going through with the green?"

"Didn't I just say that?"

"No."

"Well, we're not."

"When did you decide that?"

"A while ago."

"When were you going to tell me?"

"Look, we're wasting time. Just wash the brush, and start doing the baseboards."

Oh, no, I think, returning downstairs only minutes after I traversed Kevin's ladder bridge, it's happening to us. All the stories I've heard about couples during renovation: the bickering, the criticizing, the snapping, the whining, the not listening. I've even begun to see articles about it. Renovation dissension. Even though we haven't lived on the job site, we liked our contractor, our contractor made good after our disaster, our budget has swelled by only a few thousand, one of us is a professional, one of us has been invisible. Still, we have not escaped.

Avoiding eye contact with Kevin, I hurry to the basement, my cheeks tight. The water in the sink is so cold, even through the gloves it hurts my hands. I wash the brush, my nose and eyes running, my wet gloves finding a used tissue in my sweatshirt. I feel like a rainy drop cloth. I want to go back to the rented house. I want to get on a plane. I want to run away to the moon.

Back upstairs, I'm too upset to speak. Hal smiles as if nothing's wrong, his way, I know, of drawing me back to a place of unity. He tells me I should do a second coat of Breathtaking while he turns his attention toward the white. Then we paint in silence.

·   ·   ·

A half hour passes, then an hour. I don't know what he's thinking, and it's all I can do to fight the impulse to bolt from the third floor and go cry in my car. But I keep reminding myself: I do not just love my husband, and I am not just committed to him. I also need to act on my commitment. These are not the same thing, which I came to appreciate only after Hal and I got married. I would like to think that I could have absorbed such basic concepts by, say, voting age, and perhaps that's the case for some people. Not until I was living with Hal in my twenties, however, did I realize that I had little understanding of the connection between love and commitment. This happened when I watched friends defect from the single life into marriage and I beseeched them to explain how they'd become decisive. They said they'd finally felt ready to commit. But what did that mean? Had they found such true love that the desire to flee was eradicated? I didn't think so. They seemed to love their betrothed, but not swooningly so. Then Hal and I broke up, and my idea of true love was revealed as delusion. Oh, I thought, as I spoke with Robin, and Harriet, and struggled to learn the lessons of love, I guess that when people love their partner— not as a soul mate, but as a down-to-earth romantic friend and life-long ally—they just decide to stay. That must be what commitment is. This is the thought I carried with me when Hal and I strolled in our wedding finery through the streets of Wilmington to the justice of the peace. But even as our two witnesses threw rose petals when we left the county building that day, I still did not understand that deciding to commit was different from acting on commitment.

My epiphany came two days later, on a seasonable May afternoon when Hal and I were walking in the Brandywine Creek Park. During a conversation whose content has long faded from memory, Hal used a tone of voice that I interpreted as patronizing. Hurt, I reacted as I had when I'd taken exception to similar slights in our first thirteen years: I ceased being able to speak, and could think only of running away. We continued walking, him unaware of my jaw tensing because we were both facing forward, me thinking, *Leave! Get out of here now!*

But this time I fell into an inner dialogue, and talked back to myself in my head.

Wait a minute, I thought. I can't leave. I just got married.

Sure you can, my steaming thoughts responded. *The wedding was just two days ago. You haven't been married long enough for it to really count. And look at how he just talked to you!*

He probably doesn't even know what he sounded like.

If you just seclude yourself in your study when you get home from this walk, you won't have to talk to him anymore.

What kind of resolution is that?

The one you used to do.

But if I go off by myself, he'll get confused and I'll get angrier and the relationship will feel even worse than it feels right now. What if I just, well, talk to him?

Don't be ridiculous. You're so hurt, you'll cry if you open your mouth.

Maybe I should just force myself.

What would you say?

I'll say, "Hal, the way you just said that comment you made? It hurt me."

And there in that park, maybe just to prove my indignant side wrong, I pushed those very words out of my mouth. To my surprise, Hal listened. Then he asked a question, and listened some more. By the time we reached Edward the great blue heron, my jaw was no longer pinched, the resentful voice inside me had shut up, and the urge to run had vanished.

So this is commitment, I realized, as we walked up the hill toward our house. Pressing myself to admit my feelings aloud, and how they arose—even when I'm so convinced that he did something wrong that I'm on the verge of running. Of course, commitment requires that the other person must love and respect me enough to want to hear, and I must love and respect him enough to speak words he *can* hear. But assuming that is the case, then this is commitment: valuing our unity over my pride, the whole of our us rather than the sum of my righteousness.

Not only did I have the love thing all wrong, I thought as we reached our house. I was also wrong about commitment. Love is not just a feeling, and commitment is not just a decision. They, when intertwined, are action. Love and commitment move, and touch, and listen, and speak. They are deeds that sacrifice individual pride. Their goal is not just happiness, but mutual vulnerability.

But gee, sometimes it's just so hard to do. Tonight, for instance. After painting two hours without a word, I can't possibly talk. The hinges in my jaw have rusted shut.

Finally at nine, Kevin leaves, and I set down my brush and manage to pry my mouth open. "I think I'm heading home," I say, my voice coming out like a bent nail.

Hal turns from the wall. "Why?"

"I'm tired and hungry, and I didn't pack enough food for a whole dinner."

"I'm tired and hungry, too."

"You have to get up early tomorrow. Why don't you come back with me?"

"I still have another coat of paint."

"You can't get it all done tonight."

"I'm going to try."

"What are you going to eat for dinner?"

"Nothing."

"I can pick you up something when I leave and bring it back."

"Don't bother."

"It's not a bother. I'll go to the Japanese place—"

"No."

"Oookkkaayy." I say this with uncertainty, hoping he'll change his mind. But he just asks me to leave the brush on its can, and goes back to his painting.

Well, I think, pausing in my new study, I guess love and commitment require timing, as well as speaking and listening. There is value in waiting for better moments to talk, and the moment between two coats of paint isn't one of them.

"Bye!" I call back up the stairs. He doesn't respond.

See? He cares more about being right than he cares about you.

I step outside and get in my car. So what that the lining of my coat is getting even more paint on it? So what that it's so cold my nose is running? I might as well get my dinner at 7-Eleven. They have my number-one comfort food: pretzels. I can drown myself in crunchy saltiness.

It is bitingly cold. I raise my hood as I pull out. I angle for the turn to the next block—

Thump thump.

My breath catches in my throat. Someone's banging on my car!

Thump thump thump.

I see nothing out the windshield, through the rearview, on the passenger side. But a carjacker must be trying to blast into my car—and I can't even see him! I look around wildly.

"Hey!" I hear from outside the driver's window.

Hal is beside my car in his painting clothes, without a coat—of course without a coat. "Are you okay?" he says.

I roll down the window. "No! I thought someone was about to carjack me!"

"I don't mean now. I mean when you left the house."

"No, I—yes, I was fine. I'm fine. Everything's fine."

"I thought I heard a crash."

"You heard the front door close behind me."

"That's it?"

"As far as I know. I can't imagine what crashed."

He looks at me. I feel so sad for him, out in the cold without his coat. "When I stop off at 7-Eleven to get pretzels"—he laughs, knowing my weakness—"do you want anything?"

"You coming back?"

"I can."

"You weren't coming back."

"I can, if you're hungry. I can even go to the Japanese place if you're hungry."

"You'd do that?"

"I'll go there right now."

"Okay," he says. "That would be nice."

Late that night, after we eat dinner standing up, not talking about our fight, just speaking cautiously about banalities, I return to the rented house while he stays to paint. I have long been asleep when the bedroom door opens. "I found it," he says, and tosses something on the blanket.

I reach over. "Your winter coat! Where was it?"

"I guess a few days ago I stuck it on the bathroom sink so it wouldn't get paint on it. Then I forgot about it."

"I'm so glad you found it. Maybe everything will be good from here on in."

He says nothing. I push myself across the bed toward him. "Can we talk about what happened?" I say, too tired to argue myself back into silence. "So it doesn't happen again?"

He pauses, then says, "When you say the same thing over and over, it makes me crazy."

I say, "I understand. You still don't need to snap at me."

"Fair enough."

"And when you feel the urge to lose your patience with me saying the same thing over and over, I'd like it if you asked why it's so important to me."

He hesitates, a shadow beside the bed. "I'll try," he says.

"I'll try, too."

This resolution is just one step, and it took all night. No—it's been taking weeks. The house holds layers of history, and now it holds ours, too. I'm glad the walls can't speak.

A few nights later, after the wooden floors have been sealed and covered with protective paper, I return for another coat of paint. I've barely seen Hal for days. I'm teaching, I'm packing, he's at work, he's at Teacher's Lane, and the clock makes another rotation.

I arrive with Hal's work clothes in a bag, as well as a take-out dinner. He greets me pleasantly but quickly, and as we stand in the empty living room, strategizing about the order in which we'll accomplish our tasks this evening, we hear a knock on the window.

It's our neighbor Jim, waving to us from under a Russian-style hat. "Come in," I say. "See the house." I'm surprised I want to show it, because Hal and I are still feeling tentative around each other, and when I look around, I don't see a whole house, only parts—like the toilet and the light fixtures, just put in—and everything that's not right. Jim jumps at the chance to go through, and as Hal peels off to work on the third floor and I begin the tour, Jim keeps saying, "It's beautiful." I almost mention the tile flaw in the bathroom, then stop. He might not even notice. He doesn't.

When we reach the still-in-progress third floor, I see that Hal has, thankfully, painted over the green railing. Now it's red with plum spindles. He's also added a sponged red to the lavender accent wall, a swirl that looks like a basement from the 1970s where a local band is having their debut. "I'm doing this to learn how to tone down the Pepto-Bismol wall in the dining room," he says. "It's cool," Jim says, then asks, "Do you feel great in here?" Hal doesn't answer, and of course I haven't felt great at all. But seeing it through Jim's eyes, imagining myself as unaware of our quarrel as I am of the history of every person who has lived in this house, I look around and see things that are indeed lovely. "I'm beginning to," I say. "Well, being here," he says, "it just lifts the spirit up," and he raises his palms toward the sky.

Jim and I return downstairs, and I see that it *is* a nice house. Yes, it's easy to dwell on all that failed to be born, like the third-floor addition that would have become my study. I can also stand in the dining room—kitchen and superimpose the image of the skeletal room, with me looking up to the rafters of the second floor. But if I blink all that away, I see a hundred-year-old house with our quirky stamp on it— sustainable, colorful, eclectic: crystal doorknobs on the second floor to go with the old transoms above the doors, retro light fixture in the dining room to go with the diner-esque glass block windows, bohemian accent walls of purple and marigold and vermillion. It is ours, because it reflects our personalities. It is also not ours, because it existed before and it will exist after, and we are just passing through, as all of us do through time itself.

After I say bye to Jim, I change back into Hal's clothes—now with thermal underwear beneath, both for warmth and to keep the pants up. Then I get to work. Hal's left the radio off entirely, and the room heaves with silence. Maybe that's good. I'll just keep my opinions to myself and go about as I've been instructed, painting one more white coat on the walls.

But I'm using a roller for the first time since my terrible paint job when I was fifteen, and I'm still terrible. It keeps leaving lavender and red dots on the white wall, and dripping onto the already painted baseboards. Then I am asked to do another coat of plum on the baseboards to cover up my error. But even with a brush I'm inept. "I can't keep to a clean line," I say.

"Just do your best," he replies, without his usual warmth.

Crouching here, gracelessly pantomiming a baseboard paint job, I consider slipping out to Susan and Jim's house, though I fear I'd break down sobbing in their living room.

So I'm not looking forward to a stand-up dinner in our empty living room an hour later, and I guess Hal isn't either, because after I hand him the salad I brought and we start eating, neither of us speaks. After a few minutes, I feel too awkward to keep saying nothing, and with no desire to arouse more tension, I attempt levity. "This is bringing out my inner oaf," I say.

Hal just forks up another piece of lettuce.

Maybe I just have to say something funnier to get him to react. I search my thoughts to come up with additional self-deprecation, but something else slips between my lips instead.

"You know," I say, "you've become a different person yourself in the last few weeks."

"How?" he says, taken aback.

I guess I have to follow up now. Love and commitment, after all, speak. "You're not smiling much. You're actually being quite stern."

He eats his salad.

I say, "Maybe this is just how you are when you're at the office, so I've never seen this part of you and I just need to get used to it."

"I don't paint for a living."

"You work with deadlines and the physical world. Maybe you need to be stern for that."

He takes another bite of salad. I look at my food, and feel as if I barely fit into my body. I say, "Jim talked about the place lifting him up.

It *is* nice—I realized that when he was over. It's *fun* being here. Do you feel that way?"

"It stopped being fun for me long ago. At this point I just want it to be over."

Time to give up this line of conversation. I ask him to fill me in on his day.

He tells me, wearily, that his office was required to attend a special seminar, one of those occasional workplace requirements devoted to making office life better.

"What was the topic?" I say, pulling teeth.

"Conflict resolution."

I laugh and say, "That's what you and I need."

He looks away. "The fact is that I'm stressed out and I'm not handling it well."

I wonder if he means the skipped meals, the lack of sleep. I say, "What do you mean?"

"I'm not treating you as well as I should be, and that's what matters."

Suddenly we're folding into each other's arms and leaning in to each other. And as our breathing moves together again, his chest in to mine and mine in to his, I know that, although these walls can't speak, many other fights must have happened right in this room. If only this house could tell us all that it's seen. If only we could learn the ways of love and commitment that those before us worked out through their own lives then we might not stumble so hard, and so long, and so many times. I know the stories are right here, all around us. If only we were able to listen.

I pull out of the hug and say, "I'm terrible at painting. At anything with building."

"It's true. You are."

"But I want to help. I want to take away some of your stress."

"So stop painting."

"Will that be less stressful to you?"

"Yes."

"But what else can I do?"

"Bring me dinner while I'm here every night, and bring my work clothes."

"But I don't cook. I toss salad."

"Just make me canned soup and salad. That'll be fine."

"It seems like such a meager contribution."

"Why not just say we're a great team? I'll do what I'm good at, and you'll do what you're good at. You can bring food and clothes—and iron my shirts back at the rented house."

"I'm not good at ironing, either."

"But you're not terrible at it."

"That's correct."

"So you do what you're not terrible at, I'll do what I'm good at, and it will work."

He's right. This formula—taking actions that not only respect our differences, but accept our different proficiencies—succeeds. Over the next week, while Hal lays a cork floor on the third story, I bring dinner. While I iron twenty-seven of his shirts in the rented house, he builds shelves. While I go to the supermarket and stock up on his favorite soups, he corrects the paint I applied poorly. While he has a final job meeting with Dan, I pick up his evening coffee.

That weekend, our last before the move, on the morning before what the news predicts will be the biggest snowstorm of the season, I paint once more on the third floor. It is something I can't mess up: rolling white over the failed experiment of the red-sponged lavender. This time, Hal bought a new roller, so the color spots are gone. This time, too, the radio is playing Beatles love songs, in honor of the upcoming Valentine's Day. And while Hal sands and drills and whistles harmony, I sing. At dusk, I produce a thermos of hot lentil soup and the nicest salad I can put together. We stand in the empty living room eating and talking and laughing, friends and allies once again; and I glance toward the stairs. There lies his winter coat, which was lost in plain view, and will now keep him warm in the storm. "Here it comes," he says, pointing. I turn toward the hundred-year-old window frames, which have witnessed untold friendships and romances and marriages and communities as they've splintered apart, and maybe, if they were lucky and willing, constructed ways to come back together. I wish the windows could tell me what they've seen, and how, two by two, we can make the world a more agreeable place. We need all the good ideas we can get. But the windows can give only a reflection of us, doing what each of us does well, or at least doesn't do terribly—and enjoying each other again. I look past the reflection into the outside. Single crystals of snow are drifting down. It won't be long until they thicken, and fall closer together, and white out the blackness of the sky.

W·R·A·P·P·I·N·G   U·P

Purpose

Tuesday, February 14
2:00 P.M.:

Three days until the renovation is complete, and I have become a feral monster. I hate everyone, except Hal.

I hate Verizon, the megacorporation that provides our phone and Internet service. I've made at least eight calls to them over the last month to transfer service from the rented house to Teacher's Lane, with each call lasting nearly an hour, some disconnecting without warning. Today—my last day before my trip to Orlando—I pour two hours into more calls until I finally shriek that they should just kill the phone and Internet service at the rented house *now*. So my phone will go dead in the next few minutes, while I'm in the middle of a frenzy of renovation-related calls and Hal needs to reach me and I'm working out my itinerary with the university in Orlando.

I hate our cats. Zeebee and Peach are agitated, leaping into and out of boxes, knocking things over, attacking each other, requiring attention I have no time to give.

I hate the people I'm speaking for in Orlando. They didn't even start making my flight arrangements and scheduling my class visits until a week ago. So I don't have a guaranteed seat on my flight down—or time during my all-day campus visit for meals.

I hate Sparky and Torch, for igniting the delay that made us move this week instead of at the far more convenient time of Christmas.

I hate the burglar who kicked this whole thing into action in the first place.

I hate human frailty because yesterday, Rosalie called to say that the cold Gordon has been fighting since Christmas is still holding on, so they won't come to see me while I'm down there and I can't come to see them. After all I went through with Hal and that lighthouse, I won't even see her. I only wish that last week, when I'd called to make sure that everything was still on track before my hosts made my flight reservations, and I suggested that Gordon might feel better if we skipped it and I didn't fly in a day early after all, Rosalie hadn't insisted that we not only stick to our plan but also that I take the earliest flight possible so we could have even more time together. I only wish that when she called to cancel, she'd made some tiny acknowledgment that tomorrow, on a day when Hal would much prefer me to be here, I'll be rising at five thirty a.m. to catch a flight with no guaranteed seat to reach Orlando a day early to see no one.

I hate myself for hating everyone, especially my mother, who is old and in decline. I hate myself for wasting my life as a writer rather than becoming a lawyer or dermatologist or someone with a real income who could therefore have faced the payments for this once-in-a-lifetime renovation without them adding up to apoplexy. But instead the cost has grown by another $11,000 and Hal has made a list of other must-haves that come to $5,000, for a grand sum of $187,000, and now that we have the total we definitely have to refinance the house to keep from breaking open our IRAs, and it is the refinance guy I'm waiting to hear from. I don't want a bigger mortgage for thirty years, but what choice do we have when I am teaching students I love at a college that won't hire me full-time yet I put in full-time hours and even graded papers today and anyway if they did pay me full-time wages it still would take years to replenish our bank account and how the heck are we going to pay off a house with a mortgage double the size of the mortgage we have now and not be done until Hal's eighty-four?

And Hal? I don't hate Hal because I don't see Hal. He's working constantly on the house. Well, yes, I hate Hal, too, because I realized a whole week ago, before it had gone in, that the vestibule floor should not be the red linoleum he specced, but the blue we have in the bathroom, so it won't clash with the berry-purple door. He agreed, and said he'd bring it up with Dan, but kept forgetting, because Dan's workers and all the subs are swarming the house at this point, making sure everything gets done by Friday, February 17—when, a few hours before our moving van pulls up, the inspector is scheduled to give, or deny, the Certificate of Occupancy—and there were just so many details for Hal to think about, along with the third floor, etc., that by the time he finally remembered to leave a note for Dan about the floor, Kevin had already laid the red, and now the tiny vestibule is a phone booth of color.

I hate myself, again, for hating Hal for being too overwhelmed to tell Dan to do something as trivial as change the color of a floor.

I say all this hatred in a scream. I am screaming into the phone at a friend who had the temerity to call minutes before Verizon sends my phone into a coma, and got thanked for her effort by getting trapped in my anger pyre.

Then I pack. Last summer I gently sorted out the necessities from the mementos. Now I hurl everything into boxes. There's no time for thought. The universe is conspiring to deprive me of my senses. Renovation is not renewal. It is annihilation.

5:30 P.M.:

Late in the day, leaving our temporary neighborhood for one last trip to bring Hal his work clothes and dinner, I see one of the neighbors from a few houses down. She waves to me on the street, and as she crosses a mound of snow to ask how we're doing, I show my gratitude by sounding off. She listens with an odd smile, then says, "Maybe some good will come out of this." I have no patience for Swedenborgian piffle, so I say, "I bet it will," and then sound off some more. Finally she says, "Well, I think it means something." "It means nothing," I respond. She says, "I think it means that this neighborhood doesn't want to let you go."

The thought is so sweet and giving in the face of my rant that I laugh. "That's nice," I say, almost crying as she waves good-bye.

The spell is broken. I drive to the house. The monster has returned me to me.

Wednesday, February 15

12:30 P.M.:

My plane lands in sunny Orlando, and as I retrieve my carry-on from the overhead bin, I remember the early hours this morning. I rose at five thirty in the dark. Hal got up then, too, neither of us having slept much, as we have not for weeks. We can't—either because of a deficit of time or a surplus of anxiety. We, like Dan's crew, are going constantly: as I showered today, Hal resumed packing; as I ate breakfast and he showered, I labeled more boxes with color-coded dots. It's a failed system, though. We have too few colors for the number of rooms in the old house, and anyway, we keep forgetting which colors mean what. Is pink my study or his studio? Blue the kitchen or bathroom? I affixed dots anyway. Meaninglessness was not enough reason to stop.

Outside, in the snowdrifts left from the weekend storm, Hal helped me load my bags into my car. He was in a suit, ready for an important meeting at the office today, which, because he took off tomorrow and Friday for the move, is his final day in the office for the week, so he'll be frantically tying up loose ends until the moment he leaves. Then, late this afternoon, he'll race home, hastily change into work clothes, and, with half his team off to the minor leagues, probably not sleep for two days. We were polite as we closed my trunk, but were so worn out from exhaustion, obligation, and the determination to make our move-in deadline that we did not speak. Finally, employing a term that, I hoped, would show me to be attuned to the same stresses as he, I asked, "Do you think we'll get the Certificate of Occupancy?" "Dan says we will," Hal said. "But do you think we'll make it?" "I can't think about it at all. That's his job," he said.

Now, on the outdoor shuttle at the airport in Orlando—"The happiest place in the world," the pilot announced when we landed—and looking out the windows at the blue sky and palm trees, I think of our good-bye kiss in the snow. I was standing beside the driver's door, and we came toward each other. But unlike some recent mornings, it was not quick, as I'd expected. It was long and close, our arms around each other, our bodies instantly relaxing. How much it meant to me: an oasis of touch in the midst of turmoil.

I press my fingers to my lips. I do not hate him. I do not hate my mother, my cats, my hosts in Orlando, myself, or Verizon. I hate human imperfection, and how impossible it is to escape.

9:30 P.M.:

I am at dinner with my hosts in Orlando: teachers from the English department and sales representatives from a textbook company. Everyone is congenial and forthcoming. At my request, each shares her life story, and we form a fast, if temporary, bond over our stir-fry, commiserating over tales of families that disappointed and marriages that failed, cheering over moments of forgiveness and well-matched pairings. I usually savor such opportunities to make friends in faraway places. But behind my laughter and requests for more tea is the sense that it is wrong that I am here.

Thursday, February 16

8:00 A.M.:

I find this out later: Hal sleeps only four hours between last night and today. Then he races around the rented house packing, and, jumping back and forth over a patch of snow, fills his car to transport yet another load of boxes to the old house. Only when he powers up the car does he see that, for the first time in his car's young life, one of its tires has gone flat.

1:45 P.M.:

I stand in front of a class of English students, all dressed in climate-appropriate T-shirts and sandals, and answer questions about writing. Then I'm escorted past tropical plantings to the campus bookstore, where I shake professors' hands. I feel drawn to my hosts, all warm and fun people, and I enjoy our brief but continual exchanges. But I do not let myself forget where I should be, and what I'm not doing.

Then I return to the hotel for a brief break. The hotel is luxurious. I want to stand gazing out the window at downtown Orlando, but instead I stare at the pitiful sums in my most recent brokerage statement. If the refinancing doesn't work out, our gooses are cooked. Even if it does, we'll be living much closer to the bone.

I call Hal, but his cell phone is off, and I leave a message. Then I pull out hotel stationery and try to add up the money I'll make this year so we can start prepaying the prodigious mortgage we'll owe after the refinancing. But it is more productive to add up air.

Maybe I should try Beth. To add to my guilt about Hal, I feel guilty about my sister—we haven't spoken for a week, and for the whole last month I've kept our calls short. Fortunately she picks up. I tell her that I'm calling from Orlando, and we're moving back to the old house tomorrow, but she doesn't grasp that this means major anxiety, and I don't tell her. Instead, she tells me that a bus driver who was once a hair stylist invited her over last weekend and gave her a cut and color of her own choosing. She chose blond. Although when I see a picture later I'll think of Billy Idol, she says it looks spectacular, or, as she pronounces it, "Specacklur." This is one of the new words another bus driver taught her recently—words which he said describe her. I, using another, say, "I bet it's exuberant, too." "Thaz me," she says, and then, using her own pronunciation again, adds, "Zoomin' Beth," and her giddiness helps me smile.

As soon as we hang up, Hal calls back. Verizon, I learn, fumbled their instructions again, but we're too worn down to get angry. Hal is also undistractable. He updates me in less than sixty seconds and then has to go. There's not enough time for me to wish him a zoomin' evening before he speeds back to his labors.

8:30 P.M.:

I am standing in the outdoor amphitheater that seats one thousand, giving my talk. Although I was told that the date of this trip was immutable because this space had been reserved and hordes were expected, most professors were never informed that an author was coming, and the few flyers that were posted around campus got taken down for reasons unknown, so I am speaking to a teeming mass of fifty students, half of whom are on their cell phones. It's clear, as I trudge through my talk, dressed in a coat and gloves and scarf because Orlando nights in February are actually chilly, that Hal didn't have to be alone right now, and I didn't have to feel guilty. How will we ever recover from this? Will it break us apart, like what happened when

Hal backed the U-Haul into the neighbor's car? Isn't renovation about coming back to life, not sending each other to ruin?

Friday, February 17
8:15 A.M.:
It's our infamous moving day, and I am on a treadmill at the hotel gym in Orlando. Outside the window, the Florida sun beams down, and flowers smile toward the sky. I look at the TV on the wall and learn that it is pouring and forty-five degrees in Delaware. I pound harder on the machine and close my eyes. It's the happiest place in the world.

10:20 A.M.:
After I pass through Security in Orlando International Airport, I call my father. He says he's been trying to leave me a message at home, but my voice mail isn't working. I bemoan the long litany of errors, Verizon's and everyone else's. He says, with a joke in his voice, "Every life must have some calamity. It just so happens that you're lucky." "How's that?" I say. He says, "You're getting it all at once, so you shouldn't have any more for a while." He gets me to laugh.

Just in case Hal has left his cell phone on, I call him. Amazingly, he picks up. But he says, "The movers are here. I can't stay on the phone." He hangs up.

So I don't call an hour later to tell him the pathetic coincidence that happens as the plane backs out of the gate: the plane's wheel malfunctions, eerily echoing Hal's flat tire yesterday. I am also unable to tell him that the plane returns to the gate for maintenance, delaying our departure even more.

I don't expect perfection. By now, I don't even expect competence. Just get me home.

Whatever that means.

1:15 P.M.:
As the plane rises into the sky, I look down from the window at the thousands, then millions of houses running up the eastern seaboard, and marvel that anything *ever* works out. Renovation is

messy, unpredictable, maybe even out of control. It crawls forward through one phase after another, nurtured by the nimble-handed and the stumble-prone and the dream-thwarted, consuming far more time and going through many more compromises than anyone would imagine, until finally it matures into a house that still, for all the preparation and hope that went into it, has shortcomings. And then we move inside this flawed house, and over time, we either come to rely on its ability to protect us, and commit ourselves to protecting it, and let ourselves grow charmed by its idiosyncrasies, and learn how to conduct ourselves when its deficiencies arise—or we leave. Just as we do with love.

Clouds come between me and the topography below. But I keep my face pressed to the window, and as my watch ticks into an afternoon when Dan might or might not have received the Certificate of Occupancy, and Hal might or might not be resenting my absence, I think back to all we've been through: all the aggravation and grief and confusion and excitement and curiosity and friction and negotiation. Then I think about how, at the far end of this epic journey, having asked enough questions to fill a concrete mixer, I still don't have the answer to one of the most pressing questions I started with. What *do* I want to do with the rest of my life? I made it this far and this is all I really know:

I want to be an ally. I want to keep learning from my fellow students in life. I want to be a good wife, and good sister, and good daughter, and good neighbor, and good stranger. And, while I'm at it, I might as well add that I want to keep my anger pyre from burning anyone down.

That's still not telling me whether to take up microbiology or humanitarian relief. But I bet if I tell this to Hal later tonight, he'll laugh. "Do you really need to figure out anything more? That list sounds ambitious enough to me."

4:30 P.M.:

In the van that's shuttling me to the parking lot outside Philadelphia International Airport, I call Hal on his cell phone. Thank goodness: it's on.

"Oh, hi!" he says, his voice buoyant.

"You sound in good spirits."

"I shouldn't." He laughs.

"Why?"

"I'm toast, man!" He laughs more. "And I'm misdirecting the movers all over the place. But we're three-quarters through the move. There's a lot to go, but we're getting there."

"Which house are you at?"

"The old one. I mean, the new one. I mean, *our* house."

"Are you okay?"

"I'm great."

"I'm so glad to hear that."

"I'm so glad to *feel* it."

The van bumps down potholed Essington Avenue, and I think, The spell has broken for us both. The monster has returned him to him, too.

I look out the van window, and as Hal and I camouflage our relief as small talk, I see a house under renovation. What camaraderie I now feel for those people. Yes, renovation is a journey of bathroom fixtures and contractor haggling. But it's also an odyssey through multiple battles—permanence versus change, perfection versus imperfection, judgment versus compassion, material desire versus internal transcendence. I know, too, that our renovation is leaving me with much that I never expected: a hoarse voice from sleeping too little, a longing for hugs, and the realization that I just might play a part in things infinitely greater than I will ever be: the mending of family, the honoring of friendship, the togetherness of community, the celebration of kindred spirits, the mystery of the long education that carves the course of every life, the unbalanced duet of love. I still don't know how I would define design, but I'm enormously glad that I'm in the thick of it.

5:30 P.M.:

I park on Teacher's Lane, where early dusk is descending with midwinter swiftness. Two moving vans are sitting in front of our house, and when I get out of my car, I put my mind to living here again.

Despite all that's happened, it's easy to envision. Actually, it's not the inside of the house I picture, as I wheel my suitcase over the sidewalk. It's these sycamores, against this pink sky. It's being able to say: I'm finally home.

Hal comes running down the porch steps toward me, smiling the way he did when he approached me twenty-four years ago on a Philadelphia street, and I think about forever. I want my life here to last that long, or as close to forever as humans can imagine ourselves to be.

8:45 P.M.:
The movers gone, I use the sparkling new bathroom for the first time.

"The faucets don't work," I tell Hal when I emerge.

Collapsed on the bed, he opens one eye. "You mean you didn't get any water from them?"

"Right."

"Foot pedals," he reminds me.

Oh, yes. Sustainable Hal speced foot-controlled sinks to save water—and a two-drawer dishwasher, high-performance furnace, super-efficient insulation. He told me about all these environmentally responsible decisions when he was drawing the plans two years ago. One zoning variance, two moves, seven movers, twenty fights, fifty disappointments, a hundred epiphanies, one explosion, and five thousand nails ago.

I return to the bathroom and press the foot pedal. The water flows.

We cook dinner catatonically. When we're cleaning up, we discover that, when one of us is using the foot pedal for the kitchen sink, which Hal asked to be installed at the middle of the baseboard below, the other of us can't open the cabinet to reach the trash can inside. "That's something I'll do differently next time," Hal says. "*Next time?*" I ask.

We fall into bed. The streetlight from outside the house spills fully into the room. We have no blinds up yet, because, having lost his notebook, Hal had to remeasure the windows, a task he completed only last week. So the streetlight shoots long rectangles across the ceiling, and I can see the whole room. In one glance it is revealed as unfamiliar, in the next as deja vu. We sleep heavily and wake several times, confused about what time period we're in.

Saturday, February 18
7:00 A.M.:
I sit up. The ceiling rises way above my head. The windows are taller than I. As sunlight streams in, the Butterfield accent wall makes the room feel elegant yet playful. The marbleized texture of the light globe, beneath the maple-bladed ceiling fan, adds an artsy aura. The wooden floor stretches out like a welcoming beach. I set my feet on the floor, then cross the hall and enter my new study. It basks in southern light, which bounces off the red wall and golden light fixture as if creating an indoor dawn. Although the heights of the ceilings and windows haven't changed, the proportions altered by the removal of the walls, the warmth added by new insulation, the moods created by the application of color, the sense of care evident in each decorative element, have transformed the atmosphere entirely.

When Hal emerges from the bathroom, I raise my arms high. "Specacklur," I say.

"You really think so?" he says, almost crying.

"Yes," I say. "I do."

1:30 P.M.:
We return to the rented house—which we now call the old house—to retrieve the items Hal had the movers skip: lamps, mirrors, plants. The day is frigid, with Canadian wind. Ginny and the other neighbors we grew close to are not home. I walk around the empty house, look through the back windows at the trees in the yard. A cardinal I've been watching for two months jumps around the branches, along with two blue jays. They will leave my life now. I will miss them.

6:00 P.M.:
Darkness has slipped across the city. When we put on our new lights, the shadows on the walls are unfamiliar, the windows lit differently. I walk around in a daze, as do Peach and Zeebee, back from their overnight stay at the vet's. They appear to recognize this house, even with

the new layout, floors, windows, and turrets of unpacked boxes. They walk gingerly, not out of fear but curiosity. How could they be here again, when here looks so different from last summer?

I think I'm aware of all the changes that were made, but little by little, I start to see something more, something I hadn't realized even after our exchange this morning. My first hint comes when I say, "The kitchen and bathroom sinks are splendidly big," and Hal smiles and says, "I thought you'd like that." The next piece of evidence presents itself as I admire the sleek metal toilet paper holder, which allows a roll to be replaced with remarkable ease; the asymmetrical closet doors, allowing for a bookcase along the adjacent wall without blocking use of the closet; the way the wrought-iron ivy sconce throws a bow of shadows onto the wall of Breathtaking. Then I start seeing it at every turn: a level of Hal's creativity that I'd never suspected—even as I'd approved the plans, the choices at the stores, the paint samples. He selected everything not just with minute care, but so it all comes together magnificently.

Only when we sit down to our first real dinner do I find words. "You know, it's beautiful."

Hal makes his quiet but pleased smile. "I'm so glad you feel that way."

"It's like all the little pieces of us have come together—and are fully in harmony with each other."

He's blushing now.

I say, "If I were an architect, what would I see when I walked in here?"

"You'd immediately notice the interlocking planes."

"The what?"

He gets up from the table, stands at the cased opening between the living room and the dining room–kitchen. "See how there's a strip of chair rail that runs through the living room, and that we painted the same plum as the baseboards? And see how, even though the blues and purples of the living room don't get duplicated in the dining room, that same strip of chair rail continues right into here, at the same height, in the same color?"

I get up and look. "Yes," I say, amazed at what I hadn't seen in my own house, in my own husband, and the way it renders the two rooms continuous, even as they retain their individual identities. "You did this, and I didn't even know you were doing it."

"In here, too," he says, stepping into the dining room–kitchen and pointing near the tops of the walls. "I ran a line around this large room at the seven-foot mark to tie it all together."

I see nothing.

"Not paint," he says. "On the east wall, it's the bottom of the sof-fits, on the south wall it's the window frame, on the west wall it's the long light fixtures, and on the north wall it's a strip of molding."

I am astonished. Here I am, in the middle of a grand design, but because I didn't know how to look—no, really, because it didn't *occur* to me to look—I had no idea that a greater scheme was at work. It just seemed like an attractive, bright, environmentally sensitive house. Now I realize that it's infinitely more.

It's as if I'm finally reading a novel he wrote over the past two years, and now that it's done, I am dazzled by its hidden logic.

It's as if I am finally looking up at a night full of stars, and making sense of the patterns of the constellations.

It's as if I am falling more in love.

He's smiling broadly now, no longer hiding his delight.

I turn off the lights and look out the back windows, into the sky. How many designs are we in the middle of right now? Hal puts his arms around me, and even though I still cannot answer that question, I feel wondrously warm. I take a breath, deep into my whole self, and embrace all that I do not know and all that I'll never see.

8:00 P.M.:

After dinner, we discover that we need to adjust the newly reassem-bled dining room table. Hal climbs underneath and starts fiddling with the leg. "Would you mind getting my toolbox?" he asks. "It's in the bedroom."

I run upstairs. The toolbox isn't easy to find because the bedroom is stuffed with boxes, most of which hold Hal's clothes. But eventually I unearth it. Then I turn off the light and step out into the hall and shut the door behind me.

My hand is still on the crystal doorknob when I feel it lock.

I turn my wrist, but the knob does not turn with me. Our new knob set has apparently locked itself from the inside—and this time, it is Hal's clothes that are sealed off from our reach.

I am completely unable to move. The last time I was locked outside a bedroom, it was our second morning in the rented house—and it made me wonder how this renovation would open the door to a new me.

Now, after all of this, who am I?

I remember that, only a few days ago, archeologists broke into a previously unknown tomb near King Tutankhamun's crypt. When they discovered it—right beside priceless sites they'd scoured for eighty years—they were astounded to lay their eyes on all the treasures that had remained hidden and yet had been right where anyone could, if they knew to look, find them.

And standing here I realize, I *did* discover a whole other me. I am still the same person I was, but I am no longer as concerned about figuring out a single great purpose for my life. But that's not because I got distracted by the renovation. It's because my life, I now understand, finds its purpose day by day: as I sing songs with friends, talk with movers, care for my sisters, wave to my neighbors, share moments with strangers, struggle with my mother, comfort my husband, listen to builders, laugh with my father, remember those I'll never know who shared my house, stand in the glow of lighthouses with kindred spirits who are renovating their own lives—and learn, sometimes belatedly, sometimes immediately, stories about them all. I know this is not as grandiose as running a country or finding a cure for cancer. But it's still a purpose. It is a love of others, and of doing all I can to feel that we are not, in our deepest selves, alone. We are all under one huge roof. We need only to leave our own rooms to see.

But there is still much to be done. A foot pedal to move to one side. A house to be refinanced to cover costs. A door to be opened.

I turn the knob one more time. It won't budge.

"Hal?" I call down the stairs.

OCCUPANCY

L·A·N·D·S·C·A·P·I·N·G

Home

It's been two and a half years since we moved back to Teacher's Lane, and people still ask, "How's the house? Is it done?" I tell them that the house is lovely, and that yes, it's done, as long as no one scrutinizes details like our motley-as-ever furniture or the still-unadorned walls. But sometimes I wish they'd ask another question altogether: "How did the renovation affect you?"

If they did, I would start my answer by telling them what Hal replied to that question just a few days ago, while we toured landmark architectural sites in celebration of our seventh anniversary. As we were driving toward some Frank Lloyd Wright buildings, Hal said, "The renovation was the fulfillment of a dream. I did the design for a comfortable house that fits our needs, and that feels really good. We're much closer now, too. We confronted things we needed to confront." Then he talked about the fight over the green paint, and how it made him face his own rigidity. He brought up the explosion, and how it led him to see he'd underestimated me. Selecting paint colors and tile reinforced for him our spirit of cooperation. "It's one thing to get another person's life as a series of slits, like those old-fashioned Kinetoscope movies," he said. "It's another to watch your wife build a wall with you, and see how tough she really is."

Then I'd go on, and talk about how I finally feel that I live in a place where I belong. It is a true home, *our* home, and because our needs and desires went into everything—from the location of the walls to the style of the light fixtures—it assumes whatever role we want it to. On evenings and weekends, for example, when Hal transforms from architect to musician, our house becomes an artist's colony where he composes his unique electronic songs in his studio while I write away in my study, and even though I still don't understand his compositions, I can now hear his happiness in every note, and that's what matters to me. At other times, such as right when he returns from work, or late at night, it is our own secluded desert island. Then, we sprawl on the bed and listen to the news on the radio, or the rain out the window, or his bad puns and comedic skits; and there is no one in the world except us. We did not just renovate our house, I feel, when we are returning from a walk in the park or cooking in the kitchen or teasing each other in the hallway. We also made it into a place of tranquillity, where we can restore ourselves.

Those aren't the only answers I would give, though. There is also the one that occurs to me today, after we fly home from our vacation— passing through the glorious light tunnel in the Detroit airport on the way, which we love as much as any building we just saw—and come back, once again, to Teacher's Lane.

Houses, the renovation taught me, generate annual traditions that can be among the most pleasurable experiences in our lives. For many people, this means the gatherings of friends and relatives on Thanksgiving or Christmas. For us, it has come to mean Halloween, when children flock from all over the city to our neighborhood, and Hal puts on goofy hats that make the trick-or-treaters laugh, and I keep the candy bowl full, and we and almost all the neighbors spend hours on our porches, creating a boisterous block party with costumes. Tradition for us also means New Year's Eve, when, opting for the warmth of our house over chilly treks to city-sponsored events, we sit on the staircase to the third floor and look over the rooftops and watch fireworks dancing like spangled ball gowns in the sky.

And then there's spring, when we celebrate a tradition so small, so untethered to any holiday, so intimately linked to who we are and what our house has lived through, that someone watching us wouldn't even know we were engaging in an annual ritual. I didn't myself, even though it might be our most cherished tradition. I realized it only today.

It comes to me when, luggage in hand and our vacation fully over, we unlock the door and step back into the house. I've gotten used to the sight that greets us: one long view of the living room, followed by the dining room–kitchen, proceeding toward the back windows, beyond the infamous dry stone wall, and into the yard. But what I haven't expected to see is something that appeared in the yard while we were away. "Look," Hal says, catching it before I do.

We lower the suitcases. There is a pile of mail to go through, and phone messages to check. But this is more important.

We pass through the living room into the dining room–kitchen. We continue to the back door, and open the lock, and go outside.

"It's back again," Hal says.

The fringelike blossoms have opened on our baby tree. For three springs now, right around our anniversary, our little tree proves that it survived the explosion.

We climb up the stone steps into the yard, walk into the garden where Hal now raises vegetables, and stand beside the tree. It is not a mighty tree. It tilts far to one side, shaped by its history. But it is thriving, in spite of its past. We reach out to touch it as, I now remember, we do every year, amazed by its resilience. Then we cup our hands around the cottony white flowers, lift them to our faces, and inhale the sweet scent of the bloom.

ACKNOWLEDGMENTS

Although this book is furnished with stories about family, friends, and many others, I used real names only for those individuals who gave me permission to do so, and altered minor details for some of the pseudonymous people to further ensure their anonymity. Therefore, I cannot thank every person in these pages by name, but to each I extend my deepest gratitude. Our respect and affection for one another enriched my life in the past, and our relationship, even if now only in memory, continues to bear fruit in my present.

But there are many people I can name. Among the individuals who enliven these pages and permitted me to identify them are Deb Cameron, Lisa Hyatt Cooper, Robin Fein, Ginny and Eliza Hyde, Susan and Jim Moseley, Joyce Muwwakkil, Bonnie Neubauer, Dr. Janice Nevin, Dr. Charlie Pohl, Craig Schollenberger, Harriet and Vic Stein, William Stillman, Marni J. Tharler, and Dan Wilkins. Lainey Papageorge was my kindred spirit in the Detroit Metropolitan Airport, and Jodi Lee Larson was my ally at the Marcus Hook Rear Range Lighthouse. Others who encouraged me but who do not appear here are Katie Andraski, Bethany Broadwell, Allison Carey, Mitchell A. Cohn, Vicki Forman, Dan Gottlieb, Mary Gaut, Marshall Hill, Hannah Jacobs, Cathy Kudlick, Mary McHugh, Denise Patton-Pace, Sherina Poorman, Joseph Shapiro, Dan Simpson, Dave Simpson, Pat Smedley, Bruce Snider, Nancy Thaler, John Timpane, Gwen Waltz, and Carol Zapata-Whelan, with additional inspiration provided by

April Allridge, Katie Beals, Mark Bernstein, Mary Clayton, Rabbi Stephen Fuchs, Cynthia Romaker Fullmer, Marc Goldman, Jackie and Marc Kramer, Doug and Sharon Klepfer, Lisa Klopfer, Carla Markell, Linda Miller, Jane Mills, Marilyn Haywood Paige, Karen Sandler, and the staff of the New Castle County library system.

Once construction began, I was grateful to encounter many friends and strangers who were willing to offer their knowledge. Top on the list are the hardworking Dan Bachtle and his staff at Edge Construction, including Dave Undorf, master carpenter; Victor Belardo, assistant carpenter; and Scott Duffie, painter, as well as Ron Piechowski of Horizon Electrical. Other experts include Patrycja Doniewski of qb3 design in Philadelphia; Bob Ernst of FBN Construction in Boston; Thomas Hine; Tony Junker; Pete Maruca of Orion General Contractors in Haverford, Pennsylvania, and his master carpenter, Irv Morey; and Earl Rentz at Conectiv in Delaware.

On the occasions when spiritual and psychological supplies were needed, I was blessed with many kind and giving people. Dr. Theodore Hiebert guided me through my thoughts about adversaries and allies. Family therapist Rachel Cox provided reassurance that renovation is as much a matter of emotion as it is construction. Anne Dubuisson Anderson made sure that this project didn't explode. During the time I spent in revisions, several gifted students also helped me keep my spirits up by giving me reasons to leave the desk, including (but hardly limited to) Melissa Bromwell, Elizabeth Catanese, Renee Chastain, Julie Church, Caitlin Dowdall, Ellen Goodlett, Steve Hagenbuch, Christian Hoyt, Tara Malone, Tammy Metz, Anna Lehr Mueser, Tasneem Paghdiwala, Faith Paulsen, Nick Pentzell, Rachel Sandler, Kate Small, Shubha Sunder, Will Turnbull, Ilana Vine, Sarah Westbrook, David Williamson, and James Zoshak. And I also owe much of my sanity to both sets of neighbors, including Kim Leary, Tom and Alice Davis, Catherine Drabkin and Pahl Hluchan, Trish and Glenn Kocher, and Carol and Sandy Woolworth, with a big kiss I must blow into the wind for the late and dearly missed Mary Young-Wilson.

The process of building by hand also requires, as Hal taught me, an enduring respect for patience. I have long held my agent, Anne

Edelstein, in high regard for many reasons, including her wisdom, warmth, enthusiasm, and faith in me. Now I can add to that list her patience, as she gave me all the time I needed to construct this book while she remained steadfast in her support and generous with her friendship. Anne, this house would not be a home without you. Thanks also to Krista Ingebretson, Anne's trusty assistant, whose lovely personality makes everything easier.

Nor would this house be a home without my editors at Dutton: Trena Keating, who served for years as my interior designer extraordinaire, and Erika Imranyi, whom I met after construction was underway. In the early stages of my apprenticeship with Trena, her reliability, composure, and respect for me ensured that a light always remained on in my spirit, even in the darkest moments; once we moved into onsite work together, I felt blessed by the way these same qualities helped bring out my best on the page. My guidance from Erika has been equally gratifying, and not only because she's as knowledgeable about story and words as she is about married life with an architect. Erika's mirth, optimism, patient ear, and clear eye sustained me through the whole process. In addition, I'm deeply grateful to Brian Tart for his enthusiastic support. A bouquet of blueprints to all of you.

Finally, there would be no house without Hal. So much began that day you said good morning back to me, and, although I know that nothing is permanent but impermanence, I so hope that our good mornings continue until time has lost all of its meaning.

ABOUT THE AUTHOR

Rachel Simon is the author of the bestselling memoir *Riding the Bus with My Sister,* which was adapted for a Hallmark Hall of Fame movie. Her other books include the short story collection *Little Nightmares, Little Dreams* and the novel *The Magic Touch.* She and her husband live in Wilmington, Delaware, on a street informally known as Teacher's Lane. For more information, please see www.rachelsimon.com.